MEASURING
THE PERFORMANCE
OF THE HOLLOW
STATE

PUBLIC MANAGEMENT AND CHANGE SERIES
Beryl A. Radin, Series Editor

TITLES IN THE SERIES

Challenging the Performance Movement: Accountability, Complexity, and Democratic Values, Beryl A. Radin

Charitable Choice at Work: Evaluating Faith-Based Job Programs in the States, Sheila Suess Kennedy and Wolfgang Bielefeld

How Management Matters: Street-Level Bureaucrats and Welfare Reform, Norma M. Riccucci

Measuring the Performance of the Hollow State, David G. Frederickson and H. George Frederickson

Revisiting Waldo's Administrative State: Constancy and Change in Public Administration, David H. Rosenbloom and Howard E. McCurdy

MEASURING THE PERFORMANCE OF THE HOLLOW STATE

David G. Frederickson and H. George Frederickson

GEORGETOWN UNIVERSITY PRESS
WASHINGTON, D.C.

As of January 1, 2007, 13-digit ISBN numbers will replace the current 10-digit system.
Paperback: 978-1-58901-119-9

Georgetown University Press, Washington, D.C.

Library of Congress Cataloging-in-Publication Data

Frederickson, David G.
    Measuring the performance of the hollow state / David G. Frederickson
and H. George Frederickson.
        p.   cm. — (Public management and change series)
    Includes bibliographical references.
    ISBN 1-58901-119-8 (pbk. : alk. paper)
        1. Contracting out—United States—Evaluation—Case studies.   2. Subcontracting—
United States—Case studies.   3. Government productivity—United States—Evaluation.
4. United States. Dept. of Health and Human Services—Evaluation.   I. Frederickson,
H. George.   II. Title.   III. Public management and change.
    HD3861.U6F74 2006
    352.5′382439—dc22   2006003224

This book is printed on acid-free paper meeting the requirements of the American
National Standard for Permanence in Paper for Printed Library Materials.

13 12 11 10 09 08 07 06   9 8 7 6 5 4 3 2
First printing

Printed in the United States of America

For Julie and Mary

CONTENTS

ILLUSTRATIONS

FIGURES

ACKNOWLEDGMENTS

Authors are shaped and sustained by the institutions of which they have been a part. We are grateful for the guidance and support of our many friends and colleagues at the School of Public and Environmental Affairs (SPEA) at Indiana University and the Department of Public Administration at the University of Kansas. We especially thank Robert Agranoff at SPEA for his encouragement and thoughtful advice. At the University of Kansas we thank Sabine Jones for cheerfully and expertly processing many manuscript revisions. This book is part of the Public Management and Change series at Georgetown University Press, a series very capably edited and directed by Beryl Radin, and we extend our gratitude to her. The first draft of the manuscript was reviewed by two anonymous experts in performance measurement and public management. Their wise and thoughtful reviews guided our revisions, and the book is very much better as a result. We thank them. We express special appreciation to the many public officials who gave us their time, their opinions and insights, and their trust. Without them there would be no book. Finally, we thank our wives, Julie and Mary, for their love and support and for putting up with endless dinner table discussions of federal performance measurement.

ABBREVIATIONS AND ACRONYMS

AI/AN	American Indian or Alaska Native
CAHPS	Consumer Assessment of Health Plans Systems
CDC	Centers for Disease Control
CHS	Contract Health Services
CMS	Centers for Medicare and Medicaid Services
FDA	Food and Drug Administration
FDAMA	Food and Drug Administration Modernization Act (1997)
FTE	full-time equivalent
FY	fiscal year
GAO	General Accounting Office
GPRA	Government Performance and Results Act (1993)
GRAS	generally recognized as safe
HAACP	Hazard Analysis Critical Control Point
HCFA	Health Care Financing Administration
HPG	Hospital Preparedness Grants
HRSA	Health Resources and Services Administration
HHS	U.S. Department of Health and Human Services
IHS	Indian Health Service
MCHB	Maternal and Child Health Bureau
NIH	National Institutes of Health
NSF	National Science Foundation
OMB	Office of Management and Budget
ORPH	Office of Rural Health Policy
PART	Performance Assessment Rating Tool
PDUFA	Prescription Drug User Fee Act (1992)
SCHIP	State Children's Health Insurance Program
SSA	Social Security Administration

1

INTRODUCTION
Federal Performance Measurement

For much of the twentieth century most scholars thought that the key to improved government performance was a politically neutral, merit-based civil service and a well-managed government of expert public administrators. Indeed, both the practices of modern American public administration and the academic field of public administration emerged during the Progressive Era, and both are uniquely associated with questions of government performance. Simply put, in the classic public administration ethos, well-managed governments will perform well. Nevertheless, by the end of the twentieth century, the government performance emphasis had shifted away from professional administration toward the rigorous measurement of agency and program performance.

At the federal level the high-water mark of the performance measurement reform movement was the passage of the Government Performance and Results Act (GPRA or the Results Act) of 1993. That reform is based on the assumption that the performance of government can be measured and that such measures are essential to improved government effectiveness. Due in part to its status as law, GPRA has steadily grown in importance (Posner 2002).

We should study the federal government's implementation of GPRA for two reasons. First, GPRA is only the most recent of several attempts to improve decision making and administration through measuring the performance of federal programs and agencies. Identifying how GPRA succeeds and fails in this endeavor, and the reasons behind its successes and failures, can inform future efforts to measure government performance. The successes and failures of GPRA as a platform for performance measurement can be compared and contrasted with previous government performance measurement efforts. Such an evaluation helps identify how the federal government can best assess its performance and can determine the best uses for the resulting performance information.

Our consideration of federal performance measurement reforms raises questions rarely explored in public administration. For example, does performance measurement yield benefits equal to or greater than its costs? After all, departments, agencies, programs, and third-party providers are dedicating considerable

1

resources to meeting GPRA's requirements. Resources dedicated to performance measurement displace other priorities; are foregone priorities less important than those served by meeting GPRA's requirements? In sum, is performance measurement worth what it costs?

The second reason we should study the federal government's implementation of GPRA deals with the fact that most of the programs and services of the federal government are now carried out by third parties (Light 1999). These third parties, which include a wide range of types, operate on the basis of grants or contracts from the federal government. How is GPRA performance measurement being implemented by federal agencies that heavily rely on third parties to carry out their purposes?

The text of the 1993 GPRA legislation identifies its purposes as improving the following: the public's confidence in government; program effectiveness, customer service, and accountability; service delivery; congressional decision making; and the internal management of the federal government. Like much reform legislation, GPRA came with very high promises, the promises of dedicated reformers. The purposes and high promises of GPRA were supported for different reasons, however, depending on the supporter.

John Mercer, the self-described "father of GPRA," served as Republican counsel to the Senate Committee on Governmental Affairs in the early 1990s. Credited with writing the initial drafts of what was to become GPRA, Mercer based his advice to Congress on his earlier experiences as an elected city council member and mayor in Sunnyvale, California. These experiences became an often-cited reference in David Osborne and Ted Gaebler's popular 1992 book, *Reinventing Government,* an especially influential treatise during the Clinton administration. Ted Gaebler was a fellow city leader in California with John Mercer in the 1980s, and David Osborne served throughout the Clinton administration as the key advisor to Vice President Gore's National Performance Review. In *Reinventing Government,* the repeated references to Sunnyvale and to Mercer include advocating five-year strategic plans and annual quantitative measures of the achievement of specific goals in such plans (240–41); the need for multiyear budgeting in government (239–41); the need for performance budgeting (142–45); and the need for fees for service to replace at least some generalized government revenues (203).

Mercer describes GPRA as an effort "to improve the effectiveness of federal programs as measured by their actual results, and to do this by improving the performance of those programs through better management" (U.S. Congress 2001, 3). Performance measurement would achieve these purposes because "transparency and accountability in federal agencies is key to improving performance, particularly as measured by program efficiency and effectiveness" (3). Performance measurement is also helpful because "in my own years of experience in a government noted for its high levels of performance, I found [a] sense of competition against past performance to be an even more powerful motivator over the long term than established goals" (3).

When asked how a small city such as Sunnyvale could serve as a model for federal government management improvement, Mercer said:

I recognize it may seem to strain credibility to assert that the experience of a single city of 130,000 out in California is a meaningful lesson for an entity the size and complexity of the federal government. However, the very existence of GPRA today is evidence that Sunnyvale's example may be relevant to federal government management reform. . . . This may be the singular lesson of the Sunnyvale experience—that there are indeed certain fundamental principles of efficient, effective government that can be applied to improve the operations of any government, regardless of size, complexity or mission. In fact, for over 20 years, governments from across the country and around the world have been coming to Sunnyvale to examine its system. (U.S. Congress 2001, 3)

GPRA seeks to address the perceived inefficiency and ineffectiveness of federal agencies. GPRA posits that these shortcomings are primarily attributable to poorly defined agency missions, goals, and objectives and to inadequate performance information. Not only do these conditions breed poor performance, advocates for GPRA passage claimed, they also lead to the public's low confidence in government and hamper congressional decision making. As a remedy for inefficiency and ineffectiveness, GPRA requires that federal agencies: (1) establish strategic plans that provide broad descriptions of agency goals and objectives covering a period of three to five years; and (2) develop annual performance plans on the basis of measures, preferably quantified, by which agencies determine the extent to which goals and objectives are being met and report annually on agency performance based on these measures.

Although GPRA became law in 1993, governmentwide implementation did not begin until September 30, 1997, when the first round of strategic plans was due. Since that time several other major GPRA implementation milestones have passed. In 1998, agencies prepared and submitted to the president and Congress performance plans for fiscal year (FY) 1999. The culmination of the first round of GPRA implementation occurred on March 31, 2000, when agencies submitted their FY 2001 performance plans supplemented with data that reported on their success at meeting the goals found in their FY 1999 performance plans. Agencies have completed seven actual reports, including performance and results measures for the years 1999 through 2005.

GPRA IMPLEMENTATION IN THE DEPARTMENT OF HEALTH AND HUMAN SERVICES

To describe and evaluate the implementation of GPRA, we engaged in an in-depth consideration of the application of GPRA in five federal health care agencies within the U.S. Department of Health and Human Services (HHS). The purposes of these five agencies are highly diverse, ranging from consumer protection to the discovery of cures for diseases. In addition these agencies have varying structures, use different management tools, and have different purposes in their implementation of performance measurement. The five agencies studied are the Health

Resources and Services Administration (HRSA); the Centers for Medicare and Medicaid Services (CMS); the National Institutes of Health (NIH); the Indian Health Service (IHS); and the Food and Drug Administration (FDA). Although they are diverse in mission, all five agencies are part of the implementation of national policies designed to improve the health of Americans. Table 1.1 presents a summary of these agencies' responsibilities, policy implementation tools, and third-party policy implementation partners.

In the United States, national health policy involves a complex and elaborate set of programs, organizations, roles, and specific organizational purposes and objectives. In order to explicate this complexity and describe it in some detail, we selected these five agencies for in-depth consideration because each represents

TABLE 1.1

FEDERAL HEALTH CARE AGENCIES, RESPONSIBILITIES, POLICY IMPLEMENTATION TOOLS, AND THIRD PARTIES

Agency	Responsibility	Policy Tool	Third Parties
Food and Drug Administration (FDA)	Responsible for ensuring that food, drugs, and medical devices on the market are safe and effective and that these products reach market in a timely way.	Regulation	Regulated industries
Centers for Medicare and Medicaid Services (CMS)	Provide health insurance to Medicare, Medicaid, and State Children's Health Insurance Program beneficiaries.	Grants (Medicare), contracted services (Medicaid)	States and territories, insurance, and health care intermediaries and carriers
Health Resources and Services Administration (HRSA)	National health programs ensuring equitable access to health care services for the medically underserved.	Grants	States and territories, local governments, profit and nonprofit institutions
Indian Health Service (IHS)	Health services to American Indians and Alaska Natives belonging to 550 federally recognized tribes.	Grants, direct services	Tribes
National Institutes of Health (NIH)	Research and training to acquire new knowledge to prevent, detect, diagnose, and treat diseases and disabilities.	Grants, intramural research	Health research institutions

Note: Policy tools and third parties represent the most significant activities in terms of resources of these agencies but are by no means exhaustive.

one or more of the primary organizational and management characteristics found in other departments and agencies. Although this is hardly a random sample of federal agencies, the five selected agencies reflect much of the range and diversity of federal government organizational structures and third-party policy implementation tools.

The agencies chosen for detailed consideration were selected specifically because their programs employ a diversity of federal government policy instruments. Although all the agencies selected have a principal tool for achieving programmatic objectives, each employs at least one other tool (Salamon 1989). We will use Lester Salamon's categorization of policy tools to provide justification for each case selection. In addition, each agency uses a unique pattern of third-party service providers.

Some agencies, such as NIH and HRSA, implement policy primarily by grants. Other agencies, such as FDA, are regulatory, implementing policy through an elaborate drug approval and oversight process. Some agencies deliver services directly, such as certain functions of the IHS. Each of the five agencies studied here has unique challenges defining its mission and goals and measuring and meeting its performance objectives. HRSA is primarily a grant-making agency; CMS relies heavily on contracted services in the Medicare program and grants to states in the Medicaid program; NIH engages in scientific health research, both intramurally (research conducted by NIH scientists) and extramurally (research conducted by grant recipients at hospitals, universities, and research institutions); IHS provides grants to tribes and engages in the direct provision of health care and dental services to American Indians and Alaska natives; and FDA is primarily a regulatory agency using systematic drug approval protocols. Variations in measuring agency performance and results depend, our study shows, on the way the agency implements its policies and on the policy instrument or management tools it uses. Table 1.1 identifies and briefly describes the responsibilities of the third parties that carry out work for the agencies we evaluated for this book.

Agency selection was based on a diversity of approaches to implementation, policy tools, and type of third-party participants. HRSA was chosen because it is a granting and contracting agency, its work entirely carried out by third parties. Unlike NIH, which also is primarily a granting agency to third parties, HRSA grants go primarily to the states, and the states in turn contract with third parties to provide services. HRSA is an omnibus or holding company agency, including six offices and bureaus administering dozens of direct-service programs. HRSA, therefore, can be broadly compared with other "hollowed-out" federal agencies giving grants and contracts to direct service providers.

With regard to the selection of CMS, we note here that Medicaid is especially important to this book because the states and territories are its third-party grant recipients as well as its partners. The implementation of GPRA in CMS can, therefore, be compared with HRSA. In addition, the Medicaid program requires state contributions. Because states are both financial participants and grant recipients, Medicaid is an especially good example of the implementation of GPRA in the context of American federalism. Medicare contracts go primarily to third-party insurance companies managing the health care claims of the elderly and those with disabilities, a mixed program of elderly health care support and health care cost controls.

NIH was selected because it is the primary health research arm of the federal government. It has a unique mix of policy tools, primarily grants to third-party research scholars and teams, and funding for internal research projects. Much of this research has to do with attempting to find cures for diseases. Like the approach in this book, NIH initially chose to implement GPRA using qualitative rather than quantitative performance measures. Similarities exist between the work of NIH and the work of other research and development agencies in the federal government such as the National Science Foundation (NSF); therefore, our findings should inform possible future research on performance measurement in governmental research and development programs.

IHS was selected in part because it is one of the few HHS agencies that provides direct government services. In addition, IHS is an agency designed to serve a single identified clientele. In addition to being very different from NIH and FDA, IHS's experience with performance measurement can be usefully compared with the implementation of performance measurement in other federal agencies providing direct services to specific clientele.

The fifth agency discussed in this book, FDA, was chosen because it is the primary regulatory agency in HHS. Obviously the products of FDA are very different from the products of NIH. FDA was chosen not only because it is different but because what we learn about FDA GPRA implementation can be usefully compared with performance measurement implementation in other federal regulatory agencies.

Taken together, our detailed consideration of the application of GPRA in these five agencies is indicative of how performance measurement is carried out in the federal government, both generally and specifically. Much of the logic of performance measurement turns on an agency's choice of policy instruments and third-party service providers, and these five agencies represent a wide range of instruments—contracting with subgovernments; contracting with private third parties for service provision; and grant making for research purposes, direct services, and regulation.

We are fortunate that a firsthand account of the initial department-level HHS response to the implementation of GPRA is available. Professor Beryl A. Radin served in the upper levels of HHS for several years in both full-time and part-time consulting capacities and had especially good access to the secretary of HHS at the time, Donna Shalala. In Radin's recounting, the Office of the Assistant Secretary for Planning and Evaluation was initially charged with implementing GPRA on a departmentwide basis. The approach called for a two-part plan, one for the whole department with broad agency crosscutting goals and objectives, the other agency-specific plans that fit with crosscutting departmental goals (Radin 2002, 109). The initial strategic plan was based on a bottom-up approach that recognized the diverse nature of the agencies under the HHS umbrella. As a result, the plan included "multiple layers and large numbers of goals, objectives, and strategies that were uncoordinated, duplicative and did not flow from one another. It was described as the product of a staff-level process, resulting in goals, objectives, and strategies that satisfy major program and constituent interests but fail to articulate a vision or priorities" (Radin 2002, 109).

The varied responses to the HHS plan are both instructive and interesting. It had been the long-standing experience of senior HHS officials that the appropriations and authorizing committees in Congress were mostly interested in specific programs rather than overall departmental goals. The processes of program review and budget evaluation in the Office of Management and Budget (OMB) in the executive branch were also program based. All of this tended to reflect the point that HHS is a large, highly fragmented structure with a wide range of purposes and constituents. Because of this, the initial HHS approach to GPRA was to have some overall crosscutting departmental goals but to build the GPRA response on the basis of the unique characteristics of each departmental program.

In the early reviews of HHS objectives and proposed performance measures, the department was criticized by the General Accounting Office (GAO) (now the General Accountability Office) and congressional leadership on the basis of the assumption that HHS "was managed as a centralized command and control department. Although this model was not realistic for a department of the size and scope of HHS (nor did it comport with the secretary's personal approach), there was a danger that the criticism of the GPRA submission could cause problems for the department" (Radin 2002, 110).

In response the department developed essentially two plans. One plan was a summary document that provided a more unified picture of the department, focusing on linkages between program unit goals and the HHS strategic plan. The other plan, based on extensive interactions with HHS constituent programs, was a departmentwide standard format for all program components so that there was a common "order of presentation," which left in place much of the flexibility and specificity associated with the wide variety of HHS programs (Radin 2002, 111). As our description of GPRA implementation in five HHS agencies unfolded, themes of departmental centralization and decentralization as well as certain political themes identified in Radin's description of the department's early stage responses to GPRA turned out to be especially helpful.

According to the law's text and as discussed above, the primary objectives of GPRA include increasing citizens' confidence in government, improving budget making, improving accountability, and improving the internal management of federal agencies. As with most legislative language, the connection between GPRA's requirements—goal setting, goal measurement, and performance reporting—and its stated objectives is not made explicit. Now that GPRA has been in place for a decade, it is possible to shed some light on the larger objectives of GPRA and determine how it has performed.

THE RESULTS OF GPRA

Our examination looked at the following: (1) how these five federal agencies have gone about implementing GPRA; (2) what problems and challenges theses agencies have faced with respect to data access and reliability, goal congruence, and political and policy conflicts; (3) how these agencies have worked with third-party grantees and contractors as they have implemented agency programs; (4) what the overall effect of the strict application of performance measurement regimes was on agency leadership and management; and (5) how the study of GPRA implementation advances conceptual understandings of performance measurement in government.

Because GPRA is relatively new and because the body of extant knowledge of public sector performance measurement is still relatively limited (Jennings and Haist 2002, 2004), there has simply not been enough aggregated quantitative data over enough years to sustain reliable generalizations on the basis of statistical analysis. We chose, therefore, to use a qualitative and descriptive approach to provide narratives of processes, understandings of contextual influences on programs and people, and techniques to describe unanticipated consequences (Miles and Huberman 1994; Maxwell 1996). It is the best approach to understanding subtle political power and authority issues within bureaucratic organizations (King, Koehane, and Verba 2001). Qualitative methods have a comparative advantage in the study of organizations with multiple and conflicting objectives. Qualitative approaches are valuable in the world of practice and application because findings can be expressed in terms that enable policy makers and public managers to improve organizational performance (Maxwell 1996; Miles and Huberman 1994). (The discussion guide for field interviews is appendix A. A detailed treatment of our research methodology is found in appendix E.)

Our approach to understanding the implementation of the Government Performance and Results Act of 1993 began as a relatively straightforward consideration of federal agency implementation of the GPRA requirements for the specification of agency goals and the measurement of how well goals were being met. But as our work evolved, the subject changed to the logic of strategic planning and performance measurement in the context of what is now the dominant federal government approach to policy implementation—articulated vertical networks of third parties. Put another way, our work began as a consideration of how the federal government measures how well it performs and evolved to a consideration of how well the federal government measures the performance of third parties with whom it contracts or to whom it makes grants to implement public policy.

ARTICULATED VERTICAL NETWORKS OF THIRD PARTIES

Just what is meant by the phrase "articulated vertical networks of third parties"? "Articulation" is taken to mean jointed, as in an articulated bus or the articulation of cars in a train. The quality of articulation has to do with the extent to which separate organizations or institutions in a network are coupled, fit together, linked, or combined and the nature and quality of those connections. Articulation can take many forms, including both block and categorical grants from the federal government to the states and territories or to other subgovernments, contracts let by the federal government or by subgovernments to nonprofit or for-profit third parties, the processes of regulating third parties, and the provision of funding to third parties with clients who have claims for services from those third parties. The point is that the wide variation of arrangements between the federal government and third parties and the remarkable variation in the purposes of these arrangements cannot be understood as just grants of contracts with third parties or subgovernments. The subject of federal grants and contracts is much more complex. Although contracting out and privatization have received the bulk of public attention, contracts are only one form of the devolution of federal program implementation by third parties. Formalized contracts between the federal government and third parties are all, however, various forms of articulation, almost all of them vertical. One of the purposes of this book is to describe the nature and range of these connections as they relate to governmental performance.

OVERVIEW OF THE CHAPTERS

Before describing GPRA performance measurement applications in HHS, we believe it is important to put our work in context. Chapter 2, "Setting the Stage: Third Parties, Fiscal Federalism, and Accountability," is a somewhat detailed treatment of the application of federal performance measurement in the context of policy implementation via third-party grants and contracts. Third-party government is nested in the complex arrangements of American federalism and is laden with issues of accountability. Chapter 3, "Performance Measurement as Political and Administrative Reform," places GPRA in the context of the American tradition of management reform. Chapter 4, "Performance as Grants to Third-Party Service Providers: The Health Resources and Services Administration," is a description and analysis of the application of GPRA performance and results measurement when all aspects of service delivery are exported to states, nonprofits, and private agencies. Chapter 5 is a treatment of the Centers for Medicare and Medicaid Services. In chapter 5, "Performance as the Provision of Health Financial Security," the emphasis is on GPRA applications to Medicare performance in the context of the states and territories as third-party partners. Chapter 6, "Performance as Grants to Third-Party Research Providers," is an in-depth treatment of the influence of GPRA in the National Institutes of Health with a focus on the unique challenges associated with measuring the results of pure research, particularly when research results are often long range and speculative. Chapter 7, "Measuring the Health Performance of Sovereign Tribes as Third Parties," is a study of GPRA applications in the Indian Health Service, a case emphasizing formally designated grant recipients coupled with extensive discretion in the use of funds by third-party Indian tribes. Chapter 8, "Performance as Regulation," is a study of the influence of GPRA on the work of the Food and Drug Administration, a consideration of the application of performance measures in a politically charged regulatory setting. Chapter 9, "Measuring Performance and Results in Theory and Practice," brings the findings of chapters 4 through 8 together and applies them to the theoretical and conceptual claims made in chapter 3. Finally, chapter 10, "After the Government Performance and Results Act: Performance Measurement, Performance Budgeting, and Performance Management," is a summation and a consideration of the practical implications of what we have learned and an update on the most recent performance measurement developments.

The performance measurement movement has influenced all modern governments and could fairly be described as a fundamental reform in public administration. The Government Performance and Results Act has brought the full force of the performance measurement movement to the federal government. This movement, including its strengths and weaknesses, has been the subject of relatively extensive analysis and research (Radin 2006).

But none of this research has focused on what we believe to be the most critical factor accounting for the effectiveness of performance measurement—third-party government. We insist that to understand federal performance measurement and particularly the applications of GPRA to federal programs, one must first consider whether programs are carried out by third parties. If federal programs and policies are implemented by third parties outside of direct hierarchal control, and many are, how shall the effectiveness of those programs and policies be measured? This is the question to which we now turn.

2

SETTING THE STAGE

Third Parties, Fiscal Federalism, and Accountability

hird parties are understood to be nongovernmental organizations and institutions carrying out public purposes using granted or contracted federal
funds. States and other subgovernments are also, in this context, understood to be third parties (Salamon 1989). University groups trying to find cures
for diseases are third parties, as are pharmaceutical companies seeking new drug
approval, as are health maintenance organizations, and so forth. First parties are
elected officials and appointed and upper civil service policy makers; second parties are direct governmental agencies that implement that policy—the bureaucracy. Public activities that involve only first and second parties are now generally
referred to as direct government. At the local level, police and fire departments or
school districts would be illustrative of direct government. At the federal level the
Postal Service and the Federal Bureau of Investigation are illustrative of direct government. Third parties are profit-making or nonprofit organizations that indirectly implement public policy through grants or contracts, states and other
subgovernments that implement federal government programs by way of grants
or mandates, or organizations that are regulated by the federal government (Kettl
1988).

Networks are understood to be the extant complexes of articulated grantees,
grantors, contractors, and contractees. These networks are vertical in the form of
modern fiscal federalism, which is to say, the utilization of top-down federal grants
or contracts to subgovernments or nongovernmental organizations and the extended chain of subsequent subcontracts and grants. In the general public administration literature one finds many definitions for networks. One accepted
definition refers to "structures of interdependence involving multiple organizations, or parts thereof, where one unit is not merely the formal subordinate of others in a larger superior-subordinate arrangement" (O'Toole 2000, 22). When
applied to the study of health agencies, then, networks are continuing structural
arrangements that are tied together, based on the cases described in chapters 4
through 8, by grants, contracts, regulatory requirements, and, now, measures and
standards of performance. Following the general network literature, we can say

11

networks are structures in which managers find themselves and which require management. These days such management has greatly to do with third parties who carry out government-funded programs. "Those tasked with public management must often seek to operate on structurally uncertain terrain, firmament that can include ties with patterns of not-for-profits and profit-seeking entities as well as multiple formally governmental institutions" (O'Toole 2000, 23). It is now generally understood that modern networked third-party government requires a new kind of management, a management less associated with institutional organization and management (hierarchy) and more concerned with interjurisdictional and interinstitutional management (Agranoff and McGuire 2001, 2003).

Addressing directly the issue of grants in networked structures, a central issue in fiscal federalism, O'Toole and Meier describe a particular form of networks as

> relatively stable arrays of interdependent organizational actors characteristic of the intergovernmental system, where grant programs continue over multiyear periods, units develop elaborate formal understandings with each other, and the networked sets of institutional actors approximate a structurally identifiable cluster. [Note the use of images such as "picket fence federalism" to describe U.S. vertical linkages between or among donor and recipient agencies that jointly administer public programs, see Wright 1988.] . . . We refer to this feature as the *structural network*. . . . In addition, managers may be active in their networked environment in efforts to build support for programs, attract partners for cooperative efforts, and fend off challenges from other actors. Some of these efforts may in fact take place in concert with others involved in a structural network; some may involve other dyads and other network actors—sporadically or regularly. We refer to the set of these moves, which are in principle observable, as the *behavioral network* and the efforts of managers to be active in this way as *managerial networking*. (O'Toole and Meier 2004, 474)

For the agencies covered here, these structural arrangements are almost all vertical; they include such a wide variety of "tools," such as grants, contracts, and regulatory regimes, as to call for the description of management of these structural networks as articulations. In such articulations the network structures are relatively stable, for example, the patterns of grants to the states and territories. But the nature of management in these structures involves the administration or coordination of highly dynamic, iterative patterns of mutual adjustment between parties in vertical network structures. In this context, the formal hierarchies of many federal agencies are relatively small because so much of the work of those agencies is now carried out through grants and contracts. Therefore, it is not that grants and contracts have replaced hierarchy, because "increasing evidence suggests a shift in the structural context within which many public managers operate. It is not so much that networks have *replaced* hierarchies but more that standard hierarchical arrays, or part of them, have often been enmeshed in lattices of complex networks arrangements" (O'Toole 2000, 26; see also Agranoff and McGuire 2001).

Federal management in such settings, particularly in the context of GPRA expectations, can be especially challenging. As the material presented in the following chapters shows, and the generalized network literature predicted, "network settings provide more opportunities for free riding as well as freewheeling, fewer reliable reporting mechanisms for political overseers, and less overall clarity regarding expectations" (O'Toole 2000, 28).

Each federal program reviewed here (each of the five agencies considered administers several different programs) has unique and distinctly articulated vertical networks of third parties. And each program has approached differently the definition of its goals and the construction of measures to determine its performance in terms of those goals. This consideration of the application of GPRA to agencies with extended vertical networks of third parties is designed to determine the *results* of hollowed-out agencies and networked third-party policy implementation.

MEASURING PERFORMANCE IN THE CONTEXT OF ARTICULATED VERTICAL NETWORKS OF THIRD PARTIES

We began our consideration of performance measurement and GPRA generally informed by the public policy and public management literature on the subject. As evidence accumulated, a new set of conceptual categories emerged that account for or explain the evidence. The results described here are the consequences of an ongoing dialogue between field-based evidence on the implementation of GPRA requirements in the agencies selected for study, on one hand, and the processes of analysis and generalization, on the other. Both the explanation of findings and the development of explanations for those findings are the result of the iterative and accumulative processes of field research. On the basis of this dialogue there emerged an explanation of GPRA and its implementation described as federal government strategic goals and the measurement of agency performance in pursuit of those goals through articulated vertical networks of third parties.

In the course of our work it became increasingly evident that theories of public sector performance measurement were insufficient to an understanding of GPRA. As the unfolding of GPRA applications at the five selected agencies proceeded, the characteristics of agency goals and the measures used to determine levels of goal achievement turned out to be in part explainable by the logic of performance measurement. But most of the performance measurement literature addressed only tangentially this critically important fact—much of what the federal government does is not done directly but rather either by the states and territories as grant recipients or by federally funded grant recipients and contractors. Together, grant recipients, including states, cities and territories, and contractors are described as "third parties." Therefore, the subject of third-party government is as central to understanding GPRA as is the subject of GPRA itself—performance measurement. Because third-party arrangements for policy implementation in the federal government are broadly understood to be a part of our scheme of fiscal federalism, it became increasingly clear to us that the fiscal federalism literature is also central to explaining GPRA applications in the agencies chosen for review.

Because many parts of the national government are primarily in the business of contract and grant administration rather than direct service provision, there are important questions of accountability. Although it is clear for whom federal civil servants work and to whom they are accountable, it is often less clear for whom employees of universities and nonprofit or for-profit organizations work when they are engaged with federal grants or contracts in the implementation of federal government programs. In the world of contract and grant administration, issues of accountability are especially critical (Romzek and Dubnick 1987). The consideration of GPRA is, therefore, at the intersection of three phenomena—public sector performance measurement, third-party government, and fiscal federalism—and is informed by the literature on these three phenomena.

Considerations of government performance and results as articulated vertical networks of third parties start with the context of public sector applications of performance measurement generally. This is followed by a series of categories that frame the subject and account for or explain the findings that follow.

PERFORMANCE MEASUREMENT

Much of the extensive literature on performance measurement takes the form of presenting the principles of performance management or recommending procedures and approaches to measuring performances (Hatry 1999; Broome 1995; Newcomer and Wright 1997; Newcomer and Downey 1998). Some of this literature is the presentation of best practices, or case studies of performance measurement (U.S. General Accounting Office 1998; Governmental Accounting Standards Board 2000). Another perspective in this literature describes the challenges of devising valid, reliable, or useful measures of performance or considerations of factors that affect the use of performance measurement (Poister and Streib 1999). A much smaller part of performance measurement literature is based on systematic research or detailed field studies of the actual application of performance measurement to governmental programs.

The dominant literature on public sector performance measurement has a distinct normative or advocacy tone to it and tends to be accompanied by descriptions of how performance measurement can improve government (Mihm 2001; Bradley and Flowers 2001; Thomas 2001; Broadnax and Conway 2001). In this literature, good performance measurement is described as objective and neutral, the application of facts scientifically derived and applied to the determination of the effectiveness of government programs. In this literature performance measurement can answer questions about the effectiveness of public programs. Performance measurement can also help identify program overlap and duplication. Performance measurement can inform policy, serve as a guide to policy, and influence policy. In this literature there is no critical assessment of the assumption that baseline results or outcomes data are available or that such data can be efficiently and systematically gathered and processed. Public sector performance measurement can determine the results or outcomes of government programs and, it is assumed, provide evidence of causal linkages between government policies and their implementation, on one hand, and the improvement of social or economic circumstances on the other. Performance measurement facilitates comparisons of program effectiveness both with and between programs (Forsythe 2001; Kearney and Berman 1999; Berman 1998; DiIulio, Garvey, and Kettl 1993; Hatry 1999; U.S. General Accounting Office 1998; Broome 1995; Bouckaert and Peters 2002).

Other literature suggests a rather less-idealized understanding of performance measurement and its applications in government. Performance measurement data in the form of agency outputs or social outcomes may be more nearly factual, more nearly objective, and more neutral than are less systematically derived data but are, nevertheless, subject to interpretation. Performance measurement data may, in the eyes of agency officials, show that the agency is effective. Those who oppose the purposes of the agency or its program emphases may, however, interpret those same data differently. Measures that are thought to answer questions regarding how well an agency performs may be interpreted as the answers to questions by some but as questions themselves by others. What measures an agency chooses may be more a function of data availability than data reliability or salience. It is sometimes said in the world of performance measurement that the more easily measurable drives out the more important. The point is that some phenomena are very difficult to quantify in any sensible way (Radin 2000, 2006).

Performance measurement may help identify program overlap or duplication, but in some cases such overlap or duplication is a function of politics and the details of agency-enabling legislation and appropriations. It is argued that performance measurement in government reduces information asymmetry and thereby provides information that enables policymakers and agencies to refine or improve policy or its implementation. Information derived from performance measurement is, however, used not only to improve policy and its implementation but also to arm policy makers with arguments for or against policy. Actual policy changes tend to be as much a function of rhetoric, changing values, changing circumstances, and winning coalitions as they are a function of reasoned choices made on the basis of performance-based knowledge (Hood and Jackson 1991). Finally, performance measurement is thought to show causal associations between agency outputs and social outcomes. Variations in social outcomes, particularly outcomes associated with such loosely defined social characteristics as health, are extremely difficult to demonstrate convincingly to have been caused by government action independent of other forces. This is especially the case in the short run. Longer-run change can more easily be linked to the effectiveness of government programs (Light 2002; Glaser and Rothenberg 2001). Table 2.1 sets out in simplified form the differences between idealized conceptions of the promise of performance measurement (column 2) and less-idealized understandings of performance measurement (column 3).

Columns 2 and 3 in table 2.1 are simplified and stylized, but nevertheless broadly represent the primary differences between the advocacy literature and the less-idealized approach on the subject of performance measurement (Radin 2006, 2000, 1998a, 1998b; Barnow 1992; Bartik 1995; Bouckaert 1993; Heckman and Smith 1995; Heinrich 1999, 2000; Friedlander and Burtless 1995; Schick 2001;

TABLE 2.1 ▨▨▨▨▨▨▨▨▨▨▨▨▨▨▨▨▨▨▨▨▨▨▨▨▨▨▨▨▨▨▨▨▨▨▨▨▨▨

IDEALIZED AND LESS-IDEALIZED PERSPECTIVES ON PERFORMANCE MEASUREMENT

	Idealized	*Less Idealized*
Performance Measures Are:	Answers to questions	Can sharpen questions
	Facts	Interpretations, information, details
	Objective, neutral	Slanted
	Guides to policy	Policy arguments
	Long run	Short run
Performance Measures:	The important	The measurable
	Results	Surrogates of results
	Outcomes	Outputs
	Reduce information asymmetry	Reduce information asymmetry to a point
Assertions of Causality:	Demonstrable	Unclear
	Determined	Indeterminate
Policy Is Influenced by:	Performance measures	Rhetoric, changing values and circumstances
Budgets Are Based on:	Performance measures	Increments to the base, changing values and circumstances
Data Are:	Available	Unavailable
	Accurate	Inaccurate
	Consistent and reliable	Inconsistent and unreliable
	Inexpensive	Expensive

Source: This table is based in part on a table in Radin (2000, 133), and a table in Frederickson (2000).

Ingraham and Moynihan 2001; Blalock and Barnow 2001; Forsythe 2001; Smith and Bratton 2001; Marschke 2001; Bouckaert and Peters 2002).

Recurring themes in the less-idealized performance measurement literature point to significant difficulties in the application of the concept to third-party government. Several of these points are covered at greater length by Beryl Radin in *Challenging the Performance Movement: Accountability, Complexity, and Democratic Values* (2006). First is the problem of goal ambiguity and contradictory goals. The GPRA process asks each agency to bring as much precision as possible to goal definitions so as to reduce ambiguities. Agencies are also asked to devise measures for all goals, even those that are contradictory. Second, even if there is goal agreement, it is often difficult to find measures adequate to the determination of social conditions (Joyce 1993). To work around this problem, agencies often turn to output measures as proxies for social outcomes (Broome 1995; Cope 1995; McKinney 1996). Third, performance measurement as prescribed in GPRA can be understood as attempts to superimpose managerial processes and managerial logic on an inherently political process, a process based on the separation of powers (Wildavsky 1979). Fourth, many of the studies cited above highlight the difficulties of measuring performance in instances of direct public service provision. Indeed, the most frequently used source to assist practitioners in performance measurement and evaluation makes little mention of the complexities introduced by third-party providers or the measuring of the performance of regulatory agencies (Wholey, Hatry, and Newcomer 1994). Fifth, the text of GPRA legislation makes little reference to the diversity of challenges federal agencies face as they attempt to implement its requirements (Radin 2000).

According to public program evaluation experts, certain minimal criteria must be met for successful and useful performance measurement to take place. The feasibility and usefulness of a program evaluation can be determined through an evaluability assessment (Wholey, Hatry, and Newcomer 1994). The evaluability assessment determines whether an agency meets the following minimal criteria: well-defined program goals and objectives, plausible program goals and objectives, consideration of important side effects and priority information, availability of relevant performance data, and agreement as to how performance measures will be used (Wholey and Newcomer 1989).

Each of these recurring themes is found in the detailed treatment of GPRA implementation in the chapters that follow. In several cases, the so-called problems associated with the effectiveness of performance measurement proved to be illusory and exaggerated in particular agencies. In other cases the problems described in the less-idealized literature here were found to have seriously diminished the effectiveness of the application of performance measurement. But none of the problems described in these themes turned out to be as important as the more obvious point that most federal government programs are now carried out by third parties. The most compelling evidence regarding this point was found at the intersection of the logic of the application of performance measurement and the logic of third-party government.

The more general scholarship on the subject of contracting out and the unique American word for contracting—privatization—is useful here because it has to do directly with third-party government and with the matter of accountability. This literature falls into three general categories: the advocacy approach represented by Emanuel S. Savas (1987) and David Osborne and Ted Gaebler (1992); the so-called smart-buyer approach in standard public administration scholarship represented by Donald F. Kettl (1993) and Lester M. Salamon (1989); and the critique of privatization represented by Elliott D. Sclar (2000) and Joel Handler (1996). Although this scholarship does not deal directly with GPRA, it is especially relevant because GPRA has much to do with third-party government and because so many of the agencies of the federal government are essentially overseeing third parties.

The advocacy literature has a strongly held faith in the logic of market competition as applied to certain parts of the public sector and an equal faith in the capacity of performance measurement or program evaluation to improve the functioning of government (Forsythe 2001). In the advocacy literature, accountability is understood to mean holding third parties accountable for their conduct of the public's business. Good public management is thought to be "steering rather than rowing," "mission-driven rather than role-driven," and "markets rather than organizations" (Osborne and Gaebler 1992, 25–40).

Accountability in the smart-buyer perspective on third-party government is an experienced-based and empirically based expression of concern that, as a general rule, governments are not smart buyers of contracted services (Kettl 1993). This is especially the case as government contracting has moved away from the long-standing purchase of capital facilities, military equipment, and other physical assets toward the purchase of social services of a variety of types and a wide array of administrative, or so-called back-office, services. Government has relied on contractors not only to provide it with goods and services but also to tell it what it ought to buy, to evaluate what it has purchased, and to manage many of the steps in between, including writing testimony for government officials to present to Congress to explain the transactions. If the government is not a smart buyer, the critical responsibility for the performance of public programs passes to its contractors, which led one scholar to observe that "government cannot be sovereign if it cannot buy smart" (Kettl 1993, 204). This is especially a problem because as the government has moved increasingly toward third-party policy implementation, it has, at the same time, downsized and disinvested in its own capacity to manage third-party contracts. Third-party government—especially in the context of extended articulated vertical networks of third parties—can change the relationship between government program managers and program output. "Instead of dealing directly with the recipients of government goods and services, program managers deal with the contractors who deliver the goods and services. . . . Instead of using their substantive knowledge of the policy area, government employees find themselves dealing with the procedural features of contract monitoring and compliance" (Kettl 1993, 206).

Public administrators now have the same problem because they oversee extended chains of grants and contracts with little real leverage over contractor behavior. In addition, there are now more layers between elected officials, appointed officials, civil servants, and the public. Citizens deal increasingly with nonprofit organizations or even for-profit organizations, all spending taxpayer money, rather than governmental representatives who are directly accountable. When things go wrong, "the tendency is to see the problems that do emerge as instances of mismanagement or program abuse instead of as a generic thread that winds its way through contracting relationships" (Kettl 1993, 205).

All the elements of the smart-buyer accountability perspective are included in the critique of third-party government, but that critique goes much further. Sclar (2000) and Handler (1996) both point out several concerns with the increasing emphasis on contracting for government services. First, they claim there is little compelling or consistent evidence that contracting saves money. Second, they are concerned about the development of the functional equivalent of the military-industrial complex, as in the mental health–mental health service provider complex or the job training–job training provider complex. Nonprofit and for-profit service providers are often very effective interest groups, influential in political decisions that result in the extended funding of the services they provide as contractors or grant recipients.

Third, because of downsizing, the federal government has a sharply diminished institutional memory and a generally depleted capacity to manage contracts effectively. Fourth, there is little evidence of genuine marketlike competition among possible service providers. Service providers in a given specialization and a given geographic area tend toward either monopoly or oligopoly.

Fifth, contracting for services, as against contracting for goods or capital, occurs with a rather high degree of uncertainty regarding both the nature of the product and the consequences of the product. This is the causal assertion problem put in another language. In extended vertical articulations of third parties, all third parties act with bounded rationality and will pursue combinations of self-interest or organizational survival.

Sixth, it is illogical to assume, these critics claim, that the motives, interests, and values of contractors match the motives, interests, and values of governments contracting for services. And, finally, although privatization is argued as an improved approach to bureaucratic accountability, in third-party government who is accountable? "There is no competitive remote-control technique to make the challenges of good public management magically disappear. A self-enforcing and competitively renewable contract to perform work for the public sector is similar to the perfectly competitive market: an ideal. The reality of public work is that much of it is complex to perform, complex to administer, and complex to evaluate" (Sclar 2000, 156). In an extensive study of contracted blue-collar services "thought to be easiest to privatize because they are easiest to visually inspect," Sclar concludes that "problems of accountability and control persist. These findings do not augur well for calls to privatize larger, more complex, and less easily evaluated services such as public safety, education, corrections, health, human services, and welfare, although these services comprise the bulk of the public budget" (2000, 157).

Easily the most comprehensive synthesis of studies of applications of performance management in government is found in Edward T. Jennings, Jr., and Meg Patrick Haist's paper titled "Does Performance Measurement Perform?" (2002). They group eighteen studies according to (1) research that analyzes aspects and dimensions of measurement; (2) survey or descriptive studies that report on the use of performance measurement with little or no attention given to impact; and (3) quantitative research that examines the impact or effectiveness of performance measurement. On the basis of their review of the extant literature on performance measurement in government, Jennings and Haist develop a series of hypotheses suggested by their synthesis. Because of the limited number of studies and the variation in research approaches, their hypotheses are tentative, suggestive, and rather general. Some of their hypotheses match and confirm the primary themes found in the more-idealized literature, but many more suggest that the less-idealized literature is more reliable empirically.

On the matter of the possible impact or effectiveness of performance measurement, Jennings and Haist hypothesize that performance measures have greater impact when (1) principals give them attention, (2) principals have the resources to shape behavior, (3) principals use resources to pursue performance goals, (4) service providers and managers care about the success of their organization, (5) service providers and managers believe that performance measures are accurate reflections of organizational performance, (6) managers believe that organizational performance and measures of performance affect their own prestige and careers, (7) performance measures are consistent with professional norms, and (8) agency or organization resources are dependent on measured performance (2002, 7–8). In the presentation of our findings, certain of these hypotheses will be referred to in terms of the extent to which they appear to explain the implementation of GPRA in the agencies studied.

The Jennings and Haist review confirms the standard hypothesis that performance measurement, like almost all other aspects of effective administration, is positively correlated with the level of goal agreement among principals. Their review also supports the argument that effective performance measurement reduces information asymmetry and enhances the mechanisms of control over both policy and policy implementation available to principals.

In their review, Jennings and Haist consider the matter of the "right tool for the job" (2002, 17). The "tool for the job," in their perspective, refers to how an organization or agency measures performance. Do agencies, for example, use prescriptive measures or targets, such as expecting school districts to achieve certain levels of average student test scores? Is performance defined and measured as agency processes, agency activities, agency outputs, or social outcomes? Is performance measurement based on external measures such as independent ranking and grading systems (Gormley and Weimer 1999)? The most recent application of federal performance "measurement" is the Program Assessment Rating Tool (PART), a rating-based performance measurement instrument. (Chapter 3 includes a more fully developed description of PART.) All these approaches to measures of performance are found in the application of GPRA to the functioning of the five agencies selected for consideration.

Most remarkable in the Jennings and Haist summary of performance measurement research is the absence of a consideration of one of the primary means by which the federal government carries out its programs—third parties. Implicit in the Jennings-Haist review is an assumption of two-party, direct government and the application of performance measurement in the context of direct government. There is an implicit assumption of direct government in the GPRA legislation itself, there being no mention of third parties. Nevertheless, many of the Jennings-Haist hypotheses are, as will be shown, relevant to the application of GPRA even in the absence of specific references to third-party government. Our findings describe how agencies have adapted the implicit direct government logic of GPRA to the third-party contexts in which they operate.

THIRD-PARTY GOVERNMENT

Over the last twenty years, research on the challenges introduced by the rapid increase in the use of third parties in the delivery of public services has been a major focus of public management scholarship. The addition of third parties adds layers of complexity to policy implementation. The terms *hollow state, government by proxy,* and *shadow bureaucracy* are all used to connote a separation between the financing of government services and the provision of services. Research indicates that the skills required to manage in multiorganizational network settings are different from those required to manage in direct service provision environments (Agranoff and McGuire 1998). These networked service provision arrangements fragment power, obscure who is doing what, and sever the lines of control (Salamon 1989).

To describe third-party government, Lester Salamon uses the metaphor of government by remote control (1989). Although there is nothing new about this phenomenon—governments have contracted out their services for decades—there has been an increasing reliance on third parties to exercise administrative discretion in matters such as setting goals, financing, determining eligibility requirements, and developing and implementing accountability structures. Using the policy tools metaphor, Haider states that "federal grants are the oldest, most widely used and probably the best understood tool that the federal government has available to carry out public policy" (1989, 93).

The advantages of third-party government include flexibility, competition, and avoidance of one-size-fits-all solutions. Nevertheless, with these advantages come accountability and management challenges. A central problem of third-party government, therefore, is how to achieve its advantages without accountability deficits. Some argue that the federal government's heavy reliance on third parties allows it to mask its true size (Light 1999). To the extent that government's size is measured by the number of its employees, third-party service delivery is a way to move toward smaller agencies. A comparison of the size of the Social Security Administration (SSA) and CMS (Medicare and Medicaid), the two largest (in budgetary terms) federal health and welfare agencies, is instructive. SSA, which directly provides services, has approximately sixty-three thousand employees. CMS, which provides its services primarily through third parties, has approximately forty-six hundred employees. One should not assume, however, that the bureaucratic apparatus supporting the Medicare and Medicaid programs is significantly smaller than the bureaucratic apparatus supporting Social Security. The critical difference is not the size of the bureaucracy but the fact that CMS has externalized much of its bureaucracy to insurance companies (Medicare) and states (Medicaid), and SSA has not externalized its bureaucracy. The treatment of GPRA applications in the five agencies chosen for evaluation here indicates that the contention that contracting out masks the true size of government is primarily correct.

The necessity to coordinate with third parties to implement GPRA is not limited to intergovernmental programs such as Medicaid. Virtually all federal programs work with third parties to carry out their policy objectives. The universe of third parties includes but is not limited to states and territories, cities and counties, contractors, regulated industries, and public and private sector grant recipients. Although GPRA's requirements are uniform for all federal agencies, agencies' roles in the production and delivery of public services are highly varied (Long and

Franklin 2004). A significant portion of the work of most agencies entails the management and oversight of third-party activities. Two important aspects of GPRA implementation challenges are that, first, different third parties have various kinds and levels of responsibilities in the delivery of public services and that, second, different third parties have differing levels of autonomy. Although these differences are critical to implementing GPRA, they have gone virtually unnoticed in the extensive discussion surrounding GPRA. The application of the PART modification of GPRA by the Bush administration is the first recognition of the importance of third parties in performance measurement; it is described in greater detail in chapter 3 and in the substantive descriptions of our findings in chapters 4 through 8.

THE STATES AND TERRITORIES AS THIRD PARTIES

Research on implementing performance measurement systems in an intergovernmental administrative environment is scant but growing. The reality of increasingly devolved federal programs to state and local governments, the rapid increase in contracting out, and the passage of GPRA all suggest that such research should take on a tone of urgency. The key to effectiveness in such extensive third-party regimes is the quality of vertical articulations between networked third-party organizations (Cooper 2003).

For the past thirty-five years Martha Derthick has been one of the most thoughtful observers of federal grants to subgovernments and the challenges of accountability in such articulated vertical arrangements. Unlike contracts, grants to states and territories have a long history and a set of deeply rooted expectations on the part of both federal government leaders and state and local leaders. Several key generalizations about fiscal federalism are relevant to an understanding of performance measurement in the context of third-party government. The probability that a block grant to a state or territory will be withheld is slim; therefore, federal–state grant relations are deeply structured and require a rather special approach to their management. On one hand, the money is federal, and, as GPRA indicates, the goals are also federal. The states and territories, on the other hand, are in the position of wanting or needing the resources, recognizing that with those resources come the dreaded mandates—federal rules, regulations, and expectations. Derthick describes management in such networked structures as a diplomatic process carried out in much the same way as nation-states manage treaties.

> In these negotiations, numerous diplomatic forms and manners are observed, especially by the federal negotiators. . . . Negotiations are carried out privately. The federal negotiators refrain from making statements in public, for they want to avoid the appearance of meddling in the internal affairs of the states. They refrain from making overt threats. They are patient. Negotiations over a single issue may go on for several years and intermittently for decades. They are polite. In addressing state officials they

are usually elaborately courteous. They make small gestures of deference to the host government, as by offering to meet at times and at places of its choosing.

The objective of the negotiating process is to obtain as much conformance as can be had without the actual withholding of funds. Because federal requirements are typically stated in general terms, administrators have a high degree of flexibility in negotiating terms of conformance. Within the broad guidelines they have laid down, they have been able to adapt to the political and administrative circumstances of each state. . . . That this is done is important primarily to the federal government, for it is the aggressive, the states the defensive, actor in intergovernmental relations. It has the greater interest in seeing that change is facilitated. But perhaps the principal advantage of a diplomatic style to federal administrators (and the choice of that style is essentially their choice) is that this mode of behavior makes the best possible use of the technique of withholding funds. It enables federal officials to exploit, without actually using, this basic resource. (Derthick, in O'Toole 2000, 182–83)

GPRA reporting requirements are now built into federal grants. Our fieldwork indicates that the process of seeking state and territorial compliance to grant requirements and federal goals is not unlike the Derthick description of other forms of the management of federated, vertical networked arrangements.

Many federal programs are implemented via grants to the states and territories, which in turn give grants and contracts to local service providers at the end of vertical networks. In Donald Kettl's view, the quality of articulation between states and territories and their third-party providers is poor because states and territories tend not to know what results their contracts are buying, because competition between third-party providers is low, and because contracts tend to degenerate into what are effectively monopolies of nonprofit or for-profit vendors (1993). Before the passage of GPRA and its implementation, Kettl concluded that "state and local governments are engaged in the equivalent of a shopping trip while blindfolded, with little effort spent to squeeze the tomatoes or thump the watermelons" (1993, 175). This suggests that the salience of federal goals *attenuates the further that federal programs are implemented down* extended vertical articulations of third-party service providers.

Although GPRA performance measures might inform federal agencies regarding goal attenuation down extended vertical networked third-party articulations, performance measures do not deal with the matter of how the federal government can cause states and territories and their contractors to implement federal goals more fully in the absence of direct control. This is the problem described by Salamon as government by remote control. Cooper makes reference to federal policy makers who assumed that grants and contracts will somehow carry themselves out (Salamon 1989; Cooper 2003).

When more authority is given to third parties, it is accompanied by more complexity in the development of performance goals and measures. One example of this is the discrepancy between the number of goals for Medicaid and the numbᴴ of goals for Medicare found in CMS's GPRA performance plan. Both programs are operated through third parties—the states and territories in the case of Medicaid, and carriers and financial intermediaries in the case of Medicare. Of CMS's performance plan goals specifically related to program performance, only three are intended to assess Medicaid program performance alone, whereas twenty of these goals are intended to assess Medicare performance. This discrepancy is tied to the challenges associated with the vast differences among states' Medicaid services and the immense coordination and negotiation that would be required to establish even a rudimentary set of uniform Medicaid goals. Indeed, one of CMS's FY 1999 developmental performance plan goals was to work with states to develop Medicaid performance goals for inclusion in subsequent budget requests. The assumption that ties these budgetary reforms to each other is that if the federal budget were more logical and analytic, then the federal bureaucracy would in turn become more logical and analytic. Both reforms are based on the assumptions of management rationality. But budget making, as the research indicates, is almost always based on the assumption of political rather than managerial rationality (Wildavsky 1979; Schick 2001).

GPRA IMPLEMENTATION, FISCAL FEDERALISM, AND FISCAL INTERGOVERNMENTAL RELATIONS

On its face, GPRA does not appear to be primarily about federalism. In fact, in the five agencies studied here, GPRA has everything to do with federalism. At its core, federalism is the elaborate structures by which governmental powers and responsibilities are shared among the federal, state, and local levels of government and the processes by which policies are implemented through these structures (Wright 1988; Walker 1995; O'Toole 2000; Conlan 1988, 1998; Joyce 1993; Kelly 2002). In one form or another, each of the five agencies studied here functions through these structures, and each is profoundly shaped by them. Although this point would be regarded as obvious to any serious student of American government, a careful reading of GPRA indicates that the requirement to measure the performance of federal agencies does not assume that federal programs are actually carried out through articulated vertical networks of third parties. Instead, the language of GPRA either assumes direct hierarchical government or assumes that the implementation of federal policy by states, local governments, territories, and Indian tribes does not materially influence federal goal setting and performance measurement. Federal agency leaders charged with implementing GPRA have found it necessary, therefore, to somehow reconcile the logic of direct government with the actual third-party arrangements and practices of federalism. The PART use of the term "partnership" to describe federal agency–third party arrangements is helpful, as is the creation of a separate GPRA category for programs implemented.

Central to the study of classic fiscal federalism in economics is the matter of sorting out the forces of centralization and decentralization in federal structures (Oates 1972). On one hand, centralization facilitates the stability needed to manage monetary policy and the capacity to gather resources centrally and redistribute them locally as well as to allocate resources to pursue centralized purposes efficiently. On the other hand, decentralization increases the probability that states, territories, and localities will efficiently respond to their varying preferences and needs. In addition, it is thought that decentralization fosters a closer connection between taxation and spending policies, assuming that at the state and local level there will be more obvious linkage between taxation policy and program spending. Finally, it is also thought that decentralization encourages experimentation and innovation. In the American context, federalism, it is argued, is a designed dynamic of constantly shifting forces of centralization and decentralization. It is through federalism that we seek the advantages of both centralization and decentralization, and it is through fiscal federalism that we sort out the financial arrangements of centralization and decentralization.

The consideration of intergovernmental grants has long been a part of the study of fiscal federalism (Oates 1972). The justification for grants, in both political and economic terms, has to do with the search for equity, such as providing funds to attempt to achieve a minimum level of health support to areas particularly in need or with insufficient resources. It is also generally understood in the study of fiscal federalism that grants to subgovernments, and particularly block grants, have some important externalities, most particularly high transaction costs and the probability of free riding. In fiscal federalism it is assumed that these two problems are made more serious as the number of decision-making units increases. Wallace E. Oates puts it this way:

> Where the externality involves only a few decision-making units, particularly if they are in close proximity, the difficulties or costs of reaching a satisfactory agreement *may* be relatively small; also, each decision-maker is likely to realize that his behavior may have a significant impact on the actions of others and hence on the aggregate level of the activity. For these reasons the small group case offers promise of joint action to reduce the distortions in resource allocation resulting from external effects. . . . In contrast, where the externality involves large numbers of decision-making units, the difficulties of effective coordinated actions are likely to be much greater. In particular, there is good reason to expect widespread free-rider behavior. Since the decision-maker is only one of many, he can anticipate that his own behavior will have only a negligible effect on the aggregate level of the activity. Consequently, each individual has an incentive to ignore the external effects of his own choices and, where possible, to reduce his provision of the good (or the funds) in favor of consuming units of output provided by others. (1972, 68–69)

The problems of high transaction costs and free riding are especially relevant points because the provision of federal government grant and contract funds through articulated vertical networks of third parties ordinarily involves several layers of decision makers. In modern fiscal federalism, and particularly in the case of the application of performance measurement, the problems of achieving the efficient provision of *federal government* purposes are very likely made greater by extended networks of third-party providers. The attenuation of federal purposes at the further reaches of vertical networks seems a safe prediction, as does the likelihood that states as well as their contractors will practice the substitution of federal funds for locally raised funds to support programs that the states or their subdivisions would have otherwise been obliged to support from their own resources.

Although the fiscal federalism literature in economics is generally informative, and illustrations of its importance are found in agency applications of performance measurement, it is clear that the contemporary study of fiscal federalism does not sufficiently recognize the extent to which federal and state government functions are now primarily carried out by third parties. The extensive public administration literature on contracting out, particularly contracting with nonprofit third parties by state governments for federal government purposes, has evidently not informed the study of fiscal federalism (see especially Romzek and Johnston 2005). This is a good example of how reality can get ahead of theory.

In recent years a somewhat different and particularly promising approach to the subject has developed in political science and public administration under the banner of intergovernmental relations. Research and theory testing using the traditional fiscal federalism perspective is limited because it has tended to be focused on vertical or hierarchical national-state relations, tending to ignore lateral relations between states and relations between states and their subgovernments (Wright 1988). Fiscal federalism in economics has, with some important exceptions, focused on jurisdictional efficiencies, on externalities, and on equity. Little attention has been given to policy, and very little attention has been given to what is described by economists as cooperative federalism or democratic federalism. For example, Inman and Rubenfeld's analysis of the Welfare Reform Act of 1996 suggests that classic fiscal federalism was unable to account for how federalism based on economics was redefined by the Welfare Reform Act (1997). Concepts of cooperative federalism, particularly the concept that federalism is an iterative pattern of negotiated adjustments between governments, were far better able to account for or explain the implementation of the Welfare Reform Act (Inman and Rubenfeld 1997, 58).

Primary concepts in intergovernmental relations theory include models that accommodate local governments in federal–state relations (Wright 2000); models that approach federalism from the perspective of network theory (O'Toole 2000); and theories of intergovernmental transfer of funds (Walker 1995). All three are relevant to third-party government and to the contemporary emphasis on performance measurement. Walker uses two especially helpful continua that account for financial intergovernmental relations, continua that bear some similarities to the primary factors used in this study. The intergovernmental transfer of funds to the states and their subgovernments can be understood as ranging from (1) allocation on the basis of federal-level formulas with defined eligibility requirements to discretionary allocations with broad eligibility; and (2) narrow to broad programmatic discretion given grant recipients (Walker 1995, 235). All federal programs that use states and localities as their third-party policy implementation agents can be described in terms of where they are located along these two continua. Obviously, the performance of federal programs carried out by states, state subgovernments, territories, and Indian tribes is in part determined by the range of discretion allowed by federal principals in grant making and made available to grant recipients, the agents carrying out federal purposes.

The intergovernmental relations perspective on federalism is also useful in terms of the increasing use of concepts of governance to describe the changing arrangements between jurisdictions, including changing financial arrangements. Concepts of governance are useful to understanding the simultaneous processes of supranationalization, such as the European Union or the North American Treaty Organization; nongovernmental organizations acting governmentally, such as the International Monetary Fund; national centralization, such as the No Child Left Behind Act of 2001; and decentralization, such as the Welfare Reform Act of 1996 or proposed changes in Medicaid (Shaw 2003; Hirst 2000; Hooghe and Marks 2003).

GPRA IMPLEMENTATION AS ACCOUNTABILITY

The purposes and processes established by the Government Performance and Results Act are often described as a modern form of government accountability. "Accountability" is part of the modern language of public administration, albeit a rather imprecise part of the language and a word without an agreed-on meaning. It is, nevertheless, a particularly evocative and powerful word in the language of government. For their evaluation of the *Challenger* accident, Barbara S. Romzek and Melvin J. Dubnick developed a broad and thoughtful description of governmental accountability (1987). In it they point out that administrative actors, even in the context of third parties, are at the center of multiple accountability expectations and relationships. These expectations and relationships are grouped into legal, political, professional, and bureaucratic accountabilities. An agency or individual ordinarily operates under one or perhaps two accountability relationships, but in a time of crisis all four types of accountability expectations can be in play. Beryl A. Radin describes the role of the secretary of Health and Human Services as an "accountable juggler" who must shift back and forth between three different types of expectations—policy, political, and processes. "These three areas define the world of the cabinet secretary in the twenty-first century. They create pressure and demands that push and pull an individual in multiple directions" (Radin 2002, 23). In addition, Radin, like Paul Light, emphasizes the importance of the layering of accountability requirements, each new reform adding another layer of expectations and accountabilities to the job of the federal administrator (Light 1995). GPRA is now one of those layers, and it is an especially important one because of its statutory origins.

In their evaluation of GPRA for a Congressional Research Service report to Congress, Frederick M. Kaiser and Virginia A. McMurtry state that GPRA is meant to "encourage greater efficiency, effectiveness and accountability in federal spending by establishing a new framework for management, and subsequently budgeting in the federal agencies" (U.S. Congressional Research Service 1997, 1). In their consideration of GPRA in the political context of administrative reforms, Joel D. Aberbach and Bert A. Rockman hit on the central accountability issue—third-party government (2000). The federal government, they point out, "often has a quite limited or indirect influence in determining whether a desired goal is achieved" (152). Quoting an early General Accounting Office review of GPRA, Aberbach and Rockman made this point: "GAO work has shown that measuring the federal contribution is particularly challenging for regulatory programs [the Food and Drug Administration, for example], scientific research programs [the National Institutes of Health, for example], and programs to deliver services to taxpayers through third parties, such as state and local government [such as the Health Resources and Services Administration and the Medicaid program]" (152). GAO reservations regarding GPRA accountability are telling because the examples they use as places in the federal government that will find it difficult to measure performance are among the agencies covered in this research.

Beryl A. Radin, in her careful analysis of GPRA, raised these points:

> During the past decade, increasing attention has been paid to the devolution of responsibilities for the implementation of programs that are partially or mainly funded with federal dollars. Fewer and fewer federal domestic programs are entirely implemented by federal staff. Instead, responsibility for making allocation decisions and actually delivering services has been delegated to state and local governments or to other third parties (often nonprofit organizations).
>
> GPRA moves against these tides. Efforts to hold federal government agencies accountable for the way that programs are implemented actually assumes that these agencies have legitimate authority to enforce the requirements that are included in performance measures. . . . Third party perspectives, thus, create a major problem in the GPRA context of determining which party defines the outcomes expected. (2000, 124)

SYNTHESIS

This synthesis of the literature is guided by the theoretical explanation of GPRA and its implementation—as described early in this chapter—as "federal government strategic goals and the measurement of agency performance in pursuit of those goals through articulated vertical networks of third parties." In the same way that this theoretical explanation emerged during the course of our fieldwork, the selection of the relevant literature just reviewed changed while our work was under way. Over time the salience of the literature on third parties, fiscal federalism, and accountability became increasingly evident.

From the literature, from information based on fieldwork, and from the interaction of concepts in the literature and knowledge from ongoing fieldwork, we developed continua that account for the basic theoretical explanations for GPRA and its application in the five federal health agencies studied. Each continuum is, in the general language of social science, a variable, representing data or information in an order from lesser to greater. Each of these continua generalizes, and in most cases comprehends, key points in two or more of the four bodies of literature reviewed above. These continua or variables are used in chapters 4 through 8 to locate each of the five agencies studied at some point along each continuum. By this technique it is possible to compare the five agencies in terms of their locations along each continuum. For example, variable G is a continuum describing the characteristics and precision of agency performance measures from low to high, low being understood to represent imprecise, descriptive, or qualitative measures, high being understood to represent precise quantitative measures. In the early years of GPRA, NIH was found to be near the low end of this continuum, whereas HRSA was found to be near the high end. In this way each continuum or variable serves as a comparative heuristic, or as an aid to learning discovery or problem solving. In chapter 9 two variable-four cell contingency tables are used as simplified multivariate heuristics.

The placement of agencies along continua, as well as the arrangement of agencies in contingency tables, was a qualitative process based on the detailed study of GPRA implementation in each agency. Although this interpretive and judgmental process could be subject to possible criticism on the basis of a lack of quantitative rigor, it served to describe GPRA applications empirically and, more important, lent itself to explanations of those applications and their implications. Further details on our approach to field research are found in appendix E.

In all, there are nine continua or variables, which are summarized in figure 2.1. A description of each of these continua follows here.

The Level of Third-Party Policy Implementation (Continuum A)

The level of third-party policy implementation ranges from direct government provision to one or more forms of hollowed-out government. The definition is simple—the approximate ratio of an agency's total budget that supports human resources in third parties to the size of its directly employed civil service staff. The smaller the ratio in a given agency, the more it is hollowed out. The previous example compared the Social Security Administration's sixty-three thousand federal employees (direct government provision) to the Centers for Medicare and Medicaid Services' forty-six hundred federal employees (hollowed out), despite CMS's much larger client pool.

The Degree of Accountability to Federal Program Purposes (Continuum B)

Accountability to federal program purposes (continuum B) is defined as the extent to which third parties are likely to adhere to agency program purposes. Points along this continuum represent the extent to which the incentives for those implementing program policies are aligned with program objectives. Agency adherence to federal program policy ranges from strict adherence on one hand to the attenuation or weakening of federal program purposes associated with third-party policy implementation on the other. One major category of third parties—the

FIGURE 2.1

KEY VARIABLES IN THE SYNTHESIS OF THE INFLUENCE OF PERFORMANCE MEASUREMENT IN FIVE FEDERAL HEALTH CARE AGENCIES

A. The Level of Third-Party Policy Implementation

hollowed out   *direct government*

B. Accountability to Federal Program Purposes

attenuated   *strict*

C. The Nature and Quality of Network Articulations

remote control   *managed network*

D. The Characteristics of Goals

processes   *outputs (POM)*   *outcomes (HOM)*

E. The Level of Goal and Policy Agreement

disagreement   *agreement*
incongruence   *congruence*

F. The Level of Centralization of Policy Implementation

decentralized   *centralized*
dispersed, fragmented

G. The Precision and Characteristics of Performance Measures

qualitative   *quantitative*
descriptive   *precise*

H. The Level and Character of Client and Stakeholder Support

weak   *divided*   *strong*

I. Professional Identity

low   *high*

POM, program outcome measure; *HOM,* health outcome measure.

states and territories—have jurisdictional purposes that may or may not match federal program purposes, as intergovernmental grants research indicates, but the broad objectives in most instances are shared. The other major group of third parties—contractors—has incentives and expectations to be profitable in the case of for-profit contractors and the need to retain contracts in the case of nonprofit contractors. This variable is a comparative estimate of agency accountability to federal purposes based on the analysis of GPRA reports, on interviews, and on observations.

The Nature and Quality of Network Articulations (Continuum C)

In third-party grant and contract regimes, the form of articulation between agencies and third parties ranges from remote control to managed networks. Remote control, according to Salamon (1989), is a loosely coupled grant or contract articulation in which third parties exercise wide discretion and latitude in both the management and the substance of policy implementation. Contracts for research and development are a typical example. At the other end of the continuum, managed networks are tightly coupled articulations between agencies and grant or contract third parties. Tight network management can be exercised through agency oversight programs, auditing procedures, carefully drafted contracts, negotiated shared understandings between agencies and third parties, and so forth.

The Characteristics of Goals (Continuum D)

In the standard vernacular of performance measurement, there are process, output, and outcome agency goals. Process goals and measures of them describe internal management objectives designed to improve agency efficiency, economy, or services. Output goals and measures of them describe an agency's product or service. Outcome goals and measures of them can be the outcomes of program outcomes or actual health outcomes. In all the cases covered in this research, measurement processes and measure of outputs describe the conditions or circumstances in an agency's target population that are thought to be influenced by an agency's program. This is the so-called causal assertion—that the economic, social, health, educational, or other conditions of a target population have been made better because of an agency's programs. In the logic of performance measurement, each goal is to have an attendant quantitative measure of the level of goal performance. It is clear that the goals an agency selects, and therefore the measures attendant to those goals, determine its claims of effective performance. Performance measurement purists strongly favor outcome goals, and the language of GPRA reflects this perspective. During the course of our research we determined that the word "outcome" is used in the two relatively distinct ways in performance measurement. Because of this, and to make sense of our findings, we grouped "outcome measures" into "program outcome measures" and "health outcome measures." A program outcome measure is an "outcome" that on its face is directly linked to health outcomes but is not in fact a health outcome. The NIH target to develop an HIV/AIDS vaccine by 2010 is described as a health outcome measure because the links between the vaccine and health outcomes are clear. A measure of deaths per 100,000 people from AIDS/HIV is also an actual health outcome measure. The measure of the annual number of donor organs transplanted is not, strictly speaking, a health outcome measure but is clearly a program outcome measure. Because of the emphasis on the use of outcome measures, we found a tendency to parse the word "outcomes" carefully and to claim that outputs that are obviously linked to program outcomes can be labeled outcomes. Because of this we chose to refer to such outcomes as program outcome measures. Each of our "findings" chapters (chapters 4 through 8) has a table that categorizes the performance measures as a process measure (PM), output measure (OM), program outcome measure (POM), or health outcome measure (HOM).

The Level of Goal and Policy Agreement (Continuum E)

Most federal programs have multiple purposes. Continuum E is designed to account for variation in the level of goal agreement or congruence in an agency's statutory or regulatory foundations and the level of policy agreement among agency principals. Performance measurement is thought to be a special challenge in agencies with competing goals and competing views of agency purposes among principals. Goal and policy disagreements are more readily identifiable than are goal and policy agreements. Tensions between the states and the federal government in the Medicaid program, and certainly the competing interests in FDA's regulatory sphere, appear often in the media and are frequently discussed in the research literature. Goal disagreement between the principals is also identified and discussed in the research discussions with agency officials.

The Level of Policy Implementation Centralization (Continuum F)

In third-party government, policy implementation is, by definition, formally extended beyond the agency's hierarchy. Continuum F accounts for variation in several forms of agency centralization and decentralization, most particularly programmatic fragmentation and the geographic spread of policy implementation agents. Levels of centralization and decentralization of third-party policy implementation complicate agency performance measurement, particularly the coordination, gathering, and management of performance data. Policy implementation, centralization, and decentralization are easily identifiable. Programs that use grants or contractors to provide services are decentralized by definition. It is the extent of their use that is captured by this continuum.

The Precision and Characteristics of Performance Measures (Continuum G)

Performance measures vary not only in terms of whether they measure processes, outputs, or outcomes but also in terms of their precision. Continuum G accounts for the variation in performance measurement from qualitative and descriptive "measures" to precise quantitative measure, or so-called metrics. In this continuum, precision is identified and operationalized by the extent to which an agency's performance measures are quantitative.

The Level and Character of Client and Stakeholder Support (Continuum H)

Federal agencies vary widely in terms of their purposes, the characteristics and power of their supporters and detractors, and the characteristics and power of their clients or target populations. Continuum H accounts for this variation, ranging from weak to strong support. This continuum also accounts for competition between supporters and detractors and competition between supporters of alternative views of the purposes of an agency. This variable also accounts for the illusive but important prestige of an agency and especially of its third parties, clients, and target populations. Although this variable is difficult to operationalize, support can be identified by various methods. For example, existing knowledge from press and scholarly accounts identifies Medicare as a program with extremely high levels of client support. Medicare's recipients depend on the program for both their physical and financial safety. Although Medicaid's beneficiaries support the program, they have comparatively less political influence, and their ability to influence the program is less than the recipients of Medicare.

The Level of Professional Identity (Continuum I)

The management of networks, including performance measurement as a network tool, is influenced by the level of professional identity of those who manage (Frederickson 2000). Attributes of professionalism, including a shared cast of mind, similar educational standards, a common corpus of theory and knowledge, agreed-on ethical standards, and a formal organization that promotes its interests and sets selection standards, combine to incline professionals in the same field to think alike (Klingner and Nalbandian 2003). Professionalism in organization theory has been found to be an important determinant of individual behavior (DiMaggio and Powell 1983). High levels of shared professional identity are likewise found in this study to influence the effectiveness of performance measurement application in articulated vertical networks of third parties.

These nine continua represent the research literature just reviewed and serve as the template for the presentation of our findings. They form common threads through our descriptions of performance measurement applications in hollowed-out health care agencies. Each of the cases is unique because each agency has unique purposes and characteristics, but application to GPRA performance measurement in each agency can be reliably described and compared through the application of the variables. Unique performance measurement stories are told in chapters 4 through 8, and through the use of these common factors, the cases can be compared.

Before turning to the presentation of our findings, we think it is important to review the special features of political and administrative reform that attend the performance measurement reform. As described earlier, the performance measurement reform rests on many earlier related reforms and has been shaped by those reforms. As a piece of legislation, GPRA was supported for many reasons, not all of them compatible with each other. Some legislators saw GPRA as a cost-cutting measure. Others saw it as an accountability measure. Still others saw it as a way to form the budgeting process. This is the subject to which we turn in chapter 3.

3

PERFORMANCE MEASUREMENT AS POLITICAL AND ADMINISTRATIVE REFORM

One can better understand performance measurement in the federal government generally and GPRA specifically by first becoming familiar with the reform foundation on which it rests. Reform of the organization and management of American government is a recurring theme, in part because the foundation on which the government rests is constitutionally based on a separation of legislative, executive, and judicial powers and on the checks-and-balances model designed by the founders. Their aim was not to build an efficient government but to construct, instead, a purposely cumbersome government that pitted power against power. In this design the arrangements for the administration of the day-to-day business of government are scattered. Departments, bureaus, and offices are formally situated in the executive branch as part of the presidential cabinet hierarchy, but control of appropriations to departments and offices belongs to the legislative branch. Furthermore, in the legislative branch there is an elaborate system of congressional oversight of executive office operations and a complex array of congressional committees and subcommittees that specialize in particular aspects of public policy and the implementation of that policy by the executive branch.

The ambiguities of the awkward arrangements for federal government administration are described as a system of legislative and executive branch co-management (Gilmour and Halley 1994). Repeated patterns of executive branch reorganization and management reforms can be understood as responses to the ambiguities inherent in the unique structure of the federal government. The performance measurement reform movement and GPRA particularly are also, we shall learn, responses to the ambiguities of the separation of powers.

The key characteristics of federal government reform have changed over the course of the twentieth century. In the early years, from the turn of the century to the Depression and through World War II, the logic of Frederick Taylor's scientific management borrowed from business was applied to federal government programs (Gulick and Urwick 1937). In this era the Taft and Brownlow commissions recommended structural reforms as well as the application of the principles of public administration to strengthen the federal executive and to make agencies and bureaus more efficient. In this era a particular emphasis was placed on the development of a merit-based civil service; indeed, the word "reform" often meant civil service reform. Most aspects of pre–World War II scientific management applications were presidential executive branch initiatives based on the work of boards and commissions appointed by the president. Only one significant piece of legislation, the Reorganization Act of 1939, was a direct result of scientific management reforms. Many of these reforms were preceded by industrial reforms of the same sort and were essentially governmental applications of business reforms. They were also associated with the rapid growth of federal government public administration, what James Q. Wilson calls the rise of the bureaucratic state (1976).

Scientific managementlike government reforms reemerged in the 1990s. Led by Vice President Gore, the National Performance Review initiatives were a federal government application of the logic of reinventing governments (Osborn and Gaebler 1992; Gore 1993, 1995, 1997; Clinton and Gore 1997; Light 1997). Scientific managementlike reform initiatives in the 1990s emerged from the executive branch both as serious attempts to make government more effective and as a form of presidential politics (Radin 2000; Kettl 1994).

Some performance measurement advocates view GPRA as a means to better government. In the tradition of Frederick Taylor, these good-government advocates reason that government activities can be measured and that measurement is the most objective means to make management and even legislative decisions. Consider the testimony of Donald Kettl before a joint hearing of the House Government Reform and Oversight Committee and the Senate Governmental Affairs Committee in which he presented ten reasons why GPRA can help Congress solve problems that must be solved. As part of his testimony, he stated, "Performance is not what it could be—and the performance measurement required by the act is the keystone for solving this problem" (U.S. Senate, Joint Hearing, 1996, 78).

Others view GPRA as primarily a means or rationale for cutting government spending. This view is espoused by many Republicans in Congress and has spawned a small but vocal industry of professional government accountability experts. The budget-cutting view of GPRA is epitomized by comments made by Senator Ted Stevens (R-AK), who stated in a joint meeting of the Senate Appropriations Committee and the Senate Government Affairs Committee that "if properly implemented, the Results Act will assist Congress in identifying and eliminating duplicative and ineffective programs. We intend to monitor compliance with the Results Act at every step of the way to ensure that agencies are providing us with the information necessary to do our jobs, spending the taxpayers' money more wisely" (U.S. Senate 1997, 2).

Other supporters of GPRA argue that it can be used to justify contracting federal services out to the private sector or shedding current federal responsibilities to state and local governments. The Heritage Foundation's Virginia Thomas expressed this view in her testimony to the Subcommittee on Rules and Organization of the House Rules Committee, arguing that GPRA performance information should be used to answer the following questions: "What can and should the federal government be doing? Is it staying within its proper boundaries? Does the agency have evidence of objective, fact-based effectiveness? Is the private sector or state or local government in a better position to accomplish the stated goal?" (Thomas 2001).

Still others see in performance measurement possible means by which to improve agency public relations or agency budgets. For example, IHS used this reasoning to get support from tribal leadership to participate in GPRA. Tribal leadership initially balked at the idea of GPRA participation, with some suggesting it was tantamount to an unfunded mandate. IHS leadership encouraged tribal leaders to help create GPRA performance goals and to participate by submitting GPRA performance goal data to IHS leadership. They did this, in part, by making the case to tribal leaders that GPRA compliance helps tribes to speak with a more unified voice and that a unified voice might result in better information by which to support future budget requests. One IHS manager put it simply, stating, "GPRA-related stuff was seen as a way to bring about more funding."

Management reform has proved to be very good presidential politics in both the Clinton and Bush administrations, and the president is sometimes now referred to as the manager in chief (Kettl 2002). Contemporary applications of scientific management to government are described by Paul Light as a form of "liberation management," a pattern of reform that encourages entrepreneurial, risk-taking public managers who steer departments, bureaus, and agencies (1997b, 36–43). The logic of liberation management is captured in the reform mantra that government is comprised of good people trapped in bad systems.

GPRA is the biggest and most important application of a wider performance measurement reform movement. As is the case in all reform movements, performance measurement advocates are often determined promoters who see in performance measurement the promise of improved government (Light 1997). Public sector performance measurement is thought to provide information that will enable policymakers

> to judge the success of programs and to hold both public managers and contracting service providers accountable for the outcomes of their activities. The emphasis on outcomes rather than inputs shifts attention from resource commitments and processes to the consequences of those commitments and activities. The focus is on results rather than processes and activities. Thus, the movement to foster attention to performance has come to be called results oriented government. (Jennings and Haist 2002, 1)

Another characteristic of federal government reform is described by Paul Light as a war on waste (1997b). Rather than an emphasis on efficiency, roughly understood to be getting better or more effective service per dollar, the emphasis of the war on waste is economy, or simply spending less. The war-on-waste approach to reform is associated with such popular political slogans as "the era of big government is over," "a government that works better and costs less," and "it is time to stamp out fraud, waste and abuse."

War-on-waste reforms have been most evident as a response to the dramatic growth of the national government associated with the New Deal and World War

11. The Budget and Accounting Procedures Act of 1950, based in part on the work of the two Hoover commissions, clarified accounting responsibilities between Congress and the executive branch. In response to federal government scandals, the Inspector General Act of 1978, which established departmental-level officials charged with looking for waste, fraud, and abuse, is evidence of war-on-waste reforms (Light 1997).

Nothing represents reforms of this type better than the Grace Commission, or the Private Sector Survey on Cost Control in the Federal Government, and its report aptly titled *War on Waste* (Grace 1984). Appointed by President Reagan to head the commission, J. Peter Grace was a high-profile corporate executive with the well-known opinion that the federal government was far too big and was riddled with waste (Downs and Larkey 1986). Among the commission's recommendations was the sale or privatization of the national parks. According to the most serious study of the Grace Commission, its proposals were based on the hubris of commissioners with little understanding of either the federal government or the processes of government reform (Downs and Larkey 1986). Virtually none of the commission's sweeping and controversial recommendations were adopted. Although generally regarded as a failed reform effort, the work of the Grace Commission could be described as a precursor of the 1990s' emphasis on contracting out government services and on privatization.

Whereas earlier reforms emphasized structural reorganization or improved management, GPRA has an emphasis on goal achievement. The GPRA statute assumes that both the organization and structure of the federal government and the characteristics of federal management are given. The GPRA formula is rational and linear, starting with agency mission definition. Once an agency's mission or missions are precisely described and put in order of priority, agency goals and activities are rationalized or justified in terms of its mission or missions. Finally, measures of goal performance and mission achievement are to be devised, and data are to be annually collected. Once this formula is established, annual GPRA reports will update agency strategic plans and indicate to policy makers and mangers how well the agency is doing, goal by goal, and, in aggregate, how well the agency is carrying out its mission or missions. Although measures of government performance and the logic of strategic management have been around since the 1930s, GPRA is certainly the most ambitious and comprehensive approach to measuring government performance and results ever attempted.

Performance measurement as reform, especially as embodied in GPRA, roughly coincided in time with the Clinton administration's program of reinventing government. By the end of the Clinton administration in early 2001, GPRA implementation was well along, most agency goals and their attendant performance measures into their third year of application. Still, performance measurement advocates had, by 2000, identified what they regarded to be problems with GPRA implementation. Many agencies had not set the performance bar high enough, they believed. Too many performance measures were not outcome measures but were, instead, process or output metrics. And too little attention had been given to measuring the performance of third-party policy implementation.

For the advocates of stronger performance measurement, the distinctions among measures of input, management processes, outputs, and outcomes are critical. Inputs include agency budget, policy directives, staff resources, and the like, which are thought to be easy to measure and representative of out-of-date ways of thinking about agency performance. Measures of managerial process—the time it takes to complete a task, for example—are likewise thought to be old-fashioned and of little interest. Agency and program outputs are the classic subjects of performance measurement and performance measurement's cousins—program evaluation and policy analysis. Measures of program outputs would include the number of persons enrolled in Medicaid or the percentage of ninth-grade students passing mathematics examinations. Such measures are more acceptable to performance measurement enthusiasts than measures of inputs or management processes but still do not rise to the level of measure of outcomes—the performance measurement pinnacle. Outcome measures, such as decreasing rates of breast cancer, are the preferable form of performance measurement. The GPRA legislation calls for outcome measures, and in the implementation of GPRA and particularly the PART application in the Bush administration, there is heavy pressure on agencies to devise and use outcome measures. To the casual observer, these distinctions may seem arcane, but in the real world of performance measurement they are very important. In the presentation of our findings on the use of performance measurement in the context of third-party policy implementation, the distinctions among kinds of "performance" being measured are especially important.

From the beginning of the managing-for-results movement in the United States in the early 1990s, a series of implementation challenges have yet to be resolved. The early years of GPRA implementation focused on creating the overall goal-setting, performance-measurement, and reporting framework. Today, the challenges are centered more on the use of performance information. The federal government, states, and localities are making progress, but they still face some common challenges in making their "managing for results" systems work.

☐ How do federal managers obtain and use information from grantees and other third parties to leverage performance?

☐ How do program managers set reasonable performance targets?

☐ How do federal managers lead when the federal government is a minority partner in solving a major public challenge?

☐ How much should elected leaders emphasize performance versus performance measures in the budget process?

☐ How do senior leaders create a governing structure that integrates performance information and strategies horizontally across agencies and levels of government to achieve a common outcome? (Kamensky and Morales 2005)

FROM CLINTON TO BUSH AND FROM GPRA TO PART

One of the key qualifications George W. Bush brought to the presidency was a management perspective; indeed, he is the first president with an MBA degree. An evaluation of President Bush's early incumbency, based almost entirely on the management perspective, pointed out that good management was also good politics (Kettl 2002). "Bush has carefully honed a style, based on building an effective team, to make strong decisions. He doesn't try to master the complexity of decisions. Rather, he builds a team, he makes *them* master the complexities, he has them frame the issues, and *then he decides,* firmly and without second thoughts" (Kettl 2002, 1). In considering the Bush presidency, Kettl claims that Bush "has proven himself a surprisingly effective executive—a 'reformer with results,' as he promised during his 2000 presidential campaign" (2002, 4). The Bush management perspective on the presidency may be "living proof that strategic, disciplined, team-based MBA strategy can work in government" (Kettl 2002, 6).

Although GPRA was still relatively new and not yet entirely implemented when the Bush administration took office, in the early stages of the Bush presidency a rather different approach to performance measurement was developed. At the direction of the White House, the Office of Management and Budget assembled a team to reform or augment GPRA, and in July 2002, OMB introduced the Program Assessment Rating Tool, a large questionnaire designed to be answered by agencies. PART includes twenty-five to thirty questions grouped into the following four categories: program purpose and design; strategic planning; program management; and program results/accountability. The first questions in each category are as follows: Is the program purpose clear? Does the program have a limited number of specific long-range performance measures that focus on outcomes and meaningfully reflect the purpose of the program? Does the agency regularly collect timely and credible performance information, including information from key program partners, and use it to manage the program and improve performance? Has the program demonstrated adequate progress in achieving its long-term performance goals? On the basis of agency answers to these and the other questions, OMB assigns either a yes/no response or a response of yes/large extent/small extent/no response. Each answer is to be accompanied by an explanation.

Two factors appear to have influenced the Bush administration's decision to add PART to GPRA. First, better management is now a standard feature of executive campaigns, and once a president is elected, presidential management reform is an almost inevitable development (Aberbach and Rockman 2000). Second, by 2002 it was evident that GPRA was not meeting the expectations of leading advocates of performance management and performance measurement (Kamensky and Morales 2005). The proponents were looking for ways to strengthen it or, in the language of performance management, leverage GPRA—and PART was designed to do that.

The relationship between GPRA and PART can be described as follows. The GPRA statute provides a framework under which agencies prepare strategic plans, performance plans (now, performance budgets), and performance reports that set goals and annual targets for those goals and report on the extent to which they are achieved. PART is a systemic method of assessing performance of program activities, focusing on their contribution to an agency's achievement of its strategic and program performance goals.

PART was designed to strengthen and reinforce performance measurement under GPRA by encouraging careful development of performance measures according to the outcome-oriented standards of the law and by requiring agency or program goals or targets that are appropriately ambitious. Therefore, performance measures included in GPRA plans and reports and those developed or revised through the PART process must be consistent.

PART also extends the usefulness of performance information by defining programs that comprise activities about which management and budget decisions are made. As a matter of sound management practice, agencies will integrate operational decisions with strategic and performance planning by

☐ improving performance measures over time through the PART review,

☐ aligning budgets with programs, and

☐ aligning programs and measures with GPRA goals.

The use of PART is intended to improve agency performance by setting the bar higher through performance measurement. This is done by the PART description of the "standards of achieving a yes" answer for each PART question.

PART holds programs to high standards. Simple adequacy or compliance with the letter of the law is not enough; a program must show it is achieving its purpose and that it is well managed. PART requires a high level of evidence to justify a "yes" response. Answers must be based on the most recent credible evidence.

On the basis of agency responses to the PART questionnaire, OMB assigns a score to each question and an aggregate score for each program assessed through PART. The aggregate score is based on the application of different weights to each of PART's four sections, with the greatest weight placed on a program's performance results. After assembling the results of agency responses to the PART questionnaire, OMB assigns a rating, based primarily on the score, to each program. Programs can be rated "effective," "moderately effective," "adequate," "ineffective," or "results not demonstrated." The PART responses and ratings are published in the subsequent year's submission of the president's budget. For example, PART assessments conducted in 2004 were published the following January with the release of the president's fiscal year 2006 budget. The last rating, "results not demonstrated," is reserved for those programs whose performance measures are judged to be insufficiently results-oriented and those programs with insufficient performance data to demonstrate their results. In the initial year of PART assessments, 2002, about half of the programs assessed were rated "results not demonstrated."

In both of the subsequent years of PART assessments, the percent of programs rated "results not demonstrated" has declined. In other words, fewer programs have inadequate performance measures and data. Following the logic of PART leveraging GPRA and the connection between performance and accountability, OMB decided to publish performance information, believing that making such information public would encourage compliance and move the federal government further in the direction of performance measurement. Keeping in mind that those who developed PART are ultimately those who assign PART scores and ratings, we do see some evidence to support the use of publishing performance information to encourage greater cooperation and compliance in performance measurement.

PART also addressed what were believed to be two important shortcomings in the GPRA law. First, to respond to the "one size fits all" criticism of GPRA, PART set up a "types of program" format with each agency slotted into one of the following types of programs:

☐ Directed federal programs

☐ Competitive grant programs

☐ Block/formula grant programs

☐ Regulatory-based programs

☐ Capital assets and service acquisition programs

☐ Credit programs

☐ Research and development (R&D) programs

Second, in response to the widespread criticism of GPRA for failing to recognize that much of the work of the federal government is in fact carried out by contract- or grant-financed third parties, PART makes an explicit consideration of third parties. The phrase "key program partners" is used throughout the PART guidance document to bring grantees and contractors into the performance measurement arena. For example, in the "program management" section of PART, the first question is, "Does the agency regularly collect timely and credible performance information, including information from key program partners, and use it to manage the program and improve performance?"

PART has received some good reviews. In the summer of 2005 Harvard University announced that PART was one of ten recipients of its Innovations in American Government Award.

GPRA IMPLEMENTATION, POLICY TOOLS, THIRD PARTIES, AND DATA CHALLENGES

Despite the diversity of agency strategic purposes, the variety of policy instruments used within the federal government, and the individual challenges faced by agencies attempting to measure their performance, GPRA seeks to fit everything into a common format. PART, as a Bush administration modification of GPRA, recognizes the need for a range of approaches to agency-level goal setting and performance measurement. The only exception to uniform GPRA requirements was allowing some agencies to use qualitative measures and report their performance in narrative form. Each agency represents a unique challenge to the protocols of goal setting, performance management, and performance budgeting required by GPRA. These challenges relate not only to the different policy instruments used but also to the unique accountability relationships between agencies and the third parties they rely on to carry out their work.

Health care programs are a good example of the difficulties of implementing performance management initiatives in a grant- and contract-based federal system. All government programs need to be financed, need to set policy, and need to be administered (Dilulio and Kettl 1995). Although the federal government shoulders much of the health care financing and policymaking burden, in many instances the administration of these programs is left to third parties (Dilulio and Nathan 1994). Decentralized policy implementation results in desired qualities of redistribution, puts decisions closer to service area delivery, and produces public goods at locally desired levels (Oates 1972). Decentralized policy implementation, however, compounds the number of administrative transactions involving a complex environment for implementing programs (Pressman and Wildavsky 1984). This makes it more difficult to set and measure goal attainment. One need only consider the agencies selected as cases for this book to see the diverse array of shared or thoroughly devolved administrative arrangements. "Third parties" in these cases included Native American tribal leaderships (IHS), medical schools (NIH), scientists (FDA and NIH), states, and commercial or nonprofit health "intermediaries" and "carriers" (CMS).

If there is a universal challenge associated with the implementation of GPRA in health programs, it is the matter of data. There has always been extensive data on the quality of health care, but until recently most of that information was private. The modern era of reporting about public health care quality started when CMS first published hospital mortality rates in the early 1990s. One of the most recent advances is the development of the Consumer Assessment of Health Plans Systems (CAHPS) project, supported by the Agency for Health Care Policy and Research. CAHPS assesses patients' experiences based on "reports" about events that did or did not happen during a clinical encounter, rather than merely asking patients to assess abstract notions of satisfaction or excellence (Cleary and Edgman-Levitan 1997).

The Health Plan Employer Data and Information Set, developed by the National Committee for Quality Assurance, holds some promise. The development of these performance and quality measures, and their possible use for GPRA purposes, depends on the extent to which they measure health outcomes and the extent to which these measurements can link health outcomes to the health agencies and the programs to which money is appropriated.

Several problems are associated with the measurement of health care performance and results. Health care performance is most frequently referred to as "quality of care." The difficulties encountered in determining health care performance and results are similar to those encountered in the public sector broadly. First, the definition of "quality" is a moving target, subject to differences according to who is asked and when they are asked. Opinions about the quality of goals and objectives are not uniform but dependent on constituency and time. Second, even when there is general agreement regarding what constitutes quality care, correlations between quality care and health outcomes are not entirely clear. Positive outcomes can be a problem because they may not always result from quality care, and it is possible that low-quality care can result in some positive outcomes (Eddy 1998). For example, one of CMS's performance goals intends to "improve satisfaction of Medicare beneficiaries with the health care services they receive" (U.S. Department of Health and Human Services, Centers for Medicare and Medicaid Services 2002). This goal defines quality care according to beneficiary perception, with no clear connection between these perceptions and actual positive health care outcomes. The matter of data quality is given further specific considerations in the later treatment of the application of GPRA to particular agencies.

GPRA, PART, AND PERFORMANCE BUDGETING

GPRA called for the selection of five pilot agencies to integrate their measures of agency performance and results with their annual budget requests. The logic of these pilot programs was to set up a system of performance budgeting so as to make spending decisions better or more wisely. Performance budgeting was identified in the text of the GPRA legislation as one of the law's purposes. In 2003 OMB moved the performance budgeting initiative associated with GPRA forward by requiring all agencies to integrate their performance results into their FY 2005 budget requests. By causing agencies to put performance measures together with budget requests, OMB reasoned, Congress would make budgetary decisions informed by agency performance and policy results. At minimum, in addition to the typical workload and output information provided in budget requests, federal appropriators would now have access to outcome-based performance information. Indeed, the justification for a program's budget was now to be based, in theory, on the performance the budgetary dollars would purchase.

Using the PART-derived summations of how well agencies were implementing performance measurement and GPRA performance measures, the fiscal year 2005 budget, published in January 2004, was the first in history to bring together agency budget requests, PART evaluations of agency performance, and actual measures of program performance. With these data it is easy to tie the administration's budget request for a specific federal program to that program's performance according to PART-based performance assessment. The linkage between agency and program performance and the administration's budget request is now an accomplished fact in the federal budget. We are on the threshold of the era of federal performance budgeting. With this development it will soon be possible to determine whether and how performance budgeting will influence congressional appropriations decisions. These patterns are described in some detail in chapter 9.

The link between funding and performance and the difficulty of measuring the outcomes of public programs are aspects of GPRA that have received the most scholarly attention (Radin 1998a, 1998b, 2000; Mihm 2001; Thomas 2001). Some of this literature is optimistic about the capacity of improved agency performance information so as to inform the budgetary process rationally (Mihm 2001). The dominant view based on past attempts to implement performance budgeting would be best described as tempered and skeptical (McNab and Melese 2003; Courty and Marschke 2003; U.S. General Accounting Office 1993).

The general research literature on linkages between program performance measurement and budget decision making in the context of third-party government is not promising (McNab and Melese 2003; Courty and Marschke 2003; U.S. Government Accounting Office 1993). The GPRA-required strategic plans suggest a deductive process approach to decision making in which specific elements flow from broader goals and objectives. By contrast, the annual budget process is usually viewed as inductive, building on past incremental decisions. Similarly, the congressional approach to budget making is a synoptic process in which specific budget marks are used as shorthand to represent and simplify program complexity (Radin 2000, 129–30).

Furthermore, others argue that GPRA imposes the rational management logic of performance measurement on the inherently political process of federal appropriation decisions. Also, agencies are subject to the oversight of multiple and diverse congressional committees and subcommittees. Some substantive committees and subcommittees may have some interest in agency performance measures, but appropriations committees are likely to be much more concerned with political distributive issues (Radin 2000, 133). Because GPRA's home is in the executive branch and specifically in OMB, there is often a wide gap between executive branch assumptions and interests, usually driven by presidential and cabinet-level policy and political interests, on one hand, and congressional interests in the distributive politics of spending, on the other hand (Handler 1996). This is true even when the presidency and Congress are controlled by the same party. Finally, the long history of attempts to bring management rationality to the budgeting process, from program-planning-budgeting systems in the Kennedy-Johnson era to zero-based budgeting in the Carter era, has had little effect on actual appropriations outcomes (Schick 1966).

Perhaps the most lasting positive impact of GPRA, however, may be its potential to improve the internal management of federal agencies. Performance and results measures have become the modern language of policy implementation, particularly within the agencies and between agencies and their contract or grant service providers (Kettl 1993). Indeed, the phrase "performance management" is currently popular, a phrase roughly taken to mean managing on the basis of goal clarification and the measurement of the achievement of agency goals. Specifically, GPRA may lead to improvements in the relationship between federal agencies and the third parties they oversee or with whom they collaborate to provide public services. The results orientation of GPRA coupled with the development of performance indicators to measure agencies' success in achieving these results may bring about better communication and coordination between agencies and third parties. And there are prospects that the performance measurement process required by GPRA can serve to improve federal agency internal management.

We now turn to the presentation of the results of our study of the application of GPRA to five agencies of the Department of Health and Human Services. Our interpretations of these findings are based in part on changing patterns of performance measurement reform and the influence of these changes on agency implementation of GPRA. In chapter 10 we return to performance measurement reform themes and discuss our findings in terms of the factors described in this chapter.

4

PERFORMANCE AS GRANTS TO THIRD-PARTY SERVICE PROVIDERS

The Health Resources and Services Administration

How does a multipurpose federal agency that relies entirely on extended chains of third parties to carry out its work meet the challenges of performance measurement? How do geographic decentralization, programmatic fragmentation, and widely varying levels of goal and policy agreement influence the implementation of GPRA? How do variations in the characteristics of client and stakeholder support influence federal agency implementation of the requirements of GPRA? An analysis of the Health Resources and Services Administration can begin to answer these questions because HRSA relies almost exclusively on the use of third-party grants and contracts to implement federal policy. Because HRSA is third-party government, the study of HRSA's implementation of GPRA is indicative of the characteristics and qualities of performance measurement and performance improvement that are likely to be found in other federal agencies that use contractors and the states and territories as third parties to achieve federal policy goals. HRSA also serves to illustrate the application of GPRA performance measurement processes as applied to health services provided by other kinds of third parties, including cities, counties, medical schools, and nonprofits such as community health centers.

To understand the management and performance measurement challenges associated with the application of GPRA to HRSA, one must understand that HRSA is the prototype of government by third parties described in the literature as "hollow government" (Milward, Provan, and Else 1993), "government by proxy" (Kettl 1988), or "government by remote control" (Salamon 1989). "Hollow government" is borrowed from the "hollow corporation" metaphor made famous by a 1986 *Business Week* article that describes manufacturers that outsource their work to such an extent that they "do little to no manufacturing." In his description of the hollow state, Milward says that "the logic of joint production, carried out to the extreme, refers to a government that as a matter of public policy has chosen to contract out all of its production capability to third parties, perhaps retaining only a systems integration function responsible for negotiating, monitoring, and evaluating

47

contracts" (1996, 193). If the word "grants" is added to the word "contracts," Milward's description of the hollow state is an apt description of HRSA.

The HRSA budget in fiscal year 2002 was 6.2 billion dollars; it had 2,110 employees. The true size of government is, however, not found in the full-time equivalent (FTE) head count of civil servants in the federal government's employment; it is found in the number of persons whose employment is supported by federal grants, contracts, and mandates (Light 1999). Therefore, the size of HRSA should not be thought of as its 2,110 civil service employees but rather as the estimated 63,000 FTE health care personnel supported by HRSA's numerous grant programs. For every person directly employed by HRSA, there are about thirty third-party persons whose employment is funded by HRSA grants or through HRSA contracts and subcontracts.[1] The illustrative point here is not precision, but to make clear the extent to which HRSA is a prototype of hollow government with a very large "shadow bureaucracy" primarily managed, as Lester Salamon refers to it, by "remote control" (1989).

HRSA is an omnibus "holding company" organization including ten bureaus and offices that provide an array of health care services that are targeted primarily to underserved, vulnerable, and special-need populations. HRSA's overall mission is to reduce inequities in the provision of health care by providing services to those who fall through the cracks of the health care market. HRSA categorizes these services into functional areas, such as rural health programs, health professions programs, primary health care programs, HIV/AIDS programs, and maternal and child health programs. HRSA grants are provided to state and local governments and their agencies, to nonprofits, and, on occasion, to individuals and for-profit organizations.

HRSA's GPRA mission is "to improve the Nation's health by assuring equal access to comprehensive, culturally competent, quality health care for all" (U.S. Department of Health and Human Services, Health Resources and Services Administration 2003). This mission is achieved through grants and contracts made by the HRSA bureaus, centers, and offices. To satisfy the GPRA requirement to set out an overall agency mission, the HRSA strategic plan has four themes: eliminate barriers to care, eliminate health disparities, assure quality of care, and improve public health and health care systems.

The operating units whose focus is primarily on eliminating barriers to health care include the Office of Rural Health Policy (ORHP) and the Office of Special Programs. ORHP seeks to improve health care quality and delivery to the nation's rural population. The Office of Special Programs funds the construction and renovation of health care facilities, coordinates the provision of uncompensated medical care, and assures quality and access to organ and bone marrow transplantation.

The operating units whose focus is primarily on eliminating health disparities include the Bureau of Primary Health Care, the HIV/AIDS Bureau, the Maternal and Child Health Bureau (MCHB), the Office of Minority Health, and the Office of Women's Health. The Bureau of Primary Health Care seeks to improve primary and preventive health care to the nation's underserved and vulnerable populations. The HIV/AIDS Bureau provides leadership in health care delivery and supporting services to uninsured and underinsured individuals and families affected by HIV and AIDS. MCHB seeks to provide health care access and to improve health care services to the nation's mothers, children, and families. The Office of Minority Health coordinates HRSA's activities that relate to the special health needs of racial and ethnic minorities. The Office of Women's Health coordinates HRSA's women's health programs and provides leadership in HRSA's response to women's health issues.

The operating units whose focus is primarily on quality of care include the Center for Quality, the Center for Managed Care, and the Bureau of Health Professionals. The Center for Quality seeks to improve the quality of health care, with a focus on HRSA programs and the populations HRSA serves. The Center for Managed Care helps ensure that when managed care is used to carry out HRSA programs there is an adequate supply of well-trained primary health practitioners and that populations served are knowledgeable about managed care practices. The Bureau of Health Professionals seeks to align the skills of the nation's health professionals with the current health care needs of the American public.

The operating units whose focus is primarily on improving public health and health care systems include the Office for the Advancement of Telehealth and the Center for Public Health Practice. The Office for the Advancement of Telehealth supports long-distance clinical health care and long-distance professional health education for the doctors and health care recipients served by HRSA. The Center for Public Health Practice works closely with state and local public health agencies and with schools of public health to strengthen public health practice throughout the country.

THE IMPLEMENTATION OF GPRA AT HRSA

A review of HRSA's GPRA performance goals provides interesting insight into the nature of the agency. First, the breadth of HRSA programs is the widest of the agencies considered in this book. In the language of public administration, HRSA is programmatically decentralized. Second, the breadth of programs administered by HRSA suggests that HRSA is the place where HHS puts health care programs that Congress wishes to fund but that have no natural or obvious home. To claim that some of these programs are closely tied to HRSA's strategic objective of improving the access and quality of health care appears to be a stretch. These programs include those for black lung disease and Hansen's disease, traumatic brain injuries, poison control, hemophilia, and compensation for those who have been harmed by large-scale childhood immunization programs. Third, HRSA is decentralized not only programmatically but also geographically. Of its approximately twenty-one hundred employees, about half are posted to the regional offices of the Department of Health and Human Services. Because virtually all of HRSA's responsibilities are carried out by the states, by their subdivisions, or by contractors and subcontractors, the geographic decentralization of directly employed HRSA staff makes sense. If there is any surprise in the matter of geographic decentralization, it is that there is not an even larger percentage of HRSA staff in the field.

GPRA implementation in HRSA is centered in the Office of Planning and Evaluation. At the administrative level, two full-time employees are dedicated entirely to GPRA and related performance measurement responsibilities, and two other employees at 0.35 FTE are partly dedicated to GPRA compliance. In addition, HRSA's bureaus and ORHP each dedicate one or two employees at 0.25–0.33 FTE. There is considerable variation in the time dedicated to GPRA by these employees, time dependent on the phase of the budget cycle. Within the programmatic offices (bureaus and ORHP), GPRA work is conducted in the Office of Program Development, not in the offices of the director or the Division of Financial Management. Even before the requirement to submit an integrated budget (with performance information included), HRSA included their Performance Report as an appendix to their budget and added their performance information wherever increments were requested in the budget.

HRSA senior management has been genuinely supportive of GPRA implementation efforts at the administrative and programmatic levels. During the last several years of the Clinton administration and the early years of the Bush administration, HRSA's administrator, Claude Earl Fox, advocated using performance measures for both assessment and accountability. He frequently used performance information during appropriations hearings to demonstrate HRSA's accomplishments. He also directed those working on GPRA to develop state profiles that identified individual state performance levels for different GPRA goals and that specified how much HRSA money would go to individual states annually. Of the five health care agencies studied here, the extent and persistence of support for GPRA by top HRSA management is by far the greatest. The enthusiasm and rhetoric in Claude Earl Fox's introduction to HRSA's 2002 GPRA plan is illustrative:

> I am proud to present the Health Resources and Services Administration's (HRSA) Strategic Plan, which charts the Agency's course for assuring 100% access to health care and health disparities for all Americans. The Plan describes this overarching goal, as well as strategies and key objectives for achieving it, in the years ahead.
>
> Through an array of grants to state and local governments, health care providers and health professions training programs, HRSA leads the Nation's efforts to open access to health care for all Americans, including poor, uninsured, and isolated individuals and families. The Agency will continue to do so in the future. With this Strategic Plan, agency priorities and program strategies are updated, specific programs are defined, and activities addressing individual problems are presented.
>
> Overall, HRSA's focus is on programs that promote its primary goal of increasing access to health care and reducing health disparities. Towards those ends, the Agency is internally strengthening its staff and positioning itself to respond as the environment changes. HRSA also works collaboratively with all agencies at the Department of Health and Human Services. Externally, the Agency will continue working with public and private agencies and organizations to bring about changes necessary to increase health care access and reduce health disparities.

I look forward to working with all of HRSA's partners on the strategies laid out in this plan. Americans want, need, and deserve health care that is both excellent and equitable—health care with access for all. (Fox 2002, 1)

Support for GPRA at lower levels in HRSA is, however, mixed. According to one HRSA insider, among those who carry out the day-to-day work of the organization, "support for GPRA is not as strong as it could or should be." GPRA requirements are seen by many as one more burden to deal with, making it a struggle to get people to participate. Simplification of the processes associated with implementing GPRA, particularly those associated with data collection, could ease GPRA-related burdens and subsequently improve attitudes. For example, in MCHB, where data collection, tracking, and analysis have been systematized, attitudes toward GPRA are more positive. Budget staff throughout HRSA has been particularly skeptical of GPRA, dubious of the notion that funding decisions will in any way be influenced by GPRA performance measures. We return to this matter at the end of this chapter.

Prior to GPRA, HRSA had already developed performance measures in several of its bureaus, but there was no overall HRSA strategic plan. The GPRA strategic plan was developed at a retreat where, with the help of a facilitator, bureau directors, in the words of one bureau insider, "battled it out." The bureau chiefs focused on the question, what major goals does HRSA want to accomplish? They used GPRA as their guide.

PERFORMANCE MEASUREMENT AND THE STATES AND TERRITORIES AS THIRD PARTIES

Most HRSA grants are based on formulas for distribution from the federal government to states and territories for specified programs. A smaller portion of HRSA grants and contracts is discretionary, either nonformula (categorical) or awarded on the basis of competition. Grants are not a single instrument, but a series of varying instruments that share the characteristic of federal payments made to subgovernments and nonprofit and quasi-governmental organizations. These grants are intended to support congressionally determined public purposes (Wright 1988; Walker 1995).

Some examples of the kinds and purposes of HRSA's grants are the following:

☐ Border Health Program. In 1994, HRSA established a task force to deal with the unique health problems associated with proximity to the U.S.-Mexico border. On the basis of the task force's analysis, HRSA established the Border Health Program in 1996 and has spent in excess of $100 million to build clinics, educate health care professionals, provide dental care, provide prenatal care, and conduct outreach programs to encourage eligible parents to enroll their children in the Children's Health Insurance Program.

☐ Rural Health Care Networks. In FY 2001, HRSA awarded $13 million in categorical project grants to improve health care access in rural communities. Following congressional direction, the Rural Network Development Grant program funds the development of rural health care consortia of at least three different providers. The consortia work together to create a network that can coordinate services to improve quality, enhance access, and achieve economies of scale. An example of such a consortium might include a hospital, local solo physicians, group medical practices, home nursing services, public health departments, and long-term care providers.

☐ Nursing Education and Practice. The Nursing Education and Practice programs make competitive grants and oversee cooperative agreements to organizations that train and educate nurses. The emphasis of these programs is to improve the geographic distribution and diversity of the health care workforce. The grants go to approximately seventeen hundred training and education institutions.

Perhaps the most important consequence of the wide range of programs under HRSA's jurisdiction and the geographic decentralization of the implementation of federal policy is the remarkable level of political support for HRSA. Virtually all the HRSA programs have a built-in constituency and a set of associated supportive professional and interest groups. Block grants to states' HRSA programs ensure a relatively high level of support from legislators, and categorical grants likewise have built-in supports and constituents. All the HRSA programs are designed to serve purposes that would ordinarily be thought of as deserving. Generally, HRSA has proved to be a politically popular agency, seldom the subject of anything other than mild criticism.

AN ANALYSIS OF HRSA'S PERFORMANCE PLAN GOALS AND THEIR MEASURES

Following GPRA guidelines, HRSA has developed a mix of process, output, and outcome goals and measures. For example, in the aftermath of the terrorism attacks of September 11, 2001, HRSA process goals now include an objective to assist hospitals with the purchase of personal protective equipment, decontamination facilities, and other biological and chemical decontamination equipment. The indicators for this goal are described as under development. In addition, HRSA will conduct a hospital bioterrorism needs assessment in the U.S. states, territories, and regions. The indicator for this goal will be the completion of a report summarizing the results of the assessment.

One example of a HRSA output goal is the aim to increase the number of uninsured and underserved persons served by health centers, with an emphasis on areas with high proportions of uninsured children to help implement the State Children's Health Insurance Program. The indicator for this goal is the total number of clients served in underserved areas. Another output goal is to increase the percentage of infants born to pregnant women who received prenatal care beginning in the first trimester. The indicator for this goal is the percentage of infants born to pregnant women who receive care in the first trimester.

One example of a HRSA outcome goal is to decrease the percentage of low-birth-weight babies born to clients of Healthy Start, ninety-six federally funded community-based projects set up to reduce the rate of infant illness and mortality. The indicator for this goal is the percent of deliveries/births of babies weighing between 1,500 and 2,499 grams. Another outcome goal requires states to set targets for reducing the incidence of fifteen-year-olds to nineteen-year-olds who contract selected sexually transmitted diseases. The outcome measure for this goal is the percentage of states that achieve their established targets.

The details of HRSA applications of GPRA goals specifications and performance measures were guided by criteria established by the Panel on Health Care Measures and Data (Perrin and Koshel 1997). The panel recommended that health care measures be specific, results oriented, meaningful, valid, reliable, responsive, and supported by adequate data. These criteria roughly match generalized criteria for quality performance measurement described in chapter 1. Overall, HRSA's performance plan/report meets these criteria. The purposes and tasks of HRSA offices and bureaus are relatively conducive to precise measures. HRSA does a commendable job of identifying, where necessary, the weaknesses of certain measures, explaining why they are weak and detailing strategies and initiatives to overcome these weaknesses.

In two areas the HRSA plan does, however, fall short—in data adequacy and in the extent to which performance measures are not genuinely results oriented. One example is the requirement that health care performance measures be supported by adequate data. The HRSA performance plan has a section devoted to data challenges in each specific program area and includes plans to overcome these challenges. The plan specifically notes that the performance measurement system "is not structured to produce a routine flow of data on grantee performance and outputs" because "grantees at the State and local level often use subgrantees or contractors to perform the work" (U.S. Department of Health and Human Services, Health Resources and Services Administration 2003, 17).

It is clear from this statement that HRSA is sensitive to the challenges of setting goals and measuring performance in the context of third-party policy implementation. HRSA indicates that it is "working to establish useful and efficient systems for gathering performance and accountability information," but does not go into further detail (U.S. Department of Health and Human Services, Health Resources and Services Administration 2003, 17). The HRSA strategic plan also points out that the Paperwork Reduction Act of 1995, which is intended to limit the reporting burden imposed by the federal government on state and local governments, conflicts with GPRA reporting requirements.

The Hospital Preparedness Grants (HPG) program is illustrative of the goal setting and data adequacy challenge. HRSA's HPG program makes grants to states to assist hospitals to improve their ability to respond to mass casualty events, including those caused by the intentional use of biological, chemical, radiological or nuclear weapons, as well as other public health emergencies. As part of OMB's implementation of PART, the HPG program achieved a score of 80 percent of the points available in Section I, for program purpose and design, and 63 percent of the points available for its strategic planning, which is mostly based on the quality and ambitiousness of its performance measures and targets. In Section III of PART, or the management section, the HPG program received 56 percent of the available points. In the final section (IV), where program results and accountability are assessed and which accounts for half of the total PART score, the HPG program received only 22 percent of the total points because "the program is relatively new, and inherently difficult of measuring preparedness against an event that does not regularly occur" (U.S. Office of Management and Budget 2005, 422–30). The result was an overall HPG PART score of 44 and a rating of "results not demonstrated." Although the HPG PART score is 20 points lower than the average PART score of 64, it is only 10 points below the average PART score for formula or block grants. As noted in the last chapter, the "results not demonstrated" rating is given when a program's performance measures do not adequately capture its intended outcomes, its performance data are not sufficient to inform the public or decision makers of its results, or both. This rating is the most common among formula and block grant programs. Because a real outcome would be a demonstration of preparedness in an actual "mass casualty event," an event to be prevented, HRSA has turned to output measures.

Annual performance measures for the HPG program are as follows.

1. Percentage of awardees who have implemented regional plans and meet all major milestones established for all the HRSA priority areas to meet the goal of a surge capacity of five hundred persons per million population.

2. Percentage of awardees who will demonstrate their ability to secure and distribute pharmaceutical resources required in emergency events, including coordinated caches of pharmaceuticals from metropolitan medical response systems, sufficient to treat five hundred persons per million population, as certified to by HRSA.

3. Percentage of awardees who have (a) assessed the existing chemical and radiological response equipment they currently possess, (b) acquired the needed additional equipment as identified in that assessment, and (c) trained hospital and emergency medical service personnel likely to respond/treat five hundred persons per million population, chemically or radiologically contaminated.

HRSA, PERFORMANCE MEASUREMENT, AND HOMELAND SECURITY

In the HRSA response to homeland security initiatives, the goals and the measures for these goals are understandably still being developed. In the plan, the achievement of these goals would be indicated merely by the successful implementation of certain organizational process or procedures. For example, the goal to assist hospitals with the purchase of personal protective equipment, decontamination facilities, and other biological and chemical decontamination equipment is a homeland security developmental process goal. Although these process goals are not ends in themselves, they imply an unstated causal assertion that their successful completion will lead to the realization of desired outcomes. In this instance the desired outcome would be hospitals that are better prepared for potential bioterrorism attacks or catastrophes that would result in large-scale casualties, defined as five hundred or more casualties. These developmental goals and measures will likely evolve into either output or outcome goals in time, that is, after the programs' specific and measurable objectives become clearer.

HRSA developmental goals in its performance plan, such as the HPG program, do provide broad, strategic objectives that will likely guide the development of more precise indicators in the future. The nature of the HPG program objectives suggests that HRSA is attempting a more strategic approach to the achievement of program objectives where certain responsibilities are either shared or exported entirely to grant recipients. For example, HRSA seeks measures of timely, systematic reporting of data on hospital bed, staff, and other resource capacities by third parties. Another example is the requirement that the states improve their capacity to communicate the status of hospital preparedness to federal health authorities in a systematic, timely, and uniform manner. We see here the evidence of the logic of so-called performance management, an approach to the "management" of third parties that builds performance requirements into grants and contracts and into the overall language of federal management.

The pressure to respond to homeland security issues provides an interesting glimpse of the use of GPRA to attempt to induce third-party grant recipients to respond to federal goals. Even before the development of measurable indicators of hospital preparedness, after September 11, 2001, HRSA goals and objectives represented a clear departure from more passive practices in the past. In the future, annual performance plans will include measures that specifically examine what happens to the money once it goes out the door. Other goals for the HPG program include such phrases as "early warning systems to alert . . . ," "timely, systematic reporting . . . ," and "the ability to effectively communicate . . . ." Given the nature of the program, its genesis in the September 11 attacks, and the subsequent anthrax attacks, it is easy to understand why the federal reins are being pulled tighter. It remains to be seen whether closer federal oversight in this instance is a function of HRSA's terrorism goals or just evidence of a broad, new direction in HRSA's attempts to achieve greater accountability on the part of third parties through GPRA performance measurement. HRSA's developmental goals and the measures attendant to them suggest that the agency may be engaging in a more heavy-handed form of top-down federalism.

THE PREVALENCE OF OUTPUT GOALS

Prior to PART, most of HRSA's approximately 120 GPRA goals could be classified as output goals or measures of HRSA's "products." Table 4.1 presents a brief list of present HRSA performance measures with an emphasis on program outcomes and health outcomes measures. As can be seen, we categorize most of those measures in either program outcomes or health outcomes. Like process goals, output goals imply causal associations between their achievement and desirable social

TABLE 4.1

HEALTH RESOURCES AND SERVICES ADMINISTRATION: 2005 REPRESENTATIVE PERFORMANCE MEASURES

Health Resources and Services Administration—Representative Performance Measures	Measure Category
Broaden access to health care services for the underserved by increasing the number of new and expanded health center sites and additional people served.	POM
Reduce rate of low-weight births among health center patients to nation's Healthy People 2010 goal of 6% of all births.	HOM
Increase the percentage of health professionals supported by the program training in underserved areas.	POM
8 maternal deaths per 100,000 live births by 2008.	HOM
Reduce infant deaths to 6.5 per 1,000 live births by 2008.	HOM
Decrease the number of uninsured children to 8 million by 2008.	POM
Reduce neonatal deaths to 4.5 per 1,000 live births by improving the quality of prenatal care by 2008.	HOM
95% increase in the number of blood stem-cell transplants facilitated by 2010.	POM
Increase the number of people served in the nation's neediest communities through the placement and retention of National Health Service Corps clinicians.	OM
Increase the annual number of deceased donor organs transplanted by 110% over the 10-year period between 2004 and 2013.	POM
Reduce percent of emergency room visits due to poisoning.	HOM
Proportion of rural residents of all ages with limitation of activity caused by chronic conditions.	POM
National rate of deaths per 100,000 people due to HIV infection.	HOM

OM, output measure; *POM,* program outcome measure; *HOM,* health outcome measure.

outcomes—or, in the GPRA/PART vernacular, results. One official charged with implementing GPRA for HRSA highlights the logic behind this approach: "Because it is difficult to sort out the impact HRSA programs have on outcomes, we focus on intermediate outcomes such as number or percentage of immunizations that will logically lead to positive final outcomes."

Because HRSA is so large and has such varied programs, the following treatment of the prevalence of output goals will use MCHB as illustrative of GPRA applications. One example is HRSA's output goal to increase the percent of infants born to mothers who have received prenatal care in the first trimester. The programs supporting this goal, funded through MCHB block grants, are authorized by Title V of the Social Security Act and by the Healthy Start program, administered by MCHB. The assertion that MCHB programs increase infant health and decrease infant mortality is treated at some length in HRSA's Performance Report, which points out that grant funding levels and improvements in infants' health and re- ductions in infant mortality are both indirect and interdependent with the possible effects of other federal programs such as Medicaid. In addition, the report notes that variations in infant mortality and health are a function of socioeconomic fac- tors and other demographic variables. One HRSA executive reflected on the diffi- culties associated with linking health care results with HRSA programs:

> Are we actually having an effect on people's health? With Healthy Start, for example, it is supposed to lead to decreases in infant mortality. We hired Mathematica (a contract research firm) to study infant mortality data and isolate the effect of the Healthy Start programs. They determined that there wasn't a big effect on infant mortality [from Healthy Start], which makes it difficult to make the case that HRSA made a difference. Despite these findings, we approach it from the standpoint that as long as there are reductions in infant mortality, we are happy to share in the success.

The HRSA 2003 Performance Plan is also candid in this regard, nevertheless letting the logical connections between HRSA's programs and the decline in in- fant mortality stand. Evidence that HRSA strikes a balance between recognizing the difficulty of identifying direct social outcomes from its programs measured in terms of positive trends in health care results and making the logical connection between HRSA's programs and these trends is found in the following statements: "For goals such as reducing the infant mortality rate, the relationship between budget resources and performance is a more . . . complex problem, as with many medical, social and economic determinants. Nevertheless, some of its determi- nants, such as low birth weight, sudden infant death syndrome, respiratory dis- tress and complications of pregnancy, can be addressed through improved access, newborn screening and other health care services" (U.S. Department of Health and Human Services, Health Resources and Services Administration 2003, 96). Because the level of HRSA funding will affect programs that provide greater health care access for expectant mothers, increased newborn screening, and other health care services, HRSA can legitimately and reasonably contend that increases in funding will result in a continuing decline in infant mortality rates.

Another section of the HRSA 2003 Performance Plan points out the steady decline in the U.S. infant mortality rate over the past few decades, from 12.6 per 1,000 in 1980 to 7.1 per 1,000 in 1999. HRSA makes the connection between this positive result and HRSA activities. "The use of timely, high-quality prenatal care can help to prevent low birth weight and infant mortality, especially by iden- tifying women who are at particularly high risk and providing counseling and as- sistance to reduce those risks" (U.S. Department of Health and Human Services, Health Resources and Services Administration 2003, 99).

The long-term targets for the goals of MCHB block grants can be found in the program's PART assessment. They are as follows:

1. The national rate of maternal deaths per 100,000 live births from 9.4 in 1980, to 8.3 in 1997, and a target of 8.0 in 2008.

2. The national rate of infant deaths per 1,000 live births from 7.6 in 1995, to 6.9 in 2000, and a target of 6.5 in 2008. (U.S. Office of Management and Budget 2005, 468–80)

The assertion of links between HRSA programs and social outcomes is complicated by the fact that whereas most HRSA programs are administered at the state and local levels, specific goals are set at the state level. Furthermore, actual service delivery is contracted out by the states to local governments, nonprofits, and other organizations at the local level. The variation in goal achievement from state to state can be great, and the ability of MCHB to demonstrate a direct effect on performance, aside from funding levels and output measures, is limited.

The prevalence of process and output measures in HRSA's performance regime follows the logic in the Panel on Performance Measures and Data for Public Health Performance Grants recommendations: "Many factors not under an agency's control can affect health outcomes, compromising the validity of measures of program effect. Consequently, the Panel recommends that health outcome measures be used in conjunction with process and capacity measures to derive appropriately conservative inferences about performance" (Perrin and Koshel 1997, 11). The panel's definition of the term "capacity measures" suggests that it can be used interchangeably with output measures.

PERFORMANCE MEASUREMENT AND THE MATTER OF DATA

Technical problems with HRSA performance data collection and analysis are extensive. For example, grants awarded to fifty-seven states and territories for one HIV/AIDS program were in turn subcontracted by the states and territories to communities, hospitals, universities, and clinics; some of these institutions, in turn, work through subcontractors. Both states and communities give these contracts and collect data on them. Each of the six HIV/AIDS programs has its own data-collecting systems. According to an HRSA executive, "We used to merely aggregate counts, leading to counting many care recipients two, three, or more times. The 57 grants can turn into upwards of 2,000 subcontractors in no time at all." Of the numerous challenges associated with data collection in the context of extended vertical networks of third parties, the effort to avoid reporting duplication is among the most daunting. When performance measures attempt to capture the number of care recipients, and there are two thousand separate and loosely connected or wholly disconnected third-party providers, how can double counting be avoided?

In addition to the problem of double counting, there is the issue of gathering performance data in settings in which different health care terms are uniquely associated with either geographic areas or different health care professions. Nevertheless, through the PART initiative, rather specific results have been set as targets. For example, PART has set a goal or target that the number of new HIV infections in the United States be reduced by 25 percent by 2010 and that the proportion of all HIV-infected people who know they are infected be increased from 70 percent in 1999 to 80 percent in 2005. Because the quality of baseline data is questionable, these results might best be described as informed estimates. OMB has pushed to improve the quality and reliability of baseline data with data-reporting protocols as part of grants, recognizing that the sources of these data are hospitals, clinics, and other nongovernmental organizations.

Even with sophisticated methods of data collection and tracking, technical data problems still exist. In MCHB, data from children's hearing tests, for instance, can come from hospital surveys in one state and surveys of statewide hearing programs in another, because hearing tests are carried out by hospitals in some states, by nonhospital contractors in others, and by statewide programs in a few states. Data collected from hospitals reflect answers from children whose parents took them there for a specific health care purpose, whereas surveys from a statewide program cast a much broader net. Another problem is low incidence. In Idaho, for example, measures of infant mortality among African Americans are skewed due to an extremely small African American population. The deaths of just a few children within this population can significantly alter state results. These data problems are of considerable concern to officials in some state offices of Maternal and Child Health, who argue that the numbers do not tell the whole story. To alleviate these concerns, MCHB assured the states that they would "work together." MCHB negotiation with the states resulted in states' ability to add "data notes," in which states provided performance data in "context" by explaining unique circumstances.

THE POLITICAL CONTEXT OF HRSA

Political, cultural, and leadership differences add to the technical problems associated with data collection. University hospitals are notorious for dragging their feet when it comes to reporting performance data. In Health Training Profession Program grants, the Bureau of Health Professions works closely with university hospitals to collect performance data. These hospitals have not historically been required to report such data, and there is a culture that, according to one HRSA official, dodges performance reporting until "we beat them over the head." The universities were somewhat helpful, however, in the development of the performance goals relating to the geographic distribution and diversity of the health care workforce. Leadership within the health professions program deliberately included university hospitals in the development of goals and their measures. Despite some reluctance, the hospitals provided help in describing how programs operate at the ground level, indicated what data were already being collected, and helped determine what additional data could be collected.

HRSA goals and the attendant measures for those goals are influenced by so-called external factors. After each external factor is listed in the strategic plan, a paragraph describes the nature of each external factor and why it is an impediment to achieving HRSA's goals. HRSA external factors include generic problems that beset health care, such as the dominance of managed care, the growing number of those without health care insurance, the changing characteristics of the health care workforce, and the aging of the American population. In addition, HRSA describes the external forces that impede its possible effectiveness: the need to partner with third parties to provide health care and the changing role of the federal government in the provision of health care services. These external factors relate directly to the importance of third parties in the provision of public health care services. Nevertheless, the HRSA strategic plan developed for HRSA does not include the effective management of third-party grant and contract recipients as an explicit goal.

What levers can be used to encourage grant recipients to collect, manage, and report performance data in the context of extended vertical networks of third parties? Highlighting the difficulties of collecting solid performance data from grant recipients, one HRSA official notes that "there is not much threat of penalty. We never have cut off funding for failure to report, so we mostly use persuasion." There are some tools that help, particularly including reporting requirements directly into grant and contract award conditions. When Title V grants were administered by MCHB, prior to GPRA, MCHB was instructed specifically not to ask for performance information from the states. This prevented MCHB from including measures of performance in grant award conditions. Then, in the 1990s and in the spirit of GPRA, Congress took the step of putting performance reporting requirements into the legislation itself. This gives grant recipients the perception that penalties could result from the failure to comply, even though there have been no actual grant rescissions due to a failure to report. In most cases, HRSA still uses "persuasion and nagging" to get performance data from grant recipients. According to the same HRSA official, "We usually tell them that if you want to justify these expenditures and protect your appropriation, it helps to report data. This approach generally works." He concludes that despite his personal belief, at the agency and unit level, "fear of getting beat up does not yet exist. Appropriations are based on interest group politics, not on GPRA."

There is also the problem of the kind of data reported. Grantees and contractors are inclined, in the interest of funding renewal, to put their agencies or organizations in the best possible light. The tendency of grantees and contractors to report good performance favorably may tend to be supportive of the purposes of giving grants or contracts because their success is closely coupled (Morini and Wolf, 2002).

OVERCOMING THIRD-PARTY GOAL AND MEASUREMENT PROBLEMS IN THE MATERNAL AND CHILD HEALTH BUREAU

Although neither the overall HRSA strategic plan nor the 2003 and 2004 performance plans considers managing the unique challenges associated with performance measurement in grant programs as a strategic imperative, the approach of HRSA's MCHB to goal development and performance reporting takes such a view.

After the passage of GPRA, HRSA administrators met with representatives from all the states' Maternal and Child Health programs, interest groups, public health experts, and health data and data systems experts. There followed a sixteen-month period of input and negotiation, which an MCHB executive referred to as a "cajoling process." This resulted in the creation of the Maternal and Child Health Performance Partnership, made up of state directors and offices of maternal and child health. The partnership jointly developed a core of eighteen measures to determine the overall performance of the state block grant program. The primary criterion for each measure is that it be clearly associated with the six broad MCHB health goals. Table 4.2 presents the agreed-on MCHB performance measures, and it is generally illustrative of the mix of process, output, and outcome indicators found in other HRSA programs.

TABLE 4.2

MATERNAL AND CHILD HEALTH CARE PARTNERSHIP PERFORMANCE MEASURES

1. The percent of state supplemental security income beneficiaries less than 16 years old receiving rehabilitative services from the state Children with Special Health Care Needs (CSHCN) program.
2. The degree to which the state CSHCN program provides or pays for specialty and subspecialty services, including care coordination, not otherwise accessible or affordable to its clients.
3. The percent of CSHCNs in the state who have a "medical/health home."
4. Percent of newborns in the state with at least one screening for each of phenylketonuria, hypothyroidism, galactosemia, hemoglobinopathies [(e.g., sickle cell disease) (combined)].
5. Percent of children through age 2 who have completed immunizations for measles, mumps, rubella, polio, diphtheria, tetanus, pertussis, Haemophilus influenza, hepatitis B.
6. The rate of birth (per 1,000) for teenagers aged 15 through 17 years.
7. Percent of third-grade children who have received protective sealants on at least one permanent molar tooth.
8. The rate of deaths to children aged 14 years and younger caused by motor vehicle crashes per 100,000 children.
9. Percentage of mothers who breastfeed their infants at hospital discharge.
10. Percentage of newborns who have been screened for hearing impairment before hospital discharge.
11. Percent of CSHCNs in the state CSHCN program with a source of insurance for primary and specialty care.
12. Percent of children without health insurance.
13. Percent of potentially Medicaid-eligible children who have received a service paid by the Medicaid program.
14. The degree to which the state assures family participation in program and policy activities in the state CSHCN program.
15. Percent of very low birth weight live births.
16. The rate (per 100,000) of suicide deaths among youths aged 15 through 19.
17. Percent of very low birth weight infants delivered at facilities for high-risk deliveries and neonates.
18. Percent of infants born to pregnant women receiving prenatal care beginning in the first trimester.

State Maternal and Child Health representatives assented to the core measures and agreed to report using these measures. The data collection and reporting procedures were detailed to such an extent that every one of the thousands of individuals recording data had a verification sheet that included exact, agreed-on definitions, down to the specific numerator and denominator for each measure. The eighteen core measures, although representing only a sample of states' maternal and child health activity, encompass the greater part of MCHB work. One MCHB official estimates that the eighteen shared MCHB measures represent between 75 percent and 90 percent of the services provided by MCHB.

The goals and agreements reached by the MCHB Performance Partnership were a significant accomplishment because they established a monitoring mechanism that protects against agents subverting the principal's intent and does so in a manner agreeable to both principals and agents. HRSA developed a uniform data collection and reporting format and provided an additional $100,000 annual grant to each state for those purposes. In the context of articulated vertical networks of third parties, the MCHB Performance Partnership is an excellent example of the "network management" approach to improved articulation between HRSA and its third parties.

In modern fiscal federalism, federal grants to state and local governments take advantage of the federal government's capacity to generate revenue, on the one hand, and provide for decentralizing service delivery for the purposes of service provision, on the other (Oates 1972). For example, MCHB partnership agreements are adjusted or adapted to local tastes and preferences in the course of accounting for the achievement of federal purposes while providing for some flexibility as to how goals are to be reached. MCHB's set of eighteen agreed-on goals, common to all states, could be thought to run counter to the logic of decentralizing service delivery in the traditional model of fiscal federalism. MCHB's implementation of GPRA takes states' tastes and preferences into account by requiring each to establish ten additional state-specific goals. Overall, however, the common eighteen partnership goals with their attended measures do provide the efficiencies needed to establish uniform measurement and reporting protocol for shared measures.

One final impediment to activating MCHB's goal measurement and reporting system was the Paperwork Reduction Act of 1995, which was intended to limit the paperwork burden imposed by the federal government on state and local governments. MCHB's efforts to meet the requirements of one law were stymied by another. MCHB dealt with this problem by engaging in extensive negotiations with OMB to obtain waivers to achieve compliance with the Paperwork Reduction Act.

MCHB implementation of GPRA could easily be thought of as a best-practice application of performance measurement in a third-party regime. How difficult would it be for other HRSA bureaus and offices to measure the performance of their grant-making programs by adopting a similar approach to cooperatively developing goals and indicators and a uniform approach to data collection and reporting? One of the weaknesses of the best-practices approach is that it fails to consider adequately the unique characteristics of best practice cases. The distinctive characteristics of MCHB that facilitated its success would need to be present in other HSRA units or other federal agencies. Four factors are distinctive and central to MCHB's success: (1) the commitment of agency leadership; (2) a belief in the logic of performance measurement as a means to improve accountability; (3) a highly developed organizational culture; and (4) adequate funding. These factors match the generalized research findings on the application of performance management to the public sector described in chapter 1 (Jennings and Haist 2002, 2004).

When asked what accounted for the success of MCHB's performance measurement system, a HRSA representative replied, "What made a difference with MCHB's success was simply the personal leadership of Peter van Dyck. Without it, even though GPRA was on the books, the performance measurement system wouldn't have been accomplished. He gathered together a group of people, dedicated staff time, and decided to do it." Peter van Dyck is the associate administrator for Maternal and Child Health of HRSA. It is important to recognize that MCHB's performance measurement system is as much a reflection of Mr. van Dyck's personally held belief in achieving accountability through performance measurement as it is a product of MCHB's response to GPRA's requirements. Indeed, the system likely would have been developed even in the absence of GPRA's passage. Van Dyck was brought up "in the system," having been the state director of Maternal and Child Health in Utah. "I worked in a state Medicaid and MCH office, and I got tired of people asking me what they were getting for all the money. . . . GPRA is about accountability, and we want greater accountability with the money that goes to the states." So firmly held is this belief that, of all the people interviewed for this research, Dr. van Dyck was the only one who was not at least somewhat dubious about the connection between performance and funding. In fact, part of what motivated van Dyck in the development of the performance measurement system was that "we thought we would get increased appropriations if we could demonstrate what we were doing with their money."

Dedicated funding is a second factor that allowed MCHB to implement its innovative performance measurement program. Aside from the money to pay for the development of the performance measures, the creation of the electronic data collection, and the Internet reporting system, the MCHB appropriation, as noted earlier, provides $100,000 annually to each state. This has gone a long way toward reducing possible resistance to performance measurement down the network of third parties. The energy applied to GPRA implementation at MCHB has resulted in a solid PART score of 73 and a rating of "moderately effective," both comparatively good for formula and block grant programs.

HRSA–THIRD-PARTY ARTICULATION AND ITS EFFECT ON PERFORMANCE MEASUREMENT

In chapter 1 performance measures were described as a means to strengthen the articulation between federal agencies and the third parties who deliver services. Increasing the strength of articulation only occurs, however, when the measures employed by third parties reinforce federal-level programmatic objectives.

The broader study of third-party federal management, as described in chapter 1, points to problems of fragmented accountability and the differences between federal and state objectives and policies (Rosenthal 1984). The manner in which MCHB developed its performance measurement regime strengthened the articulation between MCHB and the third parties that deliver the services and thereby alleviates, at least to some extent, these challenges. By design, the process of agreement on the eighteen core performance measures and their indicators reduced differing opinions between MCHB and the states about the policy purposes and objectives. Through the goal development process, agreed-on measures reflected the joint opinion of MCHB and third parties regarding policy purposes and objectives. Fragmentation in accountability was reduced, because both the states and the MCHB were clear about the goals against which their performance would be judged. Furthermore, uniform data collection and reporting procedures should reduce accountability fragmentation. Accountability is bolstered by annual face-to-face meetings with each of the state directors of Maternal and Child Health about their performance on the eighteen shared core measures and the ten individual state measures. In the end, according to one MCHB official, "all 59 states and jurisdictions agreed to collect and report data on uniform measures, using uniform methods, with the knowledge that all the performance information would be published on the Internet."

Agreements between MCHB and the states represent only two of the parties involved in extended, articulated networks in the provision of health care services. The strength of third-party articulation depends on the degree to which states convey these goals and their measures to subgrantee contractors and subcontractors. One way these goals are conveyed throughout vertical articulated networks is through data collection and reporting procedures. One MCHB executive indicated that complete public access to each state's and each jurisdiction's performance information over the Internet was selected over publishing through an internal Intranet publication because it was thought that this avenue would create "peer-pressure to improve performance."

Another HRSA agency, ORHP, faces more daunting impediments to establishing goals and measuring performance. The office works with third parties from both the public and the private sectors, including associations, foundations, health care providers, and community leaders. Much of ORHP's mission is carried out through five grant programs with a wide range of performance-measuring difficulties. Grants fund diverse rural health activities—from training emergency medical technicians to providing primary and preventive care to migrant farm workers. ORHP finds it difficult to select a sample of performance measures that is representative of the program's overall activities. Unlike other HRSA agencies, ORHP is not just one program, nor is it governed by a single piece of legislation. Unlike MCHB block grants to the states and territories, most ORHP grants are awarded directly to nonprofits and local government consortia in rural areas, particularly rural areas that lack crucial Medicaid resources. Many of these health care facilities are staffed by only one doctor, one nurse, and a part-time clerk. In these facilities all available resources are directed toward patient care, and few resources are devoted to GPRA reporting. Indeed, some ORHP grants go to help rural health care clinics meet the quality assurance reporting demands of Medicaid. One of ORHP's programs, the Rural Healthcare Network Development grant program, provides $80 million annually to support establishing managed care networks in rural areas.

The lack of funds is not the primary impediment to the functioning of managed care networks in rural areas. GPRA's uniformity seems ill-suited for programs such as those funded by ORHP. Furthermore, OHRP is not likely to be able to take advantage of GPRA's requirements to further their coordination efforts with third parties or grant recipients. The purposes of ORHP grants are so diverse and the resources of the grant recipients so limited that complying with GPRA is particularly daunting. Further complicating performance measurement, noted an HRSA representative, is that "some of the Rural Health grants recipients are so small that they don't have the staff or equipment they need to collect performance data. Many don't have LANs [local area networks/Internet connection], and some don't even have computers." The biggest problem in rural health care is the lack of a critical mass of patients and health care service practices in a reasonable geographic area. Not surprisingly, grant recipients tend to spend federal monies on health care activities, with the collection and reporting of performance data an afterthought.

At least according to the PART evaluation of HHS's rural health activities, ORHP has been able to, at least partially, overcome its performance measurement challenges. With scores of 60 percent in terms of purpose and design, 75 percent for strategic planning, 70 percent for management, and 58 percent for results and accountability, ORHP's total PART score is 63 and its rating is "adequate." ORHP's score is nine points higher than the average for competitive grants. ORHP now has new and more demanding long-term and annual performance goals, such as reducing the percentage of rural residents with limitation of activity caused by chronic conditions from 14.6 percent in 2000 to 13.9 percent in 2010.

HRSA AND PERFORMANCE BUDGETING

GRPA requires agencies to address key external factors that could significantly affect the achievement of their goals. This requirement is especially relevant to GPRA applications to HRSA, because most of HRSA's budget goes to programs implemented by third parties over which it has limited control. Despite this requirement and HRSA's fragmented organizational structure, an analysis of HRSA goals later in this chapter shows that the agency has not been sufficiently attentive to strategies to manage better the performance relationship between HRSA and its third parties, which are state and local governments, health care providers, and health professions training programs.

As with most federal programs, there is reason to believe that the connection between performance and appropriations for HRSA is tenuous at best and that these dollars go where politics, rather than performance information, dictates. One example is the health facilities construction funded by the Health Centers Program. Continued budgetary increases are likely less connected to its 85 PART score and the highest rating of "effective" and more likely due to the appeal to Congress of its distributive nature. The Health Center Program's goals are for new facilities, new satellite facilities, and the expansion of existing facilities. These are decidedly output measures. This constitutes a definition of results that will be favorable independent of any evidence of a positive correlation between facilities construction and improved health. The positive PART score and rating resulted in a substantial proposed increase for the program in the president's FY 2006 budget. The proposed increase to the program was offset by a proposed elimination of the congressional earmark portion of the Health Center Program's budget.

GPRA measures may determine that certain of HRSA's programs are not meeting their goals and are generally failing to perform. And GPRA measures may determine that third parties that are one, two, or even three steps removed from federal concerns and objectives are performing poorly. What would appropriators do with negative performance information? One HRSA official indicated that "decisions will still be made on political, not performance grounds." As described in chapter 1, federal grant customs involve negotiating, cajoling, and threatening, but rarely the actual withdrawing of a grant.

The complicated causal factors associated with health care outcomes highlight the challenges associated with integrating performance and budgetary information and the hope that budgetary resources can, at least in part, be allocated on the basis of some level of performance. Even if performance metrics were advanced to a level of sophistication that could isolate the specific effects of particular programs, it is a stretch to assume that appropriations subcommittee members will take the time to understand these complicated relationships, let alone take them into consideration while they make funding decisions.

CONCLUSIONS

Our conclusions draw together HRSA's GPRA implementation findings presented in this chapter and put those findings in the context of performance measurement theory and practice and in the context of comparison with the other four health agencies under consideration. Figure 4.1 is a graphic representation of our general conclusions.

As figure 4.1 shows, HRSA is a contract management agency that carries out federal programs through extended vertical articulations of third parties. It is the epitome of a hollowed-out, third-party federal agency, and GPRA implementation at HRSA can only be understood in this context. Much of the work of GPRA implementation at HRSA has been based on HRSA systems of grant management through cooperation with the states and territories as their policy implementation agents. GPRA implementation at HRSA has been approached the same way, through cooperation in data gathering, annual data reporting, and other forms of contract management. GPRA is one of the mechanisms by which HRSA manages third-party grants and contracts. These articulations, as the literature of federalism indicates, are most often in the form of diplomacy-like negotiations, treaties, and the like—and less often in the form of overtly threatening the sanction of grant discontinuation. But with the introduction of PART, the relationship be-

FIGURE 4.1

KEY FACTORS IN THE SYNTHESIS OF THE INFLUENCE OF PERFORMANCE MEASUREMENT IN THE HEALTH RESOURCES AND SERVICES ADMINISTRATION

A. The Level of Third-Party Policy Implementation

HRSA

hollowed out   *direct government*

B. Accountability to Federal Program Purposes

                                              HRSA

attenuated   *strict*

C. The Nature and Quality of Network Articulations

                        HRSA

remote control   *managed network*

D. The Characteristics of Goals

                               HRSA

processes   *outputs*   *(POM) outcomes (HOM)*

E. The Level of Goal and Policy Agreement

                                     HRSA

disagreement   *agreement*
incongruence   *congruence*

F. The Level of Centralization of Policy Implementation

HRSA

decentralized   *centralized*
dispersed, fragmented

G. The Precision and Characteristics of Performance Measures

                                 HRSA

qualitative   *quantitative*
descriptive   *precise*

H. The Level and Character of Client and Stakeholder Support

                                 HRSA

weak   *divided*   *strong*

I. Professional Identity

                                 HRSA

low   *high*

POM, program outcome measure; *HOM*, health outcome measure.

tween HRSA and its third parties began to shift. According to one HRSA official, PART moved the performance bar higher, and the HRSA agencies and the states are expected to be more "hard nosed with their third parties." PART has forced some states and agencies to threaten contractors and grantees with eliminating their funding if they do not take performance measurement seriously.

These managed, contract-based articulations between HRSA and its primary third parties, the state and territories, are for the most part effective in the following terms. First, grant recipients and contractees are, generally speaking, accountable to federal goals. GPRA is one mechanism by which this federal accountability is now exercised. Second, even in the context of very high program fragmentation, HRSA program goals, program by program, are generally compatible with one another, and the level of policy agreement among principals is rather high. Third, many of the programs administered by HRSA have strong stakeholder and client support. GPRA purposes have been fully and vocally supported by HRSA leadership, and this support has permeated the processes of grant and contract management at all levels of implementation. Taken together, these factors allow HRSA to be a relatively noncontroversial health agency with high levels of political and stakeholder support. HRSA staff is highly professionalized and has used professional associates to cultivate relations with state and other third-party partners. HRSA has also consciously attempted to build, state by state and program by program, a culture of goodwill and program identification. HRSA, therefore, has been a good seedbed for GPRA implementation.

HRSA is a small agency in terms of direct staff, but it has a large budget and a huge third-party shadow bureaucracy. In the context of high program fragmentation, very high geographic decentralization of policy implementation, and third-party policy implementation, HRSA has chosen to follow GPRA guidelines rather literally. All its performance measures are quantitative, and HRSA has invested heavily in performance data-gathering activities. HRSA's measures at the outset of this research were predominantly process and output performance measures. Likely due to the emphasis within PART for outcome-oriented measures, HRSA has adopted several program outcome measures and some health outcome measures. While taking GPRA seriously HRSA has, nevertheless, concluded that not only is it difficult to measure health outcomes annually, it is even more difficult to claim logically that HRSA programs, standing alone, affect measurable health outcomes calibrated annually.

Because HRSA programs support the health needs of underserved populations, populations with health problems, it could be assumed that the effects of HRSA programs should be measurable. But health is a highly complex phenomenon, subject to many influences, and in the range of these influences even the most determined effort on the part of HRSA might not produce measurable improvements in health outcomes. Is it reasonable under such circumstances to hold HRSA accountable for health outcomes? Probably not. If the policy question is, Is HRSA well managed and effective, based on annual GPRA data? the answer is yes. Is HRSA taking performance measurement more seriously under GPRA and PART? The answer is yes. If, however, the policy question is, Are HRSA programs measurably influencing the health of the underserved? the answer is probably "we don't know."

To the outsider, HRSA performance measures and its annual plan and report are a very good representation of what HRSA does and how it does it. On the inside, the biggest effect of GPRA implementation has to do with managing the processes of agency—third-party articulations. The language of performance metrics has become the language of contract management and the language of the successive patterns of interaction between HRSA principals and agents in the states and territories. In HRSA the language of performance management is increasingly the language of on-the-ground fiscal federalism.

The HRSA response to GPRA is typically bureaucratic. Like all bureaucrats, HRSA leadership is supportive of the agency's purposes and is inclined to present those purposes and the achievement of those purposes in a favorable way. It is unreasonable to expect agency leadership to purposely emphasize measures or data that reflect unfavorably on it. In the pattern of HRSA third-party articulations, it appears that grantees and contractors are likewise inclined to represent favorably the implementation of federal policy and the spending of federal dollars in their states, territories, and organizations. It is evident in the HRSA implementation of GPRA that there is a good bit of apprehension regarding how performance measures might be used, particularly by legislators and especially in the budgetary/appropriations process. This apprehension is warranted. In the president's FY 2006 budget seven HRSA programs are recommended for discontinuation because they "are similar to other activities or have failed to demonstrate results." The programs are as follows:

- ☐ Emergency medical services for children
- ☐ Health facility construction congressional earmarks (pork barrel)
- ☐ Healthy community access program
- ☐ State planning grant program
- ☐ Trauma care program
- ☐ Traumatic brain injury program
- ☐ Universal newborn hearing screening program

How Congress will respond to these purposed program eliminations remains to be seen. But it is a safe guess that when it comes to integrating performance information in its budgeting, HRSA and HHS officials will be cautious.

HRSA is also typically bureaucratic in the selection of goals, knowing that significant improvement in the health circumstances of the poor and underserved, tracing directly and primarily to its programs, is at the lower end of plausibility. Because "outcomes" plausibility is not particularly high, at least in terms of specifying HRSA's contribution, HRSA initially selected goals that were both reasonable and achievable, goals of process and output. The application of PART to HRSA's implementation of GPRA combined higher performance targets and more outcomes measures. Initially, performance measurement realists in HRSA recognized the idealized expectations of GPRA and developed a performance measurement regime that they believed was reasonably faithful to GPRA's intent. The implementation of PART and the logic of rating program performance have caused HRSA to drop some GPRA measures, tweak some others, and add some new ones that are outcome oriented and more difficult to achieve.

Because its programs are implemented at the state and local level through grants and contracts, HRSA is intergovernmental relations at work. The logic of cooperative federalism holds up well in the study of HRSA's GPRA implementation because federally funded programs are bent at the level of implementation and shaped to local conditions and circumstances. HRSA's grant and contract management model is built on flexibility, negotiations, and interjurisdictional cooperation. Because GPRA is thought to be an instrument of accountability to the purposes of the federal government, HRSA's application of GPRA is designed to accommodate variations in local application so long as federal purposes are not significantly altered. The GPRA "one size fits all" language has been wisely interpreted at HRSA to accommodate the realities of federalism.

This chapter began with a series of questions about how a federal agency that relies entirely on third parties for policy implementation responds generally to the challenges of performance measurement and specifically to GPRA. From the HRSA case it is clear that the agency responded to the imperative of GPRA performance measurement with strong leadership and with network management as a means by which to compensate for the fact that third parties carry out all of their work. In the main this approach appears to be effective, given the hollowed-out nature of GPRA. In addition, GPRA and its third parties initially selected management process and agency–third-party output goals and attendant measures while carefully steering clear of being held responsible for outcomes they believed to be beyond their control.

To some extent this cautious approach has been changed by PART, causing HRSA to attempt to meet more nearly an idealized conception of the values of strategic planning and performance measurement. HRSA has the advantage of relatively compatible goals and relatively strong clients and stakeholders. In this context their careful approach to goal and performance measure selection and their visible top-level performance measurement and managed network leadership have served the agency well. It is clear that this is a cautious and careful approach to performance measurement, a risk-averse approach generally aligned with the less-idealized perspective on performance measurement described in table 2.1. But in the larger picture, GPRA is being implemented at HRSA as part of a broader, long-term approach to cooperative federalism that emphasizes agency-state deliberation and negotiation. This approach has served the agency well for many years, and it appears that the imperatives of GPRA have simply been folded into the HRSA way of doing third-party government.

With this baseline information, the study of performance measurement and third-party government turns, in the next chapter, to two huge programs that are differently hollowed out, programs that use third-party government much like HRSA in one case and different from HRSA in the other case—Medicaid and Medicare.

NOTE

1. HRSA's FY 2002 budget provided $156.1 million for "program management," which includes personnel and administrative expenses. Members of HRSA's Planning, Evaluation, and Legislation Office indicated that other administrative and personnel expenses were scattered throughout the budget and that an estimate of $200 million for HRSA administrative costs is accurate. The estimate of the actual size of HRSA is based on the following calculations. In FY 2002, personnel and other administrative expenses accounted for approximately $200 million of the HRSA budget. When these personnel and administrative costs are divided by the number of direct HRSA employees, the result is approximately $95,000 per year per direct civil service employee. To estimate the number of third-party employees supported by the HRSA budget, the remaining $6 billion in the HRSA budget was divided by $95,000, for a total of 63,300 grant and contract FTE employees.

5

PERFORMANCE AS THE PROVISION
OF HEALTH FINANCIAL SECURITY

The Centers for Medicare and Medicaid Services

Third-party government takes many forms. From the perspective of performance measurement, what difference does the form of third-party policy implementation make? Is GPRA implemented differently, with different results, in the context of grant-based third-party operations compared to contract-based third-party policy implementation? One very significant federal agency is ideally suited to finding the answers to these questions—the Centers for Medicare and Medicaid Services. CMS, formerly the Health Care Financing Administration (HCFA), was selected as a subject for this book in part because of its extensive use of both grants (Medicaid) and contracting (Medicare) and in part because, in terms of the distribution of federal dollars, it is one of the largest and most important government agencies.

An examination of CMS's implementation of GPRA helps identify how a single agency adopts different approaches to measuring health care processes, outputs, and outcomes depending on which policy tool it uses—grants to states and territories or contracts with health insurance and service carriers.

THE CENTERS FOR MEDICARE AND MEDICAID SERVICES AND THIRD-PARTY SERVICES PROVIDERS

The Medicaid program operates almost entirely on the basis of grants to the states and territories and would appear to be similar to HRSA and to IHS. Medicare relies on contracts for service provision and has, therefore, many similarities to NIH, although the nomenclature is confusing because NIH uses the word "grant" to describe contracts given for medical research. The open-ended nature of CMS Medicaid grants to subgovernments that provide matching funds to states is unique, adding a complicating factor to GPRA applications to Medicaid. States may choose to widen or narrow eligibility to provide more or less generous services as long as they meet federally required minimal standards, a characteristic of fiscal intergovernmental relations that differentiates Medicaid from other grants programs, making the measurement of Medicaid performance particularly challenging.

Unlike HRSA, which includes many smaller programs and programs that vary greatly in character and purposes, CMS is much larger and easier to describe. CMS is best thought of as a giant governmental health financing and insurance agency. Most agencies rely on generalized federal income and other taxes for revenues, as does the federal share of CMS's Medicaid program. The Medicare program has more complicated funding, however. Medicare Part A, which covers hospital care for the elderly, is financed through a federal payroll tax, which accounts for 2.9 percent of wages, with half (1.45 percent) being paid by the employer and half being paid by the employee. Medicare Part B, which covers doctors' visits and outpatient medical services, is financed through general federal revenue and monthly insurance premiums paid Medicare beneficiaries. State funding comprises about 40 percent of total Medicaid spending.

On the expenditure side there are two primary groups of entitled CMS clients, the elderly under Medicare and the poor and disabled under Medicaid. Both Medicaid and Medicare clients are, in their language, beneficiaries, who may engage health providers, including doctors, hospitals, nursing homes, and pharmacies, having been entitled to the coverage of all or part of their services. Having rendered services to entitled beneficiaries, health providers bill "carriers" for the services provided, very much like they bill health insurers such as Blue Cross/Blue Shield. In the case of Medicare for the elderly, because all the funds are federal, the CMS contracts with very large carriers. In the case of Medicaid, because the states share in funding, carriers are ordinarily contracted for at the state level.

CMS annually engages in tens of millions of transactions, each transaction expected to comply with reams of regulations and procedures. It is clear that CMS engages in these health care financial transactions in the context of competing purposes. On one hand there are gaps between those who are eligible for CMS services and those who are actually enrolled in CMS programs—either Medicare or Medicaid. There is continuing pressure to close these gaps. On the other hand, CMS is designed to be an agency that controls costs. It is very difficult to control cost while expanding the enrollment of the eligible.

In this chapter we put the performance measurement movement and the implementation of GPRA in the context of the very unique Medicaid and Medicare articulated vertical networks of third parties. We describe some of the loose and tight coupling in Medicaid and Medicare third-party articulations and the effectiveness of attempts to measure program effectiveness at CMS.

GPRA asks agencies to consider factors that could significantly affect the achievement of their goals, factors that are external to them and beyond their control. Of the agencies reviewed here, CMS's performance plan, especially the portions dealing with the Medicare program, goes to the greatest length to take external factors into consideration in its selection of goals, measures, and strategies to improve performance. Nearly the entire CMS budget, almost $400 billion in FY 2003, goes to parties that are beyond its direct control, and CMS's performance plan reflects this reality. The goals it has selected, the measures it uses to gauge success in meeting these goals, and the strategies employed to improve goal performance all take into account its vertically articulated and highly decentralized approach to policy implementation.

CMS has by far the largest budget of the agencies considered for this book and the largest budget of any domestic agency in the federal government, yet it has the fewest performance measures. The FY 2003 Performance Plan includes thirty-seven FY 2003 measures and reports on thirty-three FY 2001 measures.

For FY 2006 the CMS budget request was just under $600 billion, an increase of nearly $200 billion in only four years. Of this budget, $394 billion, or 70 percent, would go to the Medicare program, and $193 billion, or 30 percent, would go to the Medicaid program. In 2002 Medicare received 62 percent and Medicaid received 36 percent of CMS funding, an indication that Medicare is growing more rapidly than Medicaid. In a brief comparison of the distribution of performance measures compared to the budget distribution, what stands out first is the comparatively small number of measures (four) developed to represent the Medicaid program. Federal expenditures for Medicaid make up only about 55 percent of total Medicaid spending. When state funding is included, Medicaid's total budget is more than $300 billion. The reasons underlying the vast discrepancy between Medicaid's costs and its representation in terms of performance measures are discussed later in this chapter.

Perhaps most remarkable in any description of CMS is the contrast between the huge size of its budget and the vastness of its program, on one hand, and the smallness of its staff, on the other. With forty-five hundred employees CMS is smaller than the Smithsonian Institution. The CMS budget, when state contributions to Medicaid are included, totals more than $700 billion, or more than $1 million per CMS employee. CMS is the very definition of hollowed-out government.

CMS AND GPRA IMPLEMENTATION

In the run-up to the implementation of GPRA, CMS established a technical advisory group to provide assistance in the development of its performance goals and measures. According to one CMS official, the advisory group was made up of "top notch people[;] there's five people on it from different parts of this agency, who examined every one of our performance goals in terms of possibility, feasibility, and measurability (are we measuring what we think we're measuring, and are we going to be able to report out properly on what we say we're going to do). . . . They're technicians, and they're very honest and objective."

The logic of performance measurement, at least as it is applied through GPRA, is that performance measures and indicators are selected on the basis of a program's strategic goals and objectives. Furthermore, a program's goals and objectives are derived from its mission or its parent agency's mission. GPRA requires that agency strategic plans begin with a comprehensive mission statement, and CMS's overall mission is: "We assure health care security for our beneficiaries" (U.S. Department of Health and Human Services, Centers for Medicare and Medicaid Services 2002, 6). No separate specific or individual missions have been established for the Medicare and Medicaid programs. Logic suggests that the mission for Medicare would be: "We assure health care security for Medicare beneficiaries," and for Medicaid the mission would be: "We assure health care security for Medicaid beneficiaries." The "health care security" portion of the mission is relatively straightforward, even though no definition of health care security is provided in the CMS performance plan. It could be assumed, however, that health care security refers to free or inexpensive access to health care services for the populations Medicare and Medicaid are designed to serve, primarily the elderly and the poor.

From the perspective of goal setting and performance measurement, the use of the term "beneficiaries" in the CMS mission is particularly important. Medicare and Medicaid beneficiaries are the programs' participants. Taken literally, then, the mission of these agencies is to ensure free or inexpensive health care access to Medicare's and Medicaid's participants. This is limiting, as one could assume that the CMS mission would be to provide health care access to all qualifying individuals, or those who meet Medicare's and/or Medicaid's eligibility requirements. The use of the term "beneficiaries" rather than the phrase "eligible or qualified individuals" appears to have been carefully chosen.

In the case of Medicare the distinction between beneficiaries and eligible individuals is negligible because they are nearly the same thing; virtually all the elderly are Medicare enrollees. Medicaid is another story, because the gap between the eligible population of the poor and disabled and the ranks of Medicaid enrollees is, depending on whom one listens to, small or wide. The choice of the word "beneficiary" in the overall CMS mission matters for reasons that are described later in this chapter, as are the reasons for the Medicaid beneficiaries–eligible populations gap. Related to the choice of words to describe its mission, the agency changed its name from nomenclature that highlighted its mission of generally providing health care security, the Health Care Financing Administration, to the generic and less-descriptive Centers for Medicare and Medicaid Services.

CMS performance measures for the Medicaid program, though quite limited in number and scope, do address the core mission of the agency: providing the finances by which to access care. Given this mission, and under most circumstances, "providing access to care" would be considered an agency output goal; yet at CMS it is described as an outcome goal. For example, CMS's Medicaid performance measure to increase the number of children on Medicaid through implementing the SCHIP program would, under most circumstances, be considered a measure of outputs. Increasing enrollment, however, can be defined as an outcome, at least a programmatic outcome, if the goal is simply to increase enrollment. Such an approach leaves unanswered the question of whether increased enrollment is positively associated with overall health outcomes. It can be reasonably argued, however, that there is such a causal association. For an agency whose primary mission is to "assure health care security," increased program enrollment can be plausibly defended as an outcome.

Because Medicaid is a federal program shared with the states and territories, the states and territories participate in the determination of the mix of health care services, the level of those services, and the eligibility requirements for those services. One CMS representative related the following about a Medicare goal related to mammography: "For HCFA [now CMS] the number of mammograms, or the percentage receiving mammograms, is an outcome because our purpose is to finance medical care. That makes us different from the Centers for Disease Control [CDC]. Based on their mission, an outcome related to mammography would be a reduction in the number of deaths resulting from breast cancer." In other words, CMS and Medicare are responsible for seeing that program beneficiaries get mammograms; they are not, as they see it, responsible for expanding eligibility for Medicare and thereby increasing the pool of women able to afford mammograms. The suggestion here is that the ultimate health outcomes related to mammography ought to be CDC's concern rather than CMS's concern, because the mission of CMS is to serve only its beneficiaries.

CMS's Medicare performance measures reflect this perspective. The goal is to "increase the percentage of Medicare beneficiaries age 65 years and older who receive a mammogram," which is measured by the percentage increase in biennial mammography rates. The goal is not to reduce incidence of cancer or death rates resulting from breast cancer. The narrative statement attached to the goal includes this comment: "By taking advantage of the lifesaving potential of mammography, we hope to ultimately decrease mortality from breast cancer in the Medicare population. Encouraging breast cancer screening, including regular mammograms, is critical to reducing breast cancer deaths for these populations" (U.S. Department of Health and Human Services, Centers for Medicare and Medicaid Services 2002, 80).

CMS faces the same challenges that all federal health care delivery agencies face in determining what effect their programs have on the health outcomes of their beneficiaries. A CMS official identified the challenge in this way: "We have a serious technical difficulty, which is something every agency faces, of measuring true outcomes. It's much easier to measure processes and outputs than to get an ultimate outcome, which is what GPRA intended to do. For example, it would be great to be able to determine our impact on influenza, but we can only get to that by measuring how many flu vaccinations were given. Trying to get a handle on the connection between our interventions and the ultimate outcomes as defined in the GPRA world is a challenge, a technical challenge that is not unique to HCFA [now CMS]." Of course, these challenges are exacerbated when the work of CMS is done entirely by third parties—states, insurance companies, hospitals, and doctors.

Regarding the possibility of focusing more directly on health outcomes, a CMS executive indicated that "this raises an important question. It would be valuable and we could do it. But it would cost a zillion dollars to do these evaluations. You know, it would be real silly to be trying to save money and doing things more efficiently and run[ning] the government more like a business, but should we spend a zillion dollars on evaluations? We've got to strike a proper balance between measuring or reporting all these things and just doing it. . . . We can't spend countless resources on just measuring performance, which is why we decided to stick to the vital few measures: the time, resources, and energy measuring and gathering data because it is a valuable and important thing to do. But eventually we need to do the work of running Medicare and Medicaid."

This perspective is generally reflected in the CMS approach to overall GPRA implementation. The selection of agency goals has been kept entirely in the range of the feasible, emphasizing service to beneficiaries rather than the eligible, particularly in the case of Medicaid. The selection of just a few measures that determine levels of goal achievement also indicates a cautious approach to GPRA implementation. It is clear that CMS, like HRSA, IHS, and FDA, has been careful to avoid the development of goals that are predicated on causal assertions about the association between agency program effectiveness and the quality of health in relevant populations. In addition, because CMS has defined its mission as service to its beneficiaries, it can plausibly claim that measures of its service to beneficiaries are outcomes.

MEDICAID, THIRD PARTIES, AND PERFORMANCE MEASUREMENT

CMS's performance indicators that deal exclusively with Medicaid are as follows:

☐ increase the percentage of Medicaid two-year-old children who are fully immunized;

☐ assist states in conducting Medicaid payment accuracy studies for the purpose of measuring and ultimately reducing Medicaid payment error rates;

☐ improve health care quality across Medicaid and SCHIP through the CMS/State Performance Measurement Partnership Project; and

☐ decrease the number of uninsured children by working with states to implement SCHIP and by enrolling children in Medicaid.

The measures that are categorized as "dual" are those whose performance is heavily influenced by both Medicare and Medicaid funding. All three of these goals deal with CMS's nursing home survey and certification program. In FY 2001, approximately 19 percent of Medicaid benefit dollars and approximately 6 percent of Medicare benefit dollars went to pay for care in nursing homes (U.S. Department of Health and Human Services, Centers for Medicare and Medicaid Services 2002). The nursing home measures relate to goals to reduce the use of physical restraints in nursing homes, to reduce the prevalence of pressure ulcers (bed sores) in nursing homes, and to improve the consistency of the surveys used to assess the quality of care in nursing homes.

The inclusion of these measures to gauge CMS's performance highlights how an administration's programmatic priorities are reflected in an agency's implementation of GPRA. According to one CMS manager, the Clinton administration considered nursing home quality of care, specifically the reduction of pressure ulcers, to be of such importance that the secretary of HHS, Donna Shalala, became personally involved in the development of these measures. Although this level of personal attention is rare, examples of an administration's or Congress's close involvement in the details of GPRA implementation were found in most of the agencies studied for this book. For example, the Clinton administration pushed NIH's aggressive goal to develop an AIDS vaccine; the Bush administration has been closely involved in the development of HRSA's measures relating to the development of their Consolidated Health Centers Program. The impact of Congress's preferences, as delineated in the Prescription Drug User Fee Act (PDUFA) and the Food and Drug Administration Modernization Act (FDAMA), is reflected throughout FDA's performance plan, as can be seen in measures related to reducing inspection times and other hurdles that slow the time it takes for drugs and food additives to get to the marketplace.

The Medicaid indicators by which CMS measures its performance are a mix of process, output, and outcome measures. Process measures include assisting states with payment accuracy studies, participating with the states in the Performance Measurement Partnership Project, and improving the quality of nursing home surveys. Output measures are for increasing child immunization, increasing SCHIP enrollment, and reducing the use of restraints in nursing homes. The sole outcome measure is to decrease pressure ulcers in nursing homes.

According to one CMS official familiar with the agency's GPRA challenges, "One of the difficulties we face implementing GPRA is the complexity of Medicaid. There is really only one Medicare program, but there are essentially 56 separate Medicaid programs. That means for Medicaid we have to negotiate to design and develop measures." This same official also indicated that even when a set of shared measures can be negotiated, there is still the issue of data collection, submission, and reporting. Because not everyone defines terms in the same manner, data become more difficult to aggregate and less meaningful to analyze. These realities of fiscal intergovernmental relations are very similar to those experienced by HRSA in their implementation of GPRA.

An example of these data collection challenges is highlighted in CMS's efforts to measure its success in meeting the goal to increase the percentage of the two-year-old children enrolled in Medicaid who are fully immunized. The first hurdle is the fact that states have different ways of classifying who a two-year-old is and what constitutes being fully immunized. The options available to CMS to achieve uniformity would be to have mandated definitions of these variables or to negotiate with the states until they could agree on definitions. Because both of these alternatives have drawbacks, CMS decided to do neither. "Since Medicaid is a state-run program it is best for states to determine how to measure their own immunization rates and to determine their own performance targets" (U.S. Department of Health and Human Services, Centers for Medicare and Medicaid Services 2002). CMS recognizes that this approach will impede the establishment of national targets, and, therefore, "as such, comparisons between States will not be useful or meaningful."

After an initial success with sixteen states in the first phase of measuring immunization, in the second phase CMS ran into resistance. According to one official in CMS's Center for Medicaid and State Operations, "We ran into some problems and resistance from the states in the second phase. Due to their resource constraints and other priorities, such as dealing with the Y2K problem, GPRA data collection moved down as a priority." Another official from the same center added, "Some of these states have claimed that the data responsibilities are an unfunded mandate." Eventually, however, resistance faded. According to this same official, the Center for Medicaid and State Operations helped to alleviate this sort of resistance by enlisting successful states from the first phase to assist with the data challenges encountered by some of the states struggling with data and methodological problems in the second phase.

Because the nursing home data already existed, CMS required no additional input from the states. As a result, the goals, targets, and whatever assumptions are built into variable definitions for these measures reflect a decidedly federal influence. The states were bypassed entirely. For the immunization targets, on the other hand, the existing data were not adequate for reporting at the national level. Instead of mandating or negotiating performance targets and data collection methods, CMS decided to serve as a facilitator to help the states implement the immunization targets that they had set themselves.

The measurement of immunization goals was implemented in three phases. The first phase began in 1999, when sixteen states volunteered to establish their own baselines. Since that time, the two remaining groups of states have begun to establish their baselines. By the end of the 2003 fiscal year, all fifty states had completed their baselines, and two of the three groups of states reported their annual performance. States have until their third year of remeasurement to meet performance targets they have set. CMS's role during the years of baseline development has been to assist states to overcome methodological and technical challenges. In these efforts, they have enlisted the help of CDC. CDC has specifically provided assistance to help states achieve greater immunization data reliability.

Of the three remaining measures that deal exclusively with Medicaid, two are process measures—to work with states to improve Medicaid health care quality and improve Medicaid payment accuracy—and one is an output measure—to increase children's Medicaid enrollment through SCHIP. None of these measures deals with health outcomes or even with the delivery of specific health services.

It is clear from an examination of performance measures that deal exclusively with Medicaid that CMS views itself as a partner with the states and territories, the third parties that deliver health care services to their citizens. In the common pattern found in fiscal intergovernmental relations, each of the agreed-on measures requires CMS to assist, coach, encourage, and support the states in their efforts to measure and improve performance. Medicaid as a hollowed-out program, relying on the states and territories to operate its programs, is rather like HRSA. A close look at the narrative sections accompanying each measure indicates an emphasis on cooperation rather than on oversight. By comparison, it is clear that for Medicare performance measures, specifically those in the Medicare Integrity Program and Medicare Operations, the emphasis is on federal oversight of intermediaries and carriers and on federal assumptions that their contractors are agents rather than partners with shared responsibilities.

Medicaid, because it is partially funded by the states and territories and because health care costs continue to increase faster than other costs, is at the center of very complicated politics and particularly the politics of federal–state relations.

Many states are simultaneously implementing Medicaid cost-containment programs and programs of expanded eligibility. In addition, many state leaders charge the federal government with either funding present levels of entitlement or expanding entitlements while not matching those entitlements with additional federal dollars, leaving the states to pick up those costs. Of note, many HHS programs have been recently evaluated using PART, including both Medicare and the Medicare Integrity Program. But the general Medicaid program, a substantial portion of the CMS budget, the HHS budget, and every state's budget, has not been "PARTed." PART is intended to identify which programs are producing results. Given a program with such an enormous budget, it would logically be the kind of program for which PART was established. Medicaid's absence in the first three years of the five-year PART schedule (during which all federal programs will be assessed) is likely because it is both very complex and highly political.

One element of Medicaid, SCHIP, which enrolls poor uninsured children in Medicaid, has been PARTed. SCHIP was rated "adequate" and received a score of 66—which is ten points higher than the average for formula and block grants federalwide. The section of PART in which SCHIP did poorest is Section III (management), where it received less than half the available points. Part of the identified shortcoming was found in the question relating to holding program partners accountable for performance. PART notes, "Without more extensive GPRA and annual performance measures, CMS cannot hold either its managers or the States accountable for cost, schedule, and performance results related to the SCHIP program" (U.S. Office of Management and Budget 2005, 181). SCHIP's key performance measure was to increase the number of poor uninsured children in Medicaid by one million annually until 2004 and then to maintain levels of enrollment. As of 2003, SCHIP enrollment was about 5.3 million children, having grown from fewer than 1 million in 1997 and an even earlier record of declining child enrollment in Medicaid in the early and mid-1990s. GPRA performance measures based on Medicaid's services to its enrolled beneficiaries, as against measures of the health care services to the broader range of poor without either Medicaid or other forms of health insurance, are particularly interesting in the case of SCHIP because of the state and federal emphasis on expanded SCHIP enrollment.

MEDICARE, THIRD PARTIES, AND PERFORMANCE MEASUREMENT

In assessing the differences between the Medicare and Medicaid programs, a CMS representative said, "Well, certainly in the case of Medicare, we are not a direct service supplier. In other words, we are an overseer or regulator. With our Medicaid program, that isn't the case. It's much more indirect, and it's much more diversified. There are 56 separate Medicaid programs, but with Medicare it's all one. There may be many different aspects to it, but we run it, and we're responsible for all of it."

The Medicare program contracts with two main types of third parties to carry out its work. Fiscal intermediaries, referred to simply as intermediaries, assist

CMS in Part A of Medicare by processing hospital claims. Medical carriers, referred to simply as carriers, assist CMS in Part B of Medicare by processing physician claims. The FY 2003 CMS performance plan highlights the importance and magnitude of the intermediaries' and carriers' job. "[In] FY 2003, they will process almost one billion Medicare claims; handle more than seven million appeals; respond to over 40 million inquiries from providers and beneficiaries; enroll, educate, and train providers and suppliers; educate and assist beneficiaries; and perform other responsibilities on behalf of CMS" (U.S. Department of Health and Human Services, Centers for Medicare and Medicaid Services 2002, V-104).

Absent the need to negotiate for performance goals and overcome the obstacles for data coordination, the performance measurement challenges in a contracting environment, such as Medicare, would pale in comparison to a grants program, such as Medicaid. As a few brief examples will illuminate, this is not the case.

CMS goals and accompanying performance measures for the Medicare program are most accurately described as indices of CMS's fiduciary and oversight responsibilities with regard to intermediaries and carriers, its administrative responsibilities over the program, its customer services, and some of its outcomes.

CMS goals that deal exclusively with the Medicare program are organized into the following four categories: Medicare benefits goals, quality-of-care goals, integrity program goals, and operations goals. Each will be discussed in turn.

The Medicare benefits goals are as follows:

1. Improve beneficiary satisfaction.
2. Improve timely (defined by statute) processing of Medicare+Choice enrollment transactions.
3. Improve the beneficiary appeals process.
4. Improve beneficiary understanding of Medicare's basic functions.

As table 5.1 shows, this group of goals and their attendant measures deal with customer or beneficiary service (1 and 4) and with access to Medicare services (2 and 3). Due in part to the daunting task of data collection and the extensive coordination required to collect the data, most of the measures for these goals are still in the development phase. For instance, to collect data using the Consumer Assessment Health Plans Surveys (CAHPS) tool, CMS worked with an impressive array of public sector and private sector partners, including but not limited to the SSA, state and local agencies, advocacy groups, and the American Association of Retired Persons.

This category of goals and its accompanying measures provide an ideal example of how measures that would be defined as outputs under most circumstances are thought to be outcomes in the case of CMS, given that its mission is assurance of access to health care services rather than the ultimate health of beneficiaries. For example, a measure of the efficiency of processing enrollment transactions is an agency-contractor output, but given the goals of CMS, it could be called an outcome with regard to providing access.

TABLE 5.1

MEDICARE AND MEDICAID REPRESENTATIVE PERFORMANCE MEASURES—2005

Medicare Representative Performance Measures	Measure Category
Percent of beneficiaries receiving antibiotic administration to reduce surgical site infection.	POM
Audit opinion on CMS financial statement.	OM
Percent of Medicare beneficiaries receiving influenza vaccination.	OM
Percentage of Medicare beneficiaries who are aware of the 1-800-MEDICARE toll-free number.	PM
Number of questions about Medicare out of 6 answered correctly.	POM
Erroneous payments made under the Medicare program.	OM
Percent of women who receive a biennial mammogram.	OM
Percent of diabetic beneficiaries who receive diabetic eye exams.	OM
Percent of Medicare contractors who have a 5% or better error rate.	POM
Percent of beneficiaries in (1) fee-for-service and (2) managed care who report access to care.	POM
Reduce Medicare's national fee-for-service error rate.	POM
Reduce all contractor error rates.	POM
Reduce provider compliance error rates.	POM

Medicaid Representative Performance Measures	Measure Category
Increase the number of children enrolled in regular Medicaid or SCHIP	POM
Improve health care quality across Medicaid and SCHIP through the Performance Measurement Partnership Project (PMPP)	PM
Increase the percentage of Medicaid 2-year-old children who are fully immunized.	POM
Assist states in conducting Medicaid payment accuracy studies for the purpose of measuring and ultimately reducing Medicaid payment error rates.	PM

POM, program outcome measure; *OM,* output measure; *PM,* process measure; *HOM,* health outcome measure.

The Medicare quality-of-care goals are as follows:

1. Improve heart attack survival rates.
2. Increase the percentage of beneficiaries receiving influenza and pneumococcal vaccinations.
3. Increase the percentage of beneficiaries receiving mammograms.
4. Increase the beneficiary rate of diabetic eye exams.

Peer Review Organizations, now known as Quality Improvement Organizations, are fifty-three geographically dispersed independent physician organizations that contract with CMS "to ensure that medical care paid for under the Medicare program is reasonable and medically necessary, meets professionally recognized standards of health care, and is provided in the most economical setting" (U.S. Department of Health and Human Services, Centers for Medicare and Medicaid Services 2002, V-27). This category of goals and their measures is representative of health conditions that the Peer Review Organizations deem to affect a large number of Medicare beneficiaries and therefore to be a significant burden on the health care system.

These goals deal with health outcomes (1) and access to specific health care services (2–4). Again, given CMS's mission and its definition of goals, the access goals can be reasonably thought of as outcomes. The story behind the goal concerning heart attack survival rates is interesting and instructive. This effort involved disseminating to hospitals throughout the country information about known successful heart attack interventions. These interventions include giving immediate dosages of aspirin and beta-blockers to heart attack sufferers shortly after hospital admission (to reduce blood clotting and heart workload, respectively). In this research and educational effort, CMS worked with the Peer Review Organizations; the National Heart, Lung, and Blood Institute; the American College of Cardiology; the American Heart Association; the American Medical Association; and the American Hospital Association. In a comparison of baseline data generated from a group of states that piloted this effort, CMS estimates that these interventions should save approximately three thousand lives annually.

The Medicare integrity program goals are as follows:

1. Reduce improper Medicare fee-for-service payments.

2. Develop Medicare integrity measures.

3. Improve Medicare program integrity by implementing a comprehensive program integrity plan.

4. Recover money from providers for beneficiary services for which Medicare was supposed to be the secondary (not primary) payer.

5. Assess program integrity customer service.

6. Improve *provider* enrollment process.

The Medicare operations category goals are as follows:

1. Improve beneficiary telephone customer support.

2. Ensure that payment timeliness meets statutory requirements.

3. Increase the use of electronic commerce for making claims.

4. Maintain "clean" audit report on CMS financial statements.

5. Improve oversight of Medicare fee-for-service contractors.

6. Increase delinquent debt referrals to the Department of the Treasury (for collection purposes).

7. Better disseminate monthly notices of benefits received.

Both the integrity program and operations program measures cover CMS's efforts to manage Medicare contractors. These goals are reflective of the fact that CMS is a thoroughly hollowed-out agency. The job of CMS's Medicare employees is to ensure that those with whom CMS contracts get the right amount of money into the right hands for medical services that were actually delivered. This is no small challenge. In FY 2003, intermediaries and contractors processed almost one billion Medicare claims, handled more than seven million appeals, and responded to more than forty million inquiries from providers and beneficiaries.

The Medicare program has been evaluated by OMB with the use of PART. The program was given high marks in all four PART sections and received an overall PART score of 79, with a rating of "moderately effective." Interestingly, although PART allows for assessment of various types (policy tools) of federal programs— even differentiating between competitive and noncompetitive (formula and block) grants—there is no PART instrument specifically for contracted service delivery. There is a PART instrument for capital assets and service acquisition programs, but the Medicare PART did not use that instrument. Medicare was assessed using the direct federal PART instrument. One of the measures, the Medicare payment error rate, was determined to have dropped from 11 percent in 1997 to 5.8 percent in 2003. In the Medicare PART summary document, where follow-up actions are recommended, Medicare is urged to put "greater emphasis on sound program and financial management" and to make "more effort to link Medicare payments to provider performance" (U.S. Office of Management and Budget 2005, 168).

A second related program has been evaluated by using PART, the Medicare Integrity Program (MIP). This program is set up to monitor payment error rates and other problems with third-party implementation. PART rated the MIP as "effective," with a score of 85. Interestingly, to account for the fact that Medicare is a contracted program, the MIP was evaluated using block- and formula-grant PART instruments. Although the partial intent of this chapter is to highlight the differences between services that are contracted out versus services that are provided through grants, the additional two questions included in the block- and formula-grant PART instrument are equally suited for contracted services. These questions are as follows: (1) Does the program have oversight practices that provide sufficient knowledge of grantee activities? and (2) Does the program collect grantee performance data on an annual basis and make it available to the public in a transparent and meaningful manner? If one replaces the word "grantee" with "contractor," then they are equally appropriate for evaluating the oversight of contractor activity.

Perhaps most interesting in the PART evaluation are the comments related to third-party health delivery to the elderly. "Although the program has an effective national measure, it does not require its partners (third parties) to commit to national or subnational error rates," and so "the Administration will complete development of contractor specific error rates and require contractors to commit to reducing their error rates" (U.S. Office of Management and Budget 2005, 169). The commentary goes on to call for a pilot program linking contract awards to reducing error rates.

It is clear from this brief review of the application of the PART approach to assessing program effectiveness that there is more straightforward recognition of the role of third parties in policy implementation in PART than there is with GPRA alone. This helps overcome a weakness in Medicare GPRA applications by putting federal performance measurement more squarely in the context of articulated chains of third-party carriers and health care providers.

PERFORMANCE MEASUREMENT AND CUSTOMER SATISFACTION

One interesting inclusion in the CMS performance plan and report is a performance goal that deals with telephone customer service. A short examination of this goal highlights two important points about CMS's GPRA efforts. First, the work CMS undertakes in this case is very much like customer-satisfaction work done in the private sector. The procedures for filing, processing, and payment of medical claims for Medicare, for example, are no different from the same procedures undertaken by Blue Cross/Blue Shield or Aetna. Indeed, CMS contracts with these same health insurance companies, which CMS refers to as carriers, to provide Medicare beneficiaries with the same services they provide their own customers. This work includes not only the handling of medical claims but also all the supporting customer-service activities, such as the handling of telephone inquiries. Medicare carriers field nearly fifteen million beneficiary inquiries annually, for an average of more than sixty thousand calls each business day. Second, the measurement of something as seemingly straightforward and simple as telephone customer satisfaction is a major endeavor requiring several years to establish a performance baseline.

CMS considered three performance measures of telephone customer service: accessibility (busy signals, time to answer), accuracy of response, and caller satisfaction. The FY 2001 target for this goal reads: "Continue data collection for accessibility, accuracy of response, and caller satisfaction measures" (U.S. Department of Health and Human Services, Centers for Medicare and Medicaid Services 2002, 109).

Why, after (at the time) eight years of GPRA and several iterations of the performance plan, is a goal for telephone customer service still in the developmental stage? Because measuring telephone customer service is a more challenging endeavor than it would first appear. CMS contracts with twenty carriers throughout the country. Medicare carriers process the Medicare Part B claims. Data on telephone customer service that provide for a comparison between carriers are not currently available. A review of the progress toward the goal shows the difficulties CMS has in measuring beneficiary telephone customer service, as table 5.2 indicates. The reader will note that the FY 2000 target to develop baselines and targets was not met, so Medicare backtracked to the revised target for FY 2001 to

TABLE 5.2

GOAL TO IMPROVE BENEFICIARY TELEPHONE CUSTOMER SERVICE

Baseline: Developmental. Baseline data on accessibility, accuracy of response, and caller satisfaction are being collected and will be available by the end of FY 2002.

FY 2003 Target: Using baseline data, establish call-center performance targets for accessibility, accuracy of response, and caller satisfaction. Collect monthly data from each call center, compare performance against targets, and identify where improvements are needed on national and regional levels. Take necessary actions and/or conduct training to bring about improved performance. Specific target goals to be determined.

FY 2002 Target: Complete data collection and set baselines/future targets.

FY 2001 Target: Continue data collection for accessibility, accuracy of response, and caller satisfaction measures (revised due to unavailability of accurate data until FY 2002).

Performance: Goal met. Data collection continuing.

FY 2000 Target: Develop baselines and targets by the end of FY 2000 in areas of accessibility, accuracy of response, and caller satisfaction.

Performance: Goal not met.

---

collect data on accessibility, accuracy of response, and caller satisfaction. Once the FY 2001 target was revised to include only data collection, it was met.

CMS began the process of standardizing definitions, calculating methodology, monitoring calls for quality, and collecting caller satisfaction surveys in FY 2000. But according to a CMS official, during "the first quarter startup, it became evident that additional work was needed with individual contractors concerning the processes and the data input procedures before the accuracy of the data could be ensured." On the basis of these coordination challenges, CMS extended the baseline collection from one to three years and used the baseline data to establish targets in FY 2003. The target for FY 2003 was essentially the same as the original FY 2000 target, which was to use baseline data to establish call center performance targets for accessibility, accuracy of response, and caller satisfaction.

In the midst of CMS work on telephone accuracy goals and performance, Congress passed a new Medicare prescription drug benefit involving drug discount cards for Medicare beneficiaries. Seniors now have a rather complex array of new insurance options and benefits and are invited to telephone 800-MEDICARE to get answers to those questions. The 800-MEDICARE line is operated on the basis of a CMS contract with Pearson Government Solutions, a unit of Pearson P.L.C., an international media company based in London.

Because of persistent criticisms of the help-line program, the Government Accountability Office conducted audits of the telephone call-in systems. Investigators determined that callers received no answer at all 10 percent of the time and obtained the wrong answers 30 percent of the time. In a separate audit of a help line set up to help doctors with their Medicare billing questions, the Government Accountability Office determined that more than half of the answers were wrong or incomplete.

Working with their contractors, Medicare officials prepare scripts to be used by contract employees to answer questions. The Government Accountability Office found that in more than half the cases those who answered the telephone calls either did not understand the scripts or did not know which script to use to answer particular questions.

Dr. Mark B. McClellan, the administrator of CMS, said in a 2004 interview with a reporter from the *New York Times,* "We are faced with an unprecedented volume of calls about a new part of the Medicare program that requires new training efforts and many new customer representatives. We believe we have responded as well as we reasonably could given the unique and demanding circumstances" (*New York Times* December 12, 2004). There are more than forty million Medicare beneficiaries, and during the fiscal year, which ended September 30, 2004, the Medicare help-line systems received more than sixteen million calls.

It is clear that CMS is attempting as best it can to comply with GPRA requirements regarding telephone help-line accuracy. But CMS planning and performance measurement protocols were clearly overtaken by events and overwhelmed by the emergence of a complicated new program and the need to implement it as fast as possible.

The GPRA implementation challenges that Medicare has to overcome have primarily to do with the coordination and oversight of the work done by contractors. For several reasons it has been evident that CMS, as a contractor, has a rather limited capacity to monitor contractor behavior, calling into question the efficiency gains that are supposed to accompany contracting. Although CMS can establish Medicare performance goals, as GPRA requires, Medicare's ability to meet these goals is only partially under its control. The contractor monitoring and enforcement mechanisms available to CMS are constrained by Medicare's authorizing legislation and its regulations, particularly a provision that does not allow CMS to contract with any intermediary it wishes. Instead, claims-processing intermediaries are selected by professional associations of hospitals and certain other institutional providers on behalf of their members. In addition, under the authorizing legislation, CMS can only contract on a cost basis, which does not allow for fixed-price or performance-based contracts. Another constraint is found in CMS's own regulations, which stipulate that the contractors that serve Medicare beneficiaries as carriers must be insurance companies that serve the full range of beneficiary needs. The regulations do not allow functional contracts—to respond to beneficiary questions, for example—for specific services, even if functional contractors could provide services more efficiently. Because these constraints limit the number of companies that qualify and want to contract with Medicare, the leverage CMS is able to use to enforce contract terms is limited (U. S. General Accounting Office 1999).

The development of performance measures, data collection, and coordination with third parties is a greater challenge in a grant-based program than it is in a contract-based program, according to one CMS insider who contrasted the challenges of working with the states (for Medicaid) versus working with contractors (for Medicare). She said that "contractors are in a very different position. They work for us; they're not partners. We tell them what the requirements are and then make meeting the requirements a condition of contract continuance." Although this statement makes sense logically, reality does not always bear out the comparative ease of measuring performance in a contracting environment versus a grants to subgovernments environment. Two recent examples are illustrative of this.

The partnership and cooperation model of working with states to develop Medicaid performance measures was highlighted by a CMS executive who stated that "we spend much more time and effort with the states to explain GPRA and its requirements. We are also constantly stressing the possible advantages of performance measurement. With the states we try to be partner oriented, less directive, and persuasive. Most importantly, we try to convince them that the data they provide to us won't eventually be used against them." The reality is, however, that how the data get used is not ultimately under CMS's control. Examples, anecdotes, and vignettes of poor contractor performance or state failure to comply are frequently used in congressional oversight or appropriations hearings. For this reason, some CMS employees are less sanguine about the future use of performance data. When asked what could cause GPRA to ultimately fail, a CMS executive responded, "GPRA could easily lead us to be too self-conscious about stretching ourselves. The incentives don't work in that direction. The danger about setting aggressive goals in a GPRA environment is that their nonattainment will be publicized."

Y2K COMPLIANCE, THIRD PARTIES, AND PERFORMANCE MEASUREMENT

The difficulty of achieving Y2K compliance is an interesting example of CMS's contract-monitoring challenges. CMS's Y2K compliance difficulties stemmed not from its internally managed systems but from the computer systems managed by its contractors. As she attempted to find ways to address the agency's unique Y2K compliance challenges, Nancy-Ann Min DeParle, CMS's administrator from 1998 to 2002, looked to the contracts themselves. To her surprise, she found that contract renewals were self-executing annually. Notwithstanding some debate about her ability to require contractors to be Y2K compliant, Min DeParle met with many of the contractors' chief executive officers to encourage their compliance. She helped them to understand that the contractors could not afford system failure. In the end, CMS's systems (those managed internally and externally) operated through January 1, 2000, without any major disruptions (National Academy of Public Administration 2000).

Of Medicare's ninety-nine mission-critical computer systems, twenty-four are managed internally by CMS, and the remaining seventy-five are managed by third parties (medical carriers and intermediaries). Although all the computer systems managed internally by CMS were Y2K compliant, not all those systems managed by third parties were compliant. Depending on how narrowly one defines the term "CMS computer system," it could be argued that CMS had met this goal. In practical terms, however, some mission-critical Medicare computer systems were not compliant in time. CMS's noncompliance because of the late start is partially a function of constraints found in the contracting provisions within Medicare's authorizing legislation, which ultimately had to be amended to allow CMS to direct its contractors to fix Y2K problems within a specific time.

COMPLIANCE, FRAUD, AND PERFORMANCE MEASUREMENT

Medicare fraud has plagued CMS for years, costing the agency billions of dollars. Medicare contractors, who pay claims to beneficiaries, are also charged with monitoring and reducing Medicare fraud. Since mid-1997, forty-four of these contractors have pled guilty to schemes to defraud the Medicare program, and they have paid more than $275 million to settle charges filed against them (Pear 1999; U.S. General Accounting Office 1999).

CMS's inadequate ability to monitor the compliance of their contractors traces in part to the previously mentioned constraints in Medicare's authorizing legislation and the agency's inability to "regularly check contractors' internal management controls, management and financial data, and key program safeguards to prevent payment errors" (U.S. General Accounting Office 1999, 5). CMS's inability to monitor contractor activities adequately is highlighted by the fact that the fraudulent behavior of contractors is almost never detected by CMS but by whistleblowers who work for contractors. In most instances contractor employees brought allegations of illegal activities to CMS's attention (Pear 1999).

CMS's extensive focus on contractors' customer-service activities might come at the expense of fraud detection. When CMS discovered that Blue Cross and Blue Shield of Michigan was providing inadequate service to Michigan's Medicare beneficiaries (from a customer-service standpoint), CMS replaced them with Blue Cross and Blue Shield of Illinois because of its solid customer-service reputation. Last year Blue Cross and Blue Shield of Illinois, which won the contract primarily on the basis of its strong customer-services reputation, was ordered to pay $4 million in criminal charges and $140 million in civil charges because of its fraudulent Medicare activities. CMS's hands were tied because, as noted earlier, their regulations do not permit functional contracts. Functional contracts would have allowed Blue Cross and Blue Shield of Michigan to continue its sound performance with regard to fiscal obligations, and a separate contract for related customer services could have been let.

Although it is important for CMS to have goals related to both customer service and health care outcomes, CMS's primary responsibilities with regard to Medicare are financial and fiduciary. Because CMS employees do not provide health care services or process claims for Medicare beneficiaries, they are at least one step removed from both of these activities. Although CMS has struggled with contractee-contractor relationships in the past, goals relating to fraud and abuse now appear in its performance budgets and annual reports that begin to reflect the actual nature of the relationship among the CMS, Medicare contractors, and the problems of fraud and abuse. CMS's performance plan goal number 24, to improve the efficiency of medical review claims, calls for a more extensive system of monitoring, including audits and investigations of contractor performance and independent verification of contractor claims. Until changes are made in Medicare regulations and the Medicare authorizing legislation is amended, contractor monitoring efforts will have only limited success.

CONCLUSIONS: COMPARING GRANTEES AND CONTRACTORS

This chapter began by asking how different forms of third-party policy implementation affect performance measurement and are affected by performance measurement. Easily the most interesting and informative characteristics of the application of GPRA performance measurement at CMS have to do with the core differences between the two programs. These differences are illustrated by the placement of Medicare and Medicaid on the nine continua or variables shown in figure 5.1. Both Medicare and Medicaid are entirely hollowed out, but differently hollowed out.

Medicare is a huge financial transfer agency that uses very large third-party carriers and administrative contracts. Medicare provides money in the context of a dizzying array of standards and requirements to be implemented by contract intermediaries and carriers, but it does not provide any direct services, at least in the traditional definition of governmental services. Furthermore, its primary contractors do not provide medical services but serve, instead, as funding mechanisms and standards enforcers for health care organizations, doctors, and hospitals that provide services. This is a highly unique setting for the implementation of performance measurement.

In terms of the variables or categories used in this research, Medicare exhibits the following primary characteristics:

☐ high stakeholder and client support;

☐ very decentralized arrangements for policy implementation;

☐ a "managed network" approach to articulation between the agency and its third-party partners;

☐ a managed network articulation that achieves relatively high levels of accountability to federal program proposes; and

☐ just as services are exported to contractors, so too are the difficult choices at the nexus of competing purposes—to fund health care for the elderly while simultaneously controlling the costs of health care for the elderly.

In this challenging context Medicare has chosen a unique approach to GPRA performance measurement. It is the CMS claim that the core purpose of Medicare is to fund, through contract intermediaries and carriers, health care financing for the elderly. It is specifically not the purpose of Medicare to improve directly the

FIGURE 5.1

KEY VARIABLES IN THE SYNTHESIS OF THE INFLUENCE OF PERFORMANCE MEASUREMENT IN THE CENTERS FOR MEDICARE AND MEDICAID SERVICES

A. The Level of Third-Party Policy Implementation

    MCD   *MCR*

hollowed out   *direct government*

B. Accountability to Federal Program Purposes

                                              MCD   *MCR*

attenuated   *strict*

C. The Nature and Quality of Network Articulations

                        MCD   *MCR*

remote control   *managed network*

D. The Characteristics of Goals

    MCD   *MCR*

processes   *outputs*   *(POM) outcomes (HOM)*

E. The Level of Goal and Policy Agreement

                                      MCD   *MCR*

disagreement   *agreement*
incongruence   *congruence*

F. The Level of Centralization of Policy Implementation

          MCD   *MCR*

decentralized   *centralized*
dispersed, fragmented

G. The Precision and Characteristics of Performance Measures

                                                           MCD   *MCR*

qualitative   *quantitative*
descriptive   *precise*

H. The Level and Character of Client and Stakeholder Support

                                              MCD   *MCR*

weak   *divided*   *strong*

I. Professional Identity

          MCD   *MCR*

low   *high*

MCD, Medicaid; *MCR*, Medicare; *POM*, program outcome measure; *HOM*, health outcome measure.

health circumstances of the elderly. "We assure health care security for our beneficiaries," CMS claims, and "performance and results" should only be judged by
this circumscribed mission. Therefore, the "outputs" of CMS, and particularly of
Medicare, are measures of how well Medicare finances are handled. It is interesting to compare the circumscribed CMS mission with the expansive HRSA mission
to "improve the nation's health by assuring equal access to comprehensive, culturally competent, quality health care for all" (U.S. Department of Health and
Human Services, Centers for Medicare and Medicaid Services 2002, 2).

The lesson in federal performance measurement is this: How an agency describes its mission is a predicate to the descriptive characteristics of an agency's
goals. If agency missions and goals are very carefully developed, it is possible to
"set up" performance to focus continually on questions of effective management
rather than on questions of social or economic outcomes. Even though Medicare's
goals and performance measures have to do with effective management, CMS has
carefully chosen a mission for which effective management is itself a measurable
outcome.

The thoughtful guidance of CMS through GPRA performance measurement
in this direction has not, however, solved two big CMS Medicare challenges. The
first has to do with data. Because it is hollowed out, Medicare is obliged to partially export to third parties and service providers funded through third parties
the complex challenge of finding common definitions, gathering data that fit these
definitions, managing those data, and, on the basis of annual data, producing the
performance measures called for by GPRA. Because of the size and complexity of
Medicare and its third-party contractors, it is taking much longer than was originally anticipated to develop performance measures and put them in place. Contract specifications call for development of such measures in a timely way, but the
real emphasis in Medicare is on funding services, and the real controversies in
Medicare have less to do with data and performance measurement (with the possible exception of fraud reduction and telephone help-line accuracy) and more to
do with the competing expectations of funding health care for the elderly while
controlling the costs of funding health care for the elderly.

The second challenge in GPRA implementation has to do with the nature of
Medicare as an articulated vertical network of third parties. At the agency level,
articulation is based on the specific wording of contracts. In fact, on an actual
day-to-day basis, CMS, as a contract manager, is the principal in highly dynamic
reciprocal interactions with its third parties. Once a contract is approved, contractee-contractor relations take on the form of problem solving, negotiations, and
the search for effectiveness. This effectiveness turns more on contractor-contractee
trust and less on the specific wording of the contract. Although contracts change
in significant ways only when they are fully renegotiated, continual incremental
adjustments make highly decentralized policy implementation possible. Medicare
is famous for what seems to medical providers to be constantly changing rules
and procedures. We see in this articulation relatively dynamic, tight coupling between Medicare and its third parties in term of policy detail, in the relentless in-
terplay between the health care service expectations of the elderly, on the one
hand, and the need to control costs, on the other. The actual implementation of

policy is, however, relatively loosely coupled, leaving considerable latitude with third parties to interact with service providers in locally acceptable ways, so long as general policy is followed—which is not easy. In this context GPRA performance measures are relevant.

A careful reading of Medicare program goals and attendant performance measures shows them to have almost entirely to do with improving service, expanding services to beneficiaries (almost all elders are beneficiaries, so there is no significant difference between the beneficiaries and those eligible to be beneficiaries), improving services to beneficiaries, and improving payment and approval processes. There are no goals or attendant measures having to do with cost reductions, although the goal to reduce improper Medicare fee-for-service payments might be interpreted as such a goal. Thus, cost-savings imperatives are passed on to third-party contractors; Medicare performance measures do not touch this controversial issue. If one were to look carefully at its goals, one might think that Medicare is all about improved and expanded service. In fact, improved service is only a part of the purposes or expectations of Medicare, particularly from the perspective of elected officials, because they are just as interested in cost controls.

One performance measure is notable: to improve oversight of Medicare fee-for-service contractors. As described earlier in this chapter, Medicare's authorizing legislation and its own regulations significantly reduce the prospects for improved contractor oversight because contractors are only partially under Medicare control. Nevertheless, it appears that the Medicare program and its third-party contractors are, in the main, accountable to federal program purposes, recognizing that Medicare is embedded in a context of competing purposes.

Unlike Medicare, Medicaid is best understood in terms of fiscal intergovernmental relations. Goal setting and performance measurement at Medicaid appear to be heavily influenced by changing relations regarding health care policy and implementation between the federal government and the states and territories. The salience of the states and territories is indicated by the claim that, unlike Medicare, which is one program with many third-party contractors, Medicaid is fifty-six programs, each with somewhat distinct characteristics. This confirms the fundamental generalization about American intergovernmental relations—a dynamic pattern of adjustment between federal purposes and state and territorial preferences. This point is made all the more important because, unlike HRSA, which is mostly comprised of federally funded programs carried out by states and territories, Medicaid receives about half of its funding from the states and territories.

Although subject to varying explanations, the complexity of Medicaid likely accounts for the remarkably limited number and scope of its GPRA goals and performance measures. This complexity has led CMS to a cautious approach to goal setting and performance measures. Like Medicare, Medicaid goals and measures tend to emphasize management and agency outputs. Unlike Medicare, Medicaid does have two measures of outcome, if one defines outcomes as expanded enrollment of those who are eligible and as increases in child immunization.

As would be expected in an intergovernmental program such as Medicaid, vertical network articulations tend to be loosely coupled, subject to negotiations and renegotiation, much like diplomatic relations between nation-states. In such a context, achieving a common definition of terms is a great challenge, as is the challenge of agreeing on performance goals, attendant measures, and data. It is no wonder that, like HRSA, Medicaid has developed a performance partnership, this one called the Measurement Partnership Project, through which the program works with the states and territories to sort out performance measurement data issues. Operating Medicaid in the heat of federal–state intergovernmental politics is both complicated and controversial even without GPRA-driven attempts to measure the performance of the states.

In summary terms, Medicaid

- [ ] is very decentralized;
- [ ] has limited client and stakeholder support, not unlike support associated with welfare or food stamps;
- [ ] has few and limited GPRA goals and performance measures;
- [ ] uses quantitative performance measures;
- [ ] is the least accountable to federal goals of the agencies and programs studied here, in large part because it is fiscal intergovernmental relations at work;
- [ ] enjoys fairly high levels of rhetorical policy agreement, agreement to the effect that those who have fallen through the health care financing cracks should have a federal/state safety net; and
- [ ] experiences continual tension regarding who should pay for the Medicaid safety net.

In addition to grantee third parties and contract third parties, there are research third parties. And, just as there are many forms of third parties, there are many ways to measure performance. We now turn to one of the most interesting applications of GPRA in the federal government—the National Institutes of Health.

6

PERFORMANCE AS GRANTS TO THIRD-PARTY RESEARCH PROVIDERS

The National Institutes of Health

How shall performance be measured when the tasks taken on by third parties are exploratory? How can performance be understood when the means by which objectives are achieved are decidedly unclear? How shall performance measurement be logically understood when it is evident that genuine performance almost always involves many years rather than a single year? The National Institutes of Health is uniquely suited to finding the answers to these questions.

NIH was selected as a subject for this book because the results of the work of the agency are inherently difficult to measure. The primary purpose of NIH is to fund research, usually pure or basic research carried out by third parties. Agency goals, according to GPRA legislation, are to be expressed in quantifiable and measurable form, unless authorized otherwise by the director of OMB. Much of the logic of performance metrics simply assumes that institutional goals can be made precise and specific and that reasonably formal indices of progress toward those goals can be formulated. Performance metrics further assume either that reliable annual data are available or that data can be gathered to make indices of goal achievement operational. In the case of NIH, these assumptions are questionable. Up until 2003–2004, NIH was one of only a few federal agencies that expressed substantial portions of its performance information in qualitative and narrative form. NSF, an agency rather like NIH in terms of its basic research mission, also uses qualitative measures. Indicators for the five "research outcome" goals of NIH's research program, which make up approximately 95 percent of the NIH budget, were, until recently, qualitative.

Understanding NIH's GPRA implementation is an important part of this book because the NIH application of qualitative performance measurement can be used to extrapolate or deduce how performance measurement is likely to be implemented at other research agencies, such as NSF, or other federal agencies with hard-to-quantify, long-term goals. This treatment of NIH helps identify the characteristics and qualities of performance measurement in federal agencies that support basic or pure research and give grants to third parties to do that research.

The word "grant" is used here because it is the common word used by NIH and NSF to describe contracts to third parties for research. In the other chapters of this book, the word "grant" is used to describe allocations of federal funds to states and territories to carry out federal programs or to third parties whose work does not easily lend itself to annual quantitative measures of performance.

THE NATIONAL INSTITUTES OF HEALTH AND THIRD-PARTY RESEARCH PROVIDERS

NIH is an especially good example of the workings of modern, grant-based, third-party government. Like HRSA and IHS, most of the NIH budget goes in the form of research grants to third parties. NIH operates on the basis of peer-reviewed discretionary grants, a subset of the larger class of categorical grants of both the formula and the discretionary, or project, type. Project grants are intended to spur innovation, make scientific discoveries, demonstrate scientific reliability, support scientific experimentation, and provide technical assistance. Most of these intentions lack well-defined or precise measures of need, capacity, or benefits (Salamon 1989). Project grants are competitively awarded and, in the case of NIH, given on the basis of previous expertise and estimates of the probability of success. Project grants are different from block and formula grants to the states and territories or to cities or other subgovernments because of the "much broader discretion regarding purpose and use to the recipients" (Salamon 1989, 96).

NIH has a relatively large internal staff, partially to manage the vast contract and grant oversight apparatus of the agency. It also conducts so-called intramural research, or in-house research. In all, there are about seventeen thousand NIH employees and an overall budget request of $29.5 billion for FY 2006, up from $22 billion in FY 2002. NIH is by far the largest health research organization in the world. Although the numbers are difficult to extrapolate, it is no doubt the case that NIH spends more per dollar on contract management than HRSA, CMS, or IHS. Using the logic developed by Paul Light (1999), and applied to HRSA in chapter 3, one can estimate that about $2.5 billion of the $29.5 billion NIH budget goes to support general administration, including grant management, and to support intramural research. Because health research is labor intensive, it is estimated that the remaining $27 billion supports a nationwide health research cadre of more than 190,000 FTE persons scattered among the leading American medical research centers, medical schools, and universities. Put another way, there are about eleven FTE persons engaged in NIH-funded medical and health research for every one direct NIH employee. These 190,000 FTE employees are scattered across the United States, making NIH one of the most geographically decentralized agencies in the federal government, at least in terms of its grant-based third parties. Medical schools and universities organize their research functions on the basis of NIH centers and institutes, with laboratories for cancer, AIDS, and the other diseases around which NIH is organized. In addition, medical schools and health research organizations are fully geared up to follow NIH grant criteria and protocols.

University medical schools and health research organizations and the various institutes of NIH have interdependent and symbiotic relationships that have evolved over the years. Medical schools and health research organizations are staffed by highly educated and qualified scientific researchers on the basis of assumptions of a close and continuing relationship based on staff expertise, consistent research success, and the possibility of NIH financial support. In turn, NIH serves as a consistent and usually reliable source of financial support. Although NIH grants are made on a competitive basis, using juries and forms of peer review, this competition is within the narrow "symbiotic" range of established NIH–medical school or health research organizations.

STRATEGIC GOAL SETTING AND PERFORMANCE MEASUREMENT AT NIH

NIH is not only geographically decentralized; it is also highly decentralized organizationally. Research at NIH is performed and coordinated through twenty-seven semiautonomous institutes and centers, each focused on one area of health research. NIH institutes include the National Cancer Institute, the National Institute of Neurological Disorders and Stroke, and the National Institute of General Medical Sciences. Illustrative of NIH centers are the National Center for Research Resources and the National Center for Minority Health and Health Disparities. Each institute and center prepares and submits GPRA performance data in the manner prescribed by NIH. The data are then compiled so that the performance of the entire NIH is considered in toto rather than for each individual institute or center. Although NIH is organized and managed in a highly decentralized fashion, the official NIH response to GPRA has been rather centralized.

The mission of NIH is to "uncover new knowledge about the prevention, detection, diagnosis, and treatment of disease and disability" (U.S. Department of Health and Human Services, National Institutes of Health 2002, 9). To achieve this mission the seven overall NIH goals are to

☐ add to the body of knowledge about normal and abnormal biological functions and behavior;

☐ develop new or improved instruments and technologies for use in research or medicine;

☐ develop new or improved approaches for preventing or delaying the onset or progression of disease and disability;

☐ develop new or improved methods for diagnosing disease and disability;

☐ develop new or improved methods for treating disease and disability;

☐ develop critical genomic resources, including the DNA sequences of the human genome and the genomes of important model organisms and disease-causing microorganisms; and

☐ develop an AIDS vaccine by 2007 (later changed to 2010).

With the exception of the AIDS vaccine goal, the other overall goals are cross-cutting, generally applicable to all NIH institutes and centers. At the institute level there are not any specific goals, such as a goal to cure cancer. After years of experience with the challenges of finding cures for diseases, it is clear that NIH is reluctant to set specific goals with attendant annual measures of performance to achieve cures that take years to find, if they are found at all. The exception, the goal to discover an AIDS vaccine by 2007, was politically imposed on the agency during the Clinton administration. By 2005 it became evident that the goal of an AIDS vaccine was not going to be met by 2007, so NIH simply changed the goal to developing an AIDS vaccine by 2010.

The goals of individual research projects are far less general and sweeping than finding a vaccine for AIDS, a cure for cancer, or even a cure for the common cold. Instead, most NIH grants fund basic research, which is foundational and several steps prior to developing cures for diseases. An NIH research project might seek, for example, to discover something about the behavior of a cell that might be related to the development of a disease. According to one NIH executive, "The nature of our business is to be investment oriented, where outcomes and results are long range and uncertain and can't be reported annually with much ease."

Apart from the challenges associated with measuring the performance of an agency charged with responsibility for basic research, the characteristics of research grants suggest three difficulties for performance measurement. First, NIH goals tend to be very broadly stated, such as developing new or improved methods for treating disease or disability. Because the goals are so broad, and because the contribution of a particular grant-funded research project to the achievement of particular goals is usually very narrow, it is difficult to measure the contributions of each research project toward the achievement of an overall goal.

Second, research grant–receiving organizations are given rather wide discretion regarding both overall goals and the organization of specific projects designed to achieve those goals. In simple terms, NIH makes grants to research groups that are trying to make discoveries, and this can be an untidy and unpredictable process. For example, a research team at a medical school may have a concept, an informed hunch, or an idea and may describe it to NIH officials. In the rarified world of medical and scientific research, investments in such ideas can be critically important if only to rule out possibilities, because ruling out possibilities is vitally important in scientific research. But money spent on ruling out possibilities could appear, following the strict logic of performance measurement, to have been wasted.

Third, the patterns of NIH third-party articulation are loosely coupled, granting research teams extensive discretion with regard to selecting their focus and activities. The authors of GPRA evidently did not anticipate such arrangements, because there is nothing in the GPRA's text that anticipates the problems of goal specification and performance measurement precision for agencies that fund pure or basic research.

Although the percentage of NIH's budget going to third parties is not as great as that of HRSA or Medicare, the tightness of agency–third-party articulation between the NIH and its grant recipients is not nearly as great as at HRSA or

Medicare. The "relaxed," "weak," or "loosely coupled" articulation between NIH and its grant recipients is designed rather than accidental, based on years of experience on the part of both NIH officials and third-party research organizations. Loosely coupled articulations make it difficult to convey performance objectives to grant recipients or even to monitor their performance during the course of a grant or in advance of the completion of a grant. According to an NIH official, if any of the grant recipients are aware of the goals in NIH's GPRA performance plan, it would be by accident rather than by design. NIH officials do not share agency goals with grant recipients, nor do they intend to do so. The justification for not sharing GPRA goals with grant recipients is straightforward: NIH wants to avoid even the suggestion that its grant-supported research could be biased so as to satisfy a priori performance expectations. They do not want NIH-supported researchers to "teach to the test" by "adapting" their findings so as to meet some preestablished goal or deadline.

THE USE OF QUALITATIVE PERFORMANCE MEASURES AT NIH

NIH initially devised a particularly interesting system of qualitative performance measurement and reporting regimes. There is simply no question that the NIH approach to GPRA implementation was unique. According to one NIH official with GPRA implementation responsibilities:

> Well, there was actually a lot of discussion about whether we could use these traditional quantitative methods because, in a way, it would have been easier for us to just use numbers. But we thought that just because we can count it doesn't mean we should, and doesn't mean that it would be meaningful. We felt very strongly that just counting was not going to be useful for demonstrating our accountability to the public and what they're getting for their research dollars. We needed a more descriptive way to say, "Here's the actual outcomes of our research program. Here's what we found, here's what we do, here's what's come from this." So we thought that the publication of our stories is certainly an important vehicle for this—it's the knowledge of new treatments and diagnostics that comes from our research that really needs to be demonstrated.

This system can be illustrated by giving examples taken from the pre-2004 GPRA reports of the National Institute of Mental Health. The data NIH used to demonstrate performance were science advances, science capsules, and stories of discovery. Science advances are one-page narratives that detail a specific scientific discovery published within the last year and supported by NIH funding. Narratives describe the significance of the finding to science, health, and/or the economy (see appendix B).

Science capsules are one-paragraph narratives that provide a snapshot of the breadth and scope of NIH research. Because there is a limit to the sheer number of detailed, one-page science advances, science capsules are a way to condense science advances and to describe briefly the achievements of research programs (see appendix C).

Stories of discovery are one- to two-page narratives focusing on advances in a broad topic of medical research. Stories of discovery shift the focus away from single, incremental findings described in science advances or science capsules and describe, for example, biomedical progress achieved through long-range research programs that aggregate the results of a number of smaller achievements. Each story of discovery traces major developments over several decades in particular domains of scientific research. In NIH stories of discovery, the connections between advances in science and improvements in the quality of life, health, and health care, as well as any resulting economic benefits, are also highlighted. Stories of discovery are filled with causal assertions (see appendix D).

Three points underscore the utility of the NIH use of qualitative/narrative science advances, science capsules, and stories of discovery. First, they are very well written. This skillful writing is both scientifically reliable and very readable. Indeed, the story of the development of medicines for schizophrenia is quite gripping. It is difficult to ascertain how these written accounts are developed, but NIH has either first-rate scientific writers on its staff or contracts for such services. Second, these qualitative/narrative descriptions of NIH performance have previously been used when NIH officials appear at congressional appropriations hearings. Legislators and their staffs appear to have been responsive to this approach, because there is no evidence of demands on their part for precise, quantitative measures of NIH performance. Third, the use of qualitative/narrative performance measures, at least as implemented by NIH, is a particularly clever way to get around the requirements for annual reporting. This is especially important because, given the long-range research objectives of NIH, annual reporting makes little sense. One NIH representative described NIH reasoning this way: "I think that we need to describe basic research, and it's really hard to do that on an annual basis. Asking for annual reports is really kind of farcical at times because that's not the way science works. We don't look at one-year increments; it takes many years of investment and findings build upon one another. Research does not necessarily proceed linearly. Maybe some findings we made years ago and we didn't know necessarily when, say ten years later, will fit with some other findings. Suddenly pieces of the puzzle fall into place. To ask us to tell what scientific accomplishments have been in the last year seems quite ridiculous at times."

Finally, research awards and honors are brief write-ups that describe outside evaluations of NIH research programs and recognitions given to those programs. The research/awards/honors narratives include details of scientific awards and honors received by NIH scientists and grantees during the previous fiscal year.

This system of GPRA indicators builds on earlier pre-GPRA NIH approaches used successfully for many years to provide the members of congressional appropriations committees and subcommittees favorable information about NIH's research programs in support of their budget justifications. Condensed versions of what are now GPRA science advances had been used for budget and appropriations justification for several years. With the coming of GPRA, these science advances have been made more robust, and the three other forms of qualitative indicators described here have been added to form the current battery of NIH qualitative performance indicators.

GPRA COMPLIANCE AT NIH

Although the focus of this chapter is primarily on qualitative performance measures, NIH has also had a battery of quantitative measures in the following categories:

- ☐ communication of results
- ☐ technology transfer
- ☐ research leadership and administration
- ☐ research training and career development
- ☐ research facilities program

Obviously, these goals have to do with the management processes and agency outputs of NIH rather than measures of health-quality outcomes. Goals associated with the communication of NIH results and the measures of those goals describe success in communicating scientific results to the medical research community, health care providers, patients, and the general public. Technology transfer goals and measures assess NIH's success in transferring new technology to the private sector resulting from NIH research so that these technologies can be incorporated into new drugs and other products that might benefit health. Research leadership and administration goals and measures assess NIH's success in setting priorities in health research, in administering an effective and efficient peer-review system for its grants, and in providing general agency management and administrative support. Research training and career development goals cover NIH's programs to ensure a continuing supply of well-trained health scientists. The research facilities program goals relate to NIH's efforts to modernize intramural and extramural research facilities.

In sheer numbers, NIH's quantitative measures far outnumber its qualitative measures. Indeed, the NIH performance plan states that the majority of its indicators are quantitative (U.S. Department of Health and Human Services, National Institutes of Health 2002). The plan states that "in most cases, the basis for performance assessment involves data that are uncontroversial, credible, and open to public scrutiny" (21). What NIH seems to be saying is that because the measures are quantitative, they are credible on their face. Wherever the NIH plan refers to its quantitative measures, it calls them "objective/quantitative." Although it is unintended, this language favors quantitative over qualitative measures in the same way GPRA legislation does. Given the qualitative characteristics of the measures associated with the NIH research programs, the central mission of NIH, the claim of objectivity associated with NIH quantitative measures may seem strange. But because GPRA is itself distinctly biased toward quantitative measures, the NIH wording is understandable. If quantitative measures are singled out for their lack of controversy and high credibility, one is left to wonder whether NIH believes that qualitative measures are noted for their controversy and lack of credibility. Quantitative data and the analysis of quantitative data are the foundation of much of science research, so when NIH determines that one of the best ways to assess its performance is through qualitative and narrative means, it evidently feels the need, if indirectly, to apologize.

It is important to note that although the number of quantitative measures in the NIH plan is greater than the number of its qualitative measures, all the measures that relate to its central research mission are qualitative. Furthermore, many of the goals in the quantitative section of NIH's performance plan cannot actually be classified as actual measures of health outcomes. Several of these goals begin with such phrases as "increase awareness . . . ," "increase understanding . . . ," and "increase knowledge . . . ." Other goals begin with such phrases as "identify ways . . ." and "further educate . . . ." Even though some of these goals do not include an expected quantitative level of performance, the reporting of their success does include quantitative data. For example, the communication-of-results goal includes a performance measure to "increase awareness of the effects of drug abuse among Native American Indians." The actual performance for this goal is reported quantitatively by stating that the "NIH distributed 150,000 calendars with anti-drug messages to this population via Native American Organizations and Businesses." In terms of GPRA compliance, it would be more desirable if the performance target were to become congruent (by making it also quantitative) with the actual performance reported. For instance, the goal could read "to increase awareness of the effects of drug abuse among Native American Indians by distributing 150,000 calendars with anti-drug messages to this population." With 150,000 calendars distributed, NIH could then report that its performance targets had been met. In this hypothetical case, both the performance target and the actual performance reported were expressed in quantitative terms. The more important question, however, is whether distributing antidrug calendars to American Indians is a good idea, that is, whether it worked.

The danger, as indicated in chapter 1, is the possibility of "the measurable driving out the important." If we assume that the goal of increasing the awareness of the effects of drug abuse among Native American Indians is a good objective, the important question is how best to achieve that goal. When an agency is faced with the requirement to measure and report on performance, the range of alternatives for determining what is the best approach narrows. If we assume that the goal is increasing drug awareness among Native Americans, the structured response is essentially the creation of another goal—measuring performance. Critics of the emphasis on performance measurement would suggest that this is a rather good example of goal displacement. GPRA only requires agencies to express their goals in "objective, quantifiable, and measurable form" and indicates that success in achieving performance goals must be reported annually. In the search for options to achieve program goals, one might reasonably ask whether the requirement to measure results and report results annually might bias the processes of policy implementation away from courses of action that are hard to measure and take several years to achieve and toward short-run and more easily measurable courses of action.

Just as FDA's performance plan reveals the extent to which FDA is responsive to its constituents, including Congress, NIH's responsiveness to powerful external actors is evident in its performance plan (Casamayou 2001; Springarn 1976). Six of the seven qualitative goals for NIH's research program deal with disease and disability broadly understood. The only exception to NIH's use of qualitative goals for its research program is the goal to find an AIDS vaccine within ten years. President Clinton compared the search for an AIDS vaccine with President Kennedy's challenge in the early 1960s to put a man on the moon by the end of the decade. Indeed, the moon shot metaphor appears to be a primary form of NIH rhetoric, particularly on the part of elected officials.

In NIH's first performance plan, the 1999 plan, the AIDS vaccine goal was one of two quantitative goals for the outcomes of the NIH research program; the other goal was to develop the DNA sequence and other critical genomic resources. Neither of these goals was necessarily expressed in quantitative terms; rather, the indicators on which progress was to be gauged were quantitative. In subsequent performance plans, the "AIDS vaccine by 2007" and later the "AIDS vaccine by 2010" goal was initially changed from quantitative to qualitative, and the measures for this goal were made narrative rather than numeric. For instance, progress toward the goal of the AIDS vaccine is indicated by such narratives as "progress in collaborating with scientists in developing countries and with industry . . ." and "progress in the design and development of new or improved vaccine strategies and delivery/production technologies."

Table 6.1 is a list of representative NIH performance goals prior to FY 2004 and those adopted thereafter. The most notable difference between the two lists is that the current measures are both quantitative and include specific dates for their achievement.

ACHIEVING ALL GOALS AT NIH

The annual NIH GPRA plan/report includes a considerable nod in the direction of determining the extent to which research goals are met. Each year independent units called assessment working groups review performance "data" submitted in the form of science advances, science capsules, stories of discovery, and research awards and honors. The assessment working groups are referred to as "independent" inasmuch as the members of the group are not directly employed by NIH. They are, however, experts selected from the ranks of university faculties, medical school research laboratories, health advocacy groups, and even persons with particular diseases. These assessment working groups rank NIH's performance according to the following ranking system: target substantially exceeded; target met or successfully met; target active; target not met and extended; and target not met.

Table 6.2, which shows evaluations by NIH assessment working groups of agency performance goals, is from the 2002 NIH GPRA report/plan. There are two

TABLE 6.1

NATIONAL INSTITUTES OF HEALTH PRE- AND POST-PART PERFORMANCE MEASURES

Pre-PART Representative Performance Measures	Measure Category	Post-PART Representative Performance Measures	Measure Category
Develop an AIDS vaccine by 2007.	HOM	By 2010, develop an HIV/AIDS vaccine.	HOM
Add to the body of knowledge about normal and abnormal biological functions and behavior.	POM	By 2007, evaluate the efficacy of 3 new treatments.	POM
Develop new or improved instruments and technologies for use in research and medicine.	POM	By 2006, develop one or more prototypes for a low-power, highly directional hearing aid microphone to help hearing-impaired persons better understand speech in a noisy background.	POM
Develop new or improved approaches for preventing or delaying the onset or progression of disease and disability.	POM	By 2006, integrate nanotechnology-based components into a system capable of detecting specific biomarkers (molecular signature) to establish proof of concept for a new approach to the early detection of cancer and, ultimately, cancer preemption.	POM
Develop new or improved methods for diagnosing and treating disease and disability.	POM	By 2009, expand the range of available methods used to create, analyze, and utilize chemical libraries, which can be used to discover new medications.	POM
Develop new or improved methods for diagnosing disease and disability.	POM	Specifically, use these chemical libraries to discover 10 new and unique chemical structures that could serve as the starting point of new drugs.	POM
Develop new or improved methods for treating disease and disability.	POM	By 2011, assess the efficacy of at least three new treatment strategies to reduce cardiovascular morbidity/mortality in patients with Type 2 diabetes and/or chronic kidney disease.	POM
Develop critical genomic resources, including the DNA sequences of the human genome and the genomes of important model organisms and disease-causing microorganisms.	POM	By 2013, identify at least one clinical intervention that will delay the progression of, delay the onset of, or prevent Alzheimer's disease.	HOM

HOM, health outcome measure; *POM*, program outcome measure.

TABLE 6.2

NIH GPRA RESEARCH GOALS AND TARGETS

Research Outcomes

Performance Goal	*FY Targets*	*Actual Performance*
a. Add to the body of knowledge about normal and abnormal biological functions and behavior. Subgoals: a.1. Discover innovative approaches for identifying and measuring genetic and environmental factors that contribute to common, complex diseases across populations. a.2. Develop model systems (animal models, cell lines, and so on) that will advance our understanding of disease processes.	*FY 2002–FY 2003* Annual milestones, which may include descriptions of science advances and stories of discovery; and initiatives such as Requests for Announcements, Program Announcements, conferences, and workshops. *FY 1999–FY 2001* Progress in advancing scientific understanding in key fields bearing on our knowledge of biological functions and behavior in their normal and abnormal states.	In independent Research Assessment Working Group reviewed annual progress and made the following assessments: FY 2001—Target substantially exceeded. FY 2000—Target substantially exceeded. FY 1999—Target substantially exceeded.
b. Develop new or improved instruments and technologies for use in research and medicine. Subgoals: b.1. Develop new technologies to enable greater understanding of genomic and proteomic information. b.2. Develop biocompatible materials for use in replacing or repairing damaged and nonfunctioning or missing tissue.	*FY 2002–FY 2003* Annual milestones, which may include descriptions of science advances and stories of discovery; and initiatives such as Requests for Announcements, Program Announcements, conferences, and workshops. *FY 1999–FY 2001* Progress in developing new instrumentation or technologies that enhance capabilities for investigating biological functions and diagnosing and treating diseases and disorders.	An independent Research Assessment Working Group reviewed annual progress and made the following assessments: FY 2001—Target substantially exceeded. FY 2000—Target substantially exceeded. FY 1999—Target substantially exceeded.

Source: Adapted from the U.S. Department of Health and Human Services, National Institutes of Health 2002, 31.

or three subgoals for each primary performance goal, targets for 2002–2003, and rankings of actual performance. In the case of primary goals *a* through *e,* the assessment working groups determined that NIH substantially exceeded its targets from 1999 through 2002. It is important to remember that these goals were extremely broad; primary goal *a,* for example, is to "add to the body of knowledge about normal and abnormal biological functions and behavior." It is also important to remember that these goals comprehend all the NIH centers and institutes. Therefore, we see the conclusion that, for example, in 2002–2003 the actual performance of NIH as regards primary goal *a* is "target substantially exceeded" based on "an independent research assessment working group [which] reviewed annual progress and made the following assessment." This conclusion comprehends the work of hundreds of grants to third-party research providers working on a remarkably wide range of health issues.

Primary goals *f* and *g* are far more specific and elaborate. Goal *f* is to "develop critical genomic resources, including the DNA sequences of the human genome and the genomes of important model organisms and disease causing microorganisms." Goal *g* is to "develop an AIDS vaccine by 2007." In both of these goal categories, NIH has chosen a far more elaborate set of subgoals and targets for these goals, the targets expressed in specific terms such as "complete full shotgun coverage of the sequence of the mouse genome; finish 40 percent of the mouse genome at 99.99 percent accuracy." It appears that the particular emphasis on the DNA sequence in the human genome and on the search for an AIDS vaccine in the NIH response to GPRA has to do with the rather high visibility of rapid progress in the case of unpacking the genome and the political visibility of the search for an AIDS vaccine. Notable, too, is that these two aspects of health research receive rather more detailed performance coverage than, for example, progress in cancer or diabetes research.

NIH leadership wishes to avoid the impression that the assessment working groups serve merely as rubber stamps; they state that the groups serve to review honestly and thoroughly NIH's success in achieving its goals. A quick review of the biographies of those serving in the working group reveals that their interests are hardly independent from those of NIH, however. As noted earlier, some of the members serving in the assessment working groups come from university faculties, health advocacy groups, the medical research community, hospitals, and health journalism, and others suffer from the diseases and disabilities that are the subjects of NIH research. It is hard to imagine that members of the assessment working groups can divorce themselves from personal and professional interests that are tied to NIH's interests and make independent judgments about NIH's performance. Indeed, these persons were likely selected for the assessment working group because of their expertise and their personal and professional interests in medical science research. In defense of the agency, we will note that it is extremely difficult for NIH to strike a balance between those who are sufficiently knowledgeable about health science research and those who can objectively assess NIH's achievement in reaching the goals of the research program.

THE CONTEXT OF NIH AND THE PROSPECTS
FOR PERFORMANCE BUDGETING

For several reasons, institutional, political, and cultural factors associated with NIH make performance measurement and the possibility of performance budgeting at NIH complex and unique. First, the distributive and geographically decentralized nature of NIH grant making and third-party networks is beneficial to members of Congress who benefit from federal funds spent in their states and districts. Second, the very large network of third-party research providers has a good bit of political clout. Third, the institutional decentralization of NIH, organized around institutes for particular diseases and families of disease, constitutes built-in support constituencies as well as easily identifiable bodies of expertise. Finally, although it is difficult to prove, the purposes of NIH and particularly of its separate institutes—to find the cures or at least the causes of diseases—evoke public and political concern and sympathy that can lead to a propensity for support. It is nearly impossible politically to oppose the purposes of NIH. Taken together, these contextual factors are the seedbed for a long history of NIH effectiveness in securing appropriations.

In an idealized way, NIH's implementation of GPRA is assumed to link research productivity, determined by performance measurement, to effective performance budgeting. It is difficult to imagine, however, finding a rational link between NIH performance and NIH appropriations. NIH is popular with members of Congress on both sides of the aisle, and the structure of the NIH response to GPRA requirements only enhances that popularity. NIH grants are awarded in all fifty states each fiscal year and in many congressional districts. Several members of Congress or members of their families have been personally affected by diseases for which NIH has institutes. In the face of human vulnerability, the NIH search for cures is a reasoned hope, and NIH has a good track record in finding cures, for example, both the extension of life expectancy for those with leukemia and the development of drugs to slow the progress of HIV. These success stories serve as the health equivalent of putting a man on the moon.

In the context of purposed cutbacks in domestic spending in the FY 2006 budget request, and the accompanying proposal to discontinue seven HHS programs, it is notable that the proposed NIH budget includes a 9 percent increase over FY 2005, which was a 9 percent increase over FY 2004. With so much congressional support and with such a creative response to GPRA goal setting and performance measurement, it is little wonder that performance budgeting when applied to NIH indicated that it is performance at an exceptionally high level and deserves, therefore, a sharp budget increase.

NIH AND THIRD-PARTY ARTICULATION

Congress dictates broadly how much of the NIH budget is spent on the areas of medical research. There is not a single appropriation for NIH; instead, there are separate appropriations for each of the institutes and centers. Therefore, NIH does not have discretion over the level of spending for cancer research versus diabetes research. It does, however, have discretion over how money is spent in the institutes and centers. The method that NIH developed to evaluate the performance of its research program outcomes does not allow for any assessment of how individual programs perform; the research program is only considered in its entirety. There was or is no effort to enable the assessment working groups to consider the direction of the research, only the outcomes. This was a conscious decision on the part of NIH.

According to an NIH official, "We could, potentially, with the approach we're taking, identify gaps in NIH research as well as make comments on some of the research findings. Instead, our approach was to focus completely on the research outcomes of all of NIH, not on the individual research programs. Because of the way we set it up, the assessment group wasn't going to be able to say, 'Hey, you know, you're a good program, but you've got some holes here, and you need to go in this direction as well.' We don't think that is what GPRA is about. We do this on our own. We look at our programs all the time, identify gaps, and then make course corrections." NIH does have a goal that is related to priority setting, but it is not one that is evaluated by the assessment working group. The goal, according to the NIH official, is to "ensure that NIH-supported research reflects the changing nature of scientific opportunities and public health needs." The indicator and target for this goal is to hold a number of workshops and panels to assess scientific progress and opportunities and to identify emerging public health needs. Suggestions resulting from these meetings are then incorporated into proposal submission requests. According to the NIH performance report, NIH met its priority-setting target because it held several such workshops and panels.

The logic of a grant-issuing research agency, such as NIH, is to select the best third parties to carry out research. NIH's performance in this regard is not left to the assessment working group. Instead, there are separate processes of grants administration and peer review. NIH's peer-review process, a system that has been in place for nearly fifty years, uses prominent scientists from around the country to evaluate each research proposal. These scientists provide advice to the NIH staff in their selection of grant recipients. Deciding the proper selection of grant recipients by the peer-review process ensures that the selection procedures are current and that the expertise used to advise NIH in its selection of grant recipients is "appropriate for the needs of modern science." NIH is currently undergoing a systematic review and reorganization of this process. It does not appear, however, that performance measurement broadly, or GPRA specifically, is informing these procedural and organizational processes. It is likely, however, that NIH would have made these changes absent GPRA and that the GPRA-required performance reporting only serves, in this instance, to be an additional medium by which to report these changes.

A grant-issuing research agency such as NIH is expected to interact with grant recipients and to manage the granting process to ensure that recipients meet the terms of grants. Given its relatively loosely coupled articulation with its grant recipients and its unique system of grant oversight, NIH grant management could be described as soft. As was indicated previously, the reputation that NIH enjoys is mostly attributable to the expertise of its grant recipients. The nature of scientific inquiry mitigates any action on the part of NIH that would inhibit third-party scientific objectivity. Given these two impediments, the extent to which NIH and extramural research grant recipients can be tightly articulated is limited. This does not mean, however, that there cannot be program accountability.

The grants administration and peer-review goals sections of the NIH GPRA performance report set out grant oversight goals and evaluate interaction between NIH and grant recipients. These goals include shortening the time between grant application submittals and receipt of funds, ensuring proper stewardship of publicly funded research, and simplifying the administrative processes required of grantees.

The indicators established to ensure effective grant stewardship include the following:

☐ Create an organizational component within NIH with FTEs devoted expressly to compliance-related activities.

☐ Perform a minimum of ten compliance site visits.

☐ Pilot-test ways to further simplify NIH's Streamlined Noncompeting Award Process. (This program allows grantees to reduce the number of steps and the amount of information required for noncompeting continuation of multiyear grant awards. Previously, grant-receiving institutions' business offices were required to engage in extensive financial reporting and to apply for continuing an existing grant.)

☐ Evaluate results of the simplified Streamlined Noncompeting Award Process pilots and make recommendations.

In August 2001, NIH opened the Division of Grants Compliance and Oversight, with three FTEs dedicated to compliance-related activities. After reviewing the results of the first eight site visits, the Division of Grants Compliance determined that making the additional two site visits was not necessary. Instead, "NIH determined that focusing on different types of institutions (e.g., Historically Black Colleges and Universities and Research Institute) for site visiting would be more productive and efficient than conducting all 10 site visits" (U.S. Department of Health and Human Services, National Institutes of Health 2002, 184). Aside from this explanation as to why the NIH site compliance goal was not met, this statement is indicative of the challenges associated with monitoring the compliance of NIH grant recipients. When a goal of ten compliance site visits for $20 billion in grant monies cannot be met, it would seem that there are NIH institutional and cultural factors that mitigate against the application of standard grant-monitoring protocols associated with federal grant money.

GPRA implementation at NIH shows evidence of the great respect NIH has for its grant recipients because the solid reputation of NIH comes, in part, from the stature and accomplishments of those grant recipients. "This extramural system is premised on independence, embodied in investigator-initiated research; on self-governance, embodied in peer review of scientists by scientists as the primary basis for judging the merits of research proposals and awarding funds; and on the powerful incentive of competition among the most highly trained scientists in the world" (U.S. Department of Health and Human Services, National Institutes of Health 2002, 14). NIH's justification for not sharing its GPRA goals with grant recipients is straightforward: NIH wants to avoid even the suggestion that its grant-supported research could be biased so as to satisfy performance expectations. Whereas other agencies can exploit GPRA's requirements to coordinate or manage third parties and orient all activities toward outcomes, NIH does not.

The application of GPRA requirements to the basic research mission of the institutes displays the classic methodological concerns of performance measurement in government. Many advances from current research will not be realized in practical applications for many years. This minimizes the usefulness of annual performance reporting. NIH's method of assessing its progress against the research program output goals it has set for itself cannot really be objectively called performance measurement because the reporting system is designed to yield favorable outcomes.

NIH is acutely aware that it is just one player in the processes of getting medical research and technologies to the marketplace and helping individuals with their diseases and disabilities. This has to do not only with the challenges associated with third-party implementation but also with the fact that NIH's role is basic research. According to an NIH executive, "Our goal, then, is not to improve health, per se, because we can't be directly responsible for that, but it's to generate knowledge and then real approaches to developing things like treatments and preventive methods that can later lead to better health. But we don't say directly that our mission is to improve the health of all Americans. And so we have to keep that in mind in setting realistic goals that relate to our research program because we want to make sure that our goals reflect our part of the whole process." Rather than the goals of curing diseases and improving health, the aims of NIH are better described as providing the underlying science research that others can further develop and build on to create products, services, and technologies that will ultimately benefit health care providers, patients, and the general public.

NIH is careful about the wording of its research program outcome goals. For instance, with regard to the goal to "develop new or improved approaches for preventing or delaying the onset or progression of disease and disability," one NIH official said, "We selected our words very carefully." She continued, "We use phrases such as 'new or improved approaches' because we can't be responsible for disease prevention from start to finish." This sort of wording also has an impact on what is considered to be success in meeting performance goals. According to an NIH representative, "In order to be successful in this goal, we don't have to be able to say we have prevented this many heart attacks, or that we have used this method to prevent this many diseases. We just have to determine that we have provided some information that can suggest a certain approach, or that we have done some preliminary tests, and it looks like this can lead to a successful prevention method."

FROM GPRA TO PART AT NIH

NIH's extramural research program, which accounts for roughly 85 percent of NIH's budget, was evaluated through PART in 2004. The extramural research program fared very well, receiving all possible points for program design and purpose (Section I), 78 percent of the strategic planning points available (Section II), 75 percent of the points available for the management section (III), and 92 percent for its results and accountability (Section IV). This gave NIH's extramural research program an overall PART score of 89 and a rating of "effective." In comparative terms these are very high scores.

Those familiar with NIH's approach to performance measurement find two aspects of the extramural program's PART particularly notable. First, aside from the AIDS vaccine health outcome measure, which is really a target or goal, the rest of the old and new measures are best described as program outcome measures rather than health outcome measures. But there are very big differences in NIH performance measures before and after PART, as table 6.1 illustrates. Before PART the key goals were highly generalized, such as "develop new or improved methods for diagnosing disease and disability" and "develop new or improved methods for treating disease and disability" (U.S. Department of Health and Human Services, National Institutes of Health 2002). These very general goals were especially suited to the NIH use of qualitative measures of progress toward these goals. By the time NIH was "PARTed," new NIH goals were in place, and they are almost all date specific, which is to say, "by 2010," "by 2013," and so forth. By comparison, the new NIH goals are relatively specific with respect to what is to be done and even how things are to be done—expand the development of chemical libraries so as to discover ten new unique chemical structures that could serve as the starting point of new drugs, for example. The new NIH goals and performance measures are certainly much more in the spirit of PART than were their earlier goals. It is important to remember, however, that performance measures are developed by the agencies. It is during the PART process where they are adjudicated in terms of their outcome orientation and their ambitiousness. It is, therefore, highly likely that the new NIH goals spelled out in table 6.1 are agreeable to NIH and are within the range of what it anticipates it can accomplish within the targeted dates.

Second, NIH no longer uses qualitative measures in its compliance with GPRA. We were unable to determine the reasons for this change except for the observation that NIH leadership thought it appropriate to move in the direction of quantitative measures. It is difficult to say whether NIH would have fared as exceptionally well in its extramural research PART scores had it retained the qualitative performance measurement approach. It is clear, however, that qualitative measures or not, NIH has done very well with respect to its annual appropriations. By comparison, NSF retains a qualitative measurement approach and has also done very well in its PART assessments. Most NSF programs have been rated "effective."

CONCLUSIONS

Our review of the application of performance measurement at NIH began with the question of how performance is to be measured when the work of third parties is exploratory, lacks precision, is not specific, and is inherently long term. In several ways the previous application of GPRA to NIH is unique, as figure 6.1 indicates. Although NIH is highly decentralized both geographically and programmatically, its GPRA goals and performance measures are highly centralized. The mission and goals of NIH are generalized, not specific to each of the individual institutes or centers. Annual progress toward those goals is also highly generalized, determined by a unique peer-evaluation system, which is based on the judgment and opinions of health research leaders. The achievement of NIH performance goals is described qualitatively, through narrative summaries of progress in aspects of basic research that touch on diseases and cures and through narrative summaries of whole bodies of research.

Because NIH is an outlier on some of the variables used in this book, it is useful to evaluate how well the NIH approach to GPRA implementation is working and how well it has been received. For the following reasons, the general answer to the question is positive.

First, the initial NIH qualitative performance measures appear to be at least as compelling to congressional committees and appropriators as are the quantitative measures used by the other agencies. Indeed, it appears that the NIH use of qualitative measures affirms the argument of performance measurement realists, and some skeptics, that policy is more likely to be moved by rhetoric than by data. Instead of growth in agency appropriations as the criterion, NIH qualitative performance measures are evidently used at least as effectively in appropriations decisions as are the quantitative measures used by other agencies, and they are perhaps used more effectively.

Second, the use of seven general goals indicating both incremental and broad annual progress in NIH performance is also a means by which to avoid comparison both within NIH and among its principals on the relative performance of research on, for example, cures for cancer as against AIDS.

Third, the geographic spread of grant recipients gives NIH high levels of support in the states and congressional districts. NIH has thus far successfully avoided the earmarked pork barrel appropriations now found in the annual budgets of several departments and agencies. And NIH has also avoided the continuing criticism directed toward NSF regarding the concentration of funding at a few universities and the failure of NSF to fund research at less prestigious institutions. NIH funding is already spread geographically, although, as might be expected, it is concentrated in large urban centers with important universities and hospitals.

Fourth, it is difficult to underestimate the importance of the status or prestige of NIH third parties. Highly regarded medical schools, medical research centers, and hospitals that receive significant NIH funding are located in most states and many congressional districts. The medical research centers, as part of the local economic development schemes, are now commonplace in part because such centers involve significant infusion of NIH and other federal health-related grant support.

FIGURE 6.1

KEY VARIABLES IN THE SYNTHESIS OF THE INFLUENCE OF PERFORMANCE MEASUREMENT IN THE NATIONAL INSTITUTES OF HEALTH

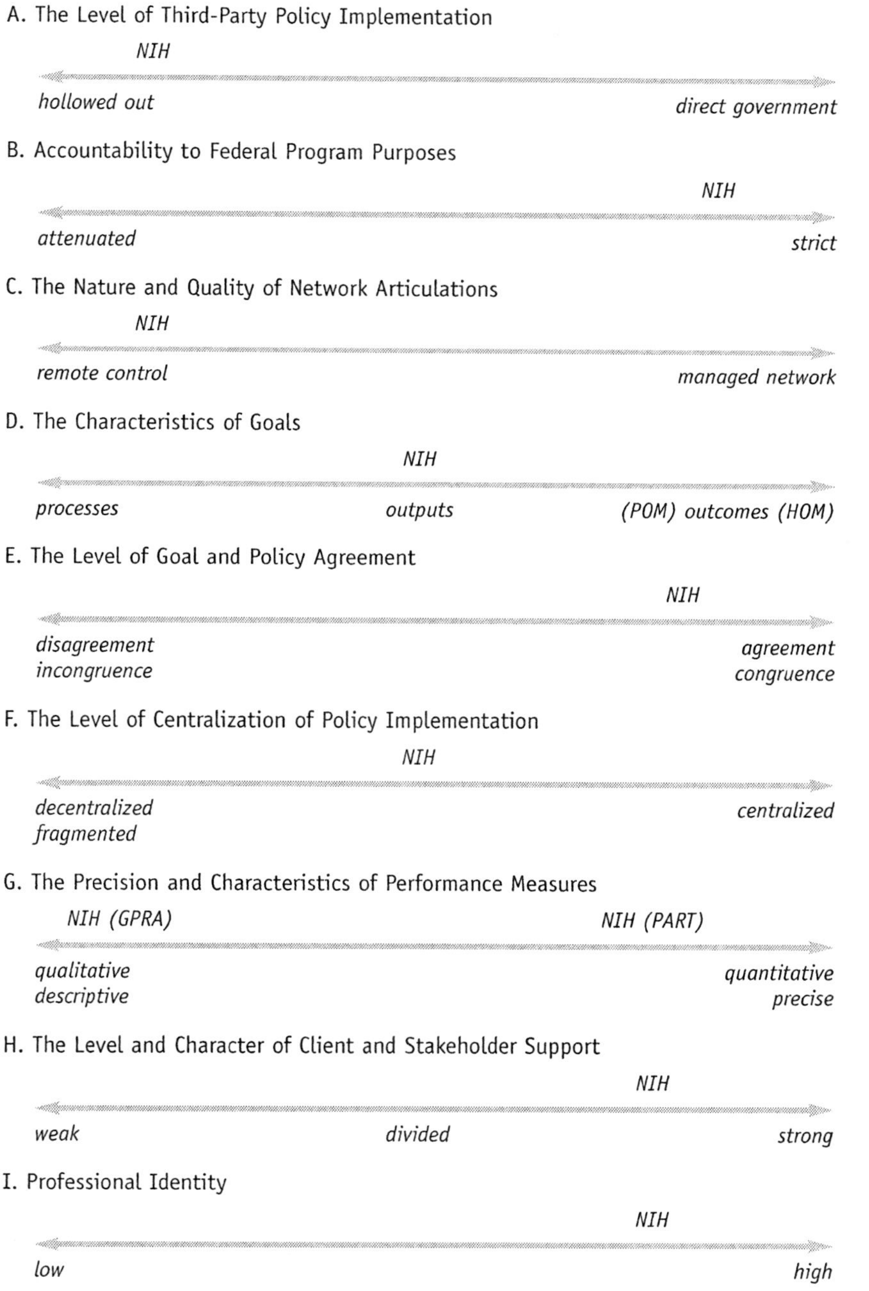

A. The Level of Third-Party Policy Implementation

NIH

hollowed out   *direct government*

B. Accountability to Federal Program Purposes

NIH

attenuated   *strict*

C. The Nature and Quality of Network Articulations

NIH

remote control   *managed network*

D. The Characteristics of Goals

NIH

processes   *outputs*   *(POM) outcomes (HOM)*

E. The Level of Goal and Policy Agreement

NIH

disagreement   *agreement*
incongruence   *congruence*

F. The Level of Centralization of Policy Implementation

NIH

decentralized   *centralized*
fragmented

G. The Precision and Characteristics of Performance Measures

NIH (GPRA)   *NIH (PART)*

qualitative   *quantitative*
descriptive   *precise*

H. The Level and Character of Client and Stakeholder Support

NIH

weak   *divided*   *strong*

I. Professional Identity

NIH

low   *high*

POM, program outcome measure; *HOM,* health outcome measure.

With regard to the questions posed at the beginning of this chapter, NIH has chosen to respond to the imperatives of GPRA and performance measurement by simply challenging the assumption that performance measurement must always be quantitative. The NIH use of narrative "science advances," "science capsules," and "stories of discovery" not only is a successful approach to performance measurement but also seems to be particularly promising as a link between agency performance and agency appropriations. The NIH qualitative approach to performance measurement also appears to be helpful as a way to get around the expectation that annual measures are meaningful. The previous relatively bold NIH approach to performance measurement in the context of third parties engaged in basic medical and scientific research is likely associated with the standing of its clients and stakeholders and its own prestige. It does not hurt that there is general political agreement regarding NIH goals and policies. Finally, even though much of the work of NIH is done by third parties, and these third parties are generally given wide latitude in their implementation of NIH grants, NIH would nevertheless be described as generally accountable to federal program purposes.

We will now turn to another question: How can performance be measured when federal purposes are being carried out by third parties who are sovereign? In the range of third parties—from states and territories to contractors or researchers—few are more interesting than Indian tribes. The agency that deals with this particular health delivery system is the subject of chapter 7.

7

MEASURING THE HEALTH PERFORMANCE OF SOVEREIGN TRIBES AS THIRD PARTIES

The Indian Health Service

Subgovernments are unique third parties in the implementation of federal health policy. They are understood to be semiautonomous partners engaged in continuous iterative patterns of mutual adjustment between accountability to federal purposes and responses to their own needs, circumstances, and preferences. This form of articulation between federal principals and state and territorial agents, as the HRSA and Medicaid cases illustrate, influences GPRA implementation by building into the details of articulation the challenges of performance measurement and, particularly, issues of data organization and management. How does this generalization change when the third parties to federal government programs are more than just semiautonomous, when they are defined in the law as sovereign? How are sovereign institutions to be held to the performance measurement requirements of GPRA? Finally, what can be learned about the implementation of GPRA in settings in which an agency may choose among direct services, grants, and contracts to do the same tasks and achieve the same objectives? The answers to these questions are found in the analysis of GPRA applications in the Indian Health Service.

IHS grants are unlike the grants made by other agencies of the Department of Health and Human Services because they are made to sovereign Indian tribes. Tribes that receive IHS grants are under no statutory obligation to provide performance information to IHS. The reasons for and consequences of this immunity are detailed below. In addition to making grants to tribes, IHS also has a comparatively large permanent staff that provides direct services to tribes and tribal members. Many IHS programs are provided both through grants to tribes (and in many cases then contracted out to third-party providers) and directly by IHS personnel. The choice between grants and direct service provision is not a function of different programs. For example, neither Congress nor IHS has made strategic decisions to provide preventive health care programs through grants and emergency medical services through direct service of IHS. Instead, decision choices between grants and direct service provision are made by those receiving the funding: for example, emergency medical services are provided directly to some tribes by IHS doctors and nurses and to other tribes by contractors funded through grants received from IHS. An examination of IHS's GPRA implementation helps to identify the characteristics and qualities of performance measurement and performance improvement in federal agencies that use both direct service provision and grants to achieve their policy goals.

Through its use of grants and third-party policy implementation, IHS is similar to HRSA, CMS, and NIH. Unlike these agencies, however, IHS makes grants to tribes whose relationship with the federal government is treaty based, which gives them wide discretion in implementation of federal health policy. In these third-party arrangements, the nature of accountability to federal goals is particularly complex.

THE INDIAN HEALTH SERVICE

According to the GPRA strategic plan, the IHS relationship with tribes is based on tribal sovereignty and a government-to-government relationship. "In this context, sovereignty means that tribes can govern their own territory and internal affairs and only Congress can override an Indian nation's authority. The government-to-government relationship is a federal policy that requires the U.S. government to consult with tribes about how federal actions may affect them" (U.S. Department of Health and Human Services, Indian Health Service 2002, 14). The overall mission of IHS is to uphold the federal government's obligation to promote healthy American Indian and Alaska Native (AI/AN) peoples, communities, and cultures and to honor and protect the inherent sovereign rights of tribes. This is the standard against which IHS performance is to be measured.

IHS has a budget of approximately $2.8 billion and employs approximately fifteen thousand people. Both numbers have been relatively stable since FY 2000. IHS has, in comparative terms, a rather large permanent staff. For example, NIH has a budget five times larger than that of IHS, but it has only two thousand more employees than IHS. Because IHS's mission is to provide health services to the AI/AN population, most IHS senior executive service staff officials are from this population. Excluding medical professionals, approximately 85 percent of all IHS staff is of American Indian or Alaska Native descent.

IHS provides a comprehensive array of health care services to approximately 1.5 million American Indians and native Alaskans, who belong to 557 different federally recognized tribes. These services include, but are not limited to, standard preventive care, emergency care, nutritional education, pharmaceutical coverage, environmental health and engineering services, alcohol and substance abuse services, and mental health services. Approximately 37 percent of the IHS budget supports the provision of health care services and the administration of these services provided directly by federal government employees. Another 44 percent of the IHS budget supports grants to Indian tribes. In almost all cases the tribes use these grants to contract with a wide range of health services providers. Finally, 16 percent of the IHS budget supports the Contract Health Services (CHS) program, a system of tertiary health care services, such as paying for major medical procedures performed at non-IHS facilities.

IHS PRINCIPALS AND AGENTS AND THIRD-PARTY ARTICULATION

IHS has a unique principal–agent problem. In the past IHS was mostly a direct service provision agency, which hired health care workers or directly contracted with health care workers to provide basic health care and dental services to American Indians and native Alaskans at IHS service units located in hospitals and clinics. The portion of the IHS budget still dedicated to direct service provision or direct contracting presents relatively few logistical data collection problems in implementing GPRA. The Indian Self-Determination and Education Assistance Act of 1975 and its subsequent amendments, however, provided tribes with the federal grant-based resources needed to enable them to act as sovereign nations. From a practical standpoint, tribes now receive IHS grant monies directly and in turn contract with the third-party health care providers of their choice.

Whereas other federal agency principals can leverage information from agents such as state and local governments, contractors, nonprofits, or other federal agencies, IHS cannot require tribal leaders to submit performance information. In 1994, the year after GPRA was passed, amendments to the Indian Self-Determination and Education Assistance Act made it even less likely that tribal leaders would comply with GPRA's reporting requirements. The express purpose of these amendments was to enable tribal leaders to influence the redesign of IHS and other federal Indian programs and prioritize their spending to suit tribal tastes and preferences. The intent of these amendments was to help tribes get out from under the dominance of federal agencies, particularly the Bureau of Indian Affairs and IHS, by providing federal grant funds, including those that were intended to be used with high levels of local discretion by local tribes. Thus the Indian Self-Determination and Education Assistance Act has significantly loosened the couplings of the federal system of grant support to AI/AN populations. This new and even looser grant articulation regime has in turn influenced IHS implementation of GPRA.

Viewing GPRA as too rigid and top down, certain tribes that choose not to comply with GPRA contend that their tribes are too small to dedicate resources to data collection and performance reporting. Their leaders argue that funds spent on GPRA compliance are funds that would otherwise be spent directly on patient care. Although this argument is neither new nor unique to IHS, when added to voluntary tribal participation in performance data collection and reporting, seeking tribal support for GPRA implementation is a particularly delicate matter. IHS must use persuasion and incentives with tribal leaders to strengthen their support and encourage participation in the development of performance goals and the submission of GPRA performance data. Although persuasion and incentives are common features of most contract-based principal–agent relations, they are usually played out in the shadow of penalties that could result from noncompliance. With contractors, there is the very real threat of contract termination for failure to perform or comply. Although such measures are not frequently used in federal contracting, the fact that funding is contingent on recipient behavior tends to fos-ter compliance. There in no such dynamic with respect to tribal grants from IHS.

The request for performance-related data to meet GPRA requirements is viewed by some tribal leaders as an unfunded mandate or, more correctly, an un-funded request. Absent the ability to back GPRA compliance requests with threats and sanctions, IHS administrators, according to one IHS executive, have responded by explaining the details of GPRA to tribal leaders and demonstrating to them that compliance helps tribes to speak with a more unified voice and that a unified voice might result in better information to support future budget requests. Although the unfunded mandate issue is present in virtually all third-party, principal–agent arrangements, because of the sovereignty of Indian tribes the unfunded mandate issue takes on greater importance.

IHS GOALS AND PERFORMANCE MEASURES

IHS implementation of GPRA IHS performance measures is organized around the following strategic goals:

1. Improve the health status of the AI/AN population. This objective focuses on reducing mortality and morbidity rates and enhancing the quality of life for eligible populations.
2. Provide health services. This goal focuses on assuring access to the full range of IHS services, including clinical, preventive, educational, and community-based services. Another focus of this objective is to provide health services in a culturally sensitive manner.
3. Assure partnerships and consultation with IHS tribal and urban-operated fa-cilities. This goal focuses on assuring tribal participants dealing with matters of policy development, budget formulation, and program management that policy and policy implementation will be conducted in the spirit of a part-nership between IHS and the tribes. It also focuses on providing sufficient in-formation to tribes so that they can make informed health care decisions.
4. Perform core functions and advocacy. This goal focuses on providing the core IHS services required of the federal government as well as serving as an ad-vocate for the health care needs of the AI/AN populations.

The IHS response to GPRA, however, is not organized around these four strategic goals. Instead, IHS GPRA performance measures are organized around the following themes:

☐ treatment
☐ prevention
☐ capital programming and infrastructure
☐ partnerships, consultation, core functions, and advocacy

If one wished to determine how IHS was performing its strategic health services goals, it would be necessary to cull the performance information from measures scattered through different parts of the performance reports. Because of this, the performance plan has frequent cross-references to the linkage between specific IHS performance measures of treatment, prevention, and so forth and the strategic goals of the Department of Health and Human Services. These two organizational flaws in the IHS performance plans make it difficult and confusing for anyone who attempts to assess IHS's performance, even according to its own criteria.

In all, there are twenty-one treatment performance indicators organized into categories based on diseases and maladies and on information technology and quality of care. The categories of treatment performance indicators are as follows: diabetes, cancer screening, well-child care, alcohol and substance abuse, oral health, abuse/neglect and violence, information technology, and quality of care. The treatment performance indicators are process and output measures, the majority being output measures. None meets the criteria for outcome measures, which is to link the functioning of IHS and the ultimate effects of public programs on their intended targets.

As table 7.1 indicates, however, it is clear that a good bit of thought and preparation has gone into the output measures developed by IHS. For most of

TABLE 7.1

INDIAN HEALTH SERVICE REPRESENTATIVE PERFORMANCE MEASURES

Representative Performance Measures	Measure Category
Percent reduction of the Years Productive Life Lost rate within 7 years of opening the new facility.	HOM
Percent increase in coverage of pneumococcal vaccinations for adults.	POM
Percent increase in screening for tobacco usage.	OM
Percent increase in the proportion of diagnosed persons with diabetes demonstrating ideal blood sugar control within 7 years of opening the new facility.	HOM
Percent of scheduled construction phases completed on time.	POM
Percent increase in alcohol screening for female patients of childbearing age.	OM
Percent increase in coverage of childhood immunizations.	POM
Percent increase in coverage of flu vaccinations for adults.	POM
Decrease obesity rates in American Indian/Alaska Native children (2–5 years).	HOM
Reduce unintentional injury mortality rates for American Indian/Alaska Native people.	HOM
Increase "ideal" blood sugar control in American Indian/Alaska Native persons with diabetes.	HOM

HOM, health outcome measure; *POM*, program outcome measure; *OM*, output measure.

them there is a clear and reasonable causal link between the output measure and desired health outcomes. The IHS performance plan does a good job of specifying these causal links and therefore justifying its heavy reliance on output as against outcome measures. One example is the diabetes treatment indicator. "During FY 2003, maintain the FY 2002 performance level for glycemic (blood sugar) control in the proportion of IHS tribal and urban clients with diagnosed diabetes" (U.S. Department of Health and Human Services, Indian Health Service 2002, pt. 2, p. 58). When compared with the other four agencies considered in this book, IHS has more actual health outcome measures.

Other than the obvious fact that IHS does not seek to improve on last year's performance in glycemic control, the GPRA performance plan and report does a good job identifying the positive health outcomes linked to glycemic control. According to the performance report and plan, on the basis of data from large clinical studies, glycemic control is associated with reducing both the medical complications of those with diabetes and the costs associated with caring for those with diabetes. The rationale and health outcome connection for the other performance indicators in the IHS performance plan that measure outputs are also thoroughly and clearly identified.

The output and process measures are chosen by IHS in part because outcome data are hard to come by. IHS considered some methods to collect traditionally difficult-to-obtain health data, such as information related to teen sexuality, alcohol and substance abuse, family abuse, tobacco use, and depression among AI/AN populations. For instance, IHS considered trying to measure tobacco use by tacking tobacco-use questions onto a list of questions in IHS dental surveys. They also considered including questions about substance-abuse levels in emergency room surveys. In the end the agency determined that neither approach was methodologically sound.

In all there are twelve prevention performance indicators in the following categories: public health nursing, immunization, injury prevention, suicide prevention, developmental prevention and treatment, HIV/AIDS, and environmental surveillance. Prevention performance indicators are also measures of IHS and third-party processes and outputs. But the ratio of process to output measures is greater for prevention than it is for treatment, which probably indicates that IHS's programs for prevention are not as developed and robust as are their measures of treatment objectives. Indeed, in many cases process measures are used because several programs have not been in place long enough to justify measuring their outputs. Examples of IHS prevention process measures include "collaborate with NIH and AI/AN sites in developing and implementing culturally sensitive community-directed pilot cardio-vascular disease prevention programs" and "develop an overall IHS tobacco control plan based on findings from CDC sponsored AI/AN tobacco control pilot sites" (U.S. Department of Health and Human Services, Indian Health Service 2002). The rationale for these measures is based on the incidence of both diabetes and smoking in the AI/AN population rates, rates that far exceed those in the U.S. population at large.

The meaning of the term "culturally sensitive" is not explained in either the IHS performance plan or strategic plan. Cultural sensitivity is not only a component of specific indicators but also a criterion of strategic objective number 2, which requires that health services be provided by culturally sensitive health professionals. In each HHS performance plan and report, the department requires a section on an agency's context for performance measurement. This section would be an ideal place to explain the benefits of cultural sensitivity in the development and delivery of health care services provided to the AI/AN population. Without this explanation, however, including the phrase "cultural sensitivity" in, for example, the cardiovascular disease prevention performance measure seems gratuitous. This is a minor point because the rationale for IHS prevention output measures and their causal linkages are both reasoned and thorough.

The two capital planning and infrastructure performance indicators measure the number of sanitation facilities provided to new, like new, and existing Indian homes and the number of new health care facilities built to serve the AI/AN population. Both of these indicators are outputs, and in both cases the GPRA reports describe clear causal linkages to positive health outcomes.

The final category of IHS performance indicators is partnerships, consultation, core functions, and advocacy. All eight measures in this category are best described as outputs, with the exception of one process indicator, a measure of IHS development of a plan to improve the retention of nurses. One example of an output measure in this category reads as follows: "Improve the level of IHS tribal and urban satisfaction with the process for consultation and participation provided by IHS, as measured by a survey of IHS tribal and urban clients" (U.S. Department of Health and Human Services, Indian Health Service 2002). As with previous output indicators, the IHS performance plan and report does a solid job of tying the output indicators to positive administrative and health outcomes.

The IHS response to GPRA reports impressive strides in AI/AN health outcomes over the last few decades. For instance, from 1972 to 1996 the following health outcomes among AI/AN populations have been achieved:

☐ Maternal mortality has been reduced from 27.7 to 6.1 per 100,000 (a 78 percent reduction).

☐ Tuberculosis mortality has been reduced from 10.5 to 1.9 per 100,000 (an 82 percent reduction).

☐ Gastrointestinal disease mortality has been reduced from 6.2 to 1.5 per 100,000 (a 76 percent reduction).

☐ Accident mortality has been reduced from 188.0 to 80.6 per 100,000 (a 57 percent reduction).

☐ Pneumonia mortality has been reduced from 40.8 to 20.2 per 100,000 (a 50 percent reduction).

☐ Infant mortality has been reduced from 22.2 to 7.6 per 100,000 (a 66 percent reduction).

Why aren't these included as indicators in the IHS performance plans and reports? The answer is that even with the substantial health care strides indicated above, there is still a significant disparity between the health conditions of the AI/AN population and the overall health conditions of the U.S. population. For instance, the overall mortality rate for the entire U.S. population is 130.5 per 100,000, whereas for the AI/AN population the mortality rate is 157.1 per 100,000—20 percent higher.

An IHS representative indicated that IHS did not include these specific outcome indicators for two reasons. First, both the mortality rate for American Indians and the disparity between American Indians and the rest of the United States is increasing. In the three-year periods of 1994–1996 and 1996–1998, the mortality rates for the AI/AN population and the disparity between the AI/AN and U.S. total population increased for diabetes, suicide, cervical cancer, heart disease, and malignant neoplasms (tumors). Between these periods the mortality rate for the AI/AN population increased from 699.3 per 100,000 to 715.2 per 100,000, or an increase of 2 percent. During the same period the disparity increased from a ratio of 1.4 to 1.5, or an increase of 7 percent.

Second, what IHS is trying to achieve, according to an IHS executive, does not lend itself to annual reporting. IHS is not trying to hide the growing disparity between U.S. and AI/AN mortality rates because these data are included in the performance reports. But the difference in mortality rates is part of the description of the context of AI/AN health circumstances; it is shown as a reference but is not used as a performance indicator. According to one IHS representative, there has been some political pressure not to include such outcome indicators in the performance report so as to avoid outcome measures that might negatively describe IHS's performance. This same IHS representative reasons that disparities between AI/AN and other American health outcome measures do not lend themselves to annual reporting. The annual reporting challenges are not, of course, limited to health care outcomes and have been found in all five of the agencies we evaluated. Indeed, the challenge of measuring and reporting the annual outcomes of public programs and the services they provide is near universal. The specific challenge this presents to the IHS and other health agencies is supported by experts in the field of health care performance measurement (Perrin and Koshel 1997).

IHS GPRA IMPLEMENTATION AND ACTUAL PERFORMANCE

As was described earlier, the CHS program accounts for 16 percent of IHS expenditures. To save IHS money, CHS negotiates special rates with frequently used health care facilities that are not managed by IHS or tribes. "Frequently used" is defined as facilities to which IHS pays at least $50,000 for inpatient services or $10,000 for outpatient services annually. Although CHS accounts for roughly 1/6 of the IHS budget, there is only one performance indicator dedicated to contract performance.

During the FY 2003 reporting period, IHS improved the level of CHS procurement of inpatient and outpatient hospital services for routinely used providers to 1 percent over the FY 2002 level of rate quote agreements, because not all health facilities that meet the definition of frequently used entered into rate agreements with CHS. This indicator measures the percentage of dollars IHS pays to frequently used health facilities that are paid through the rate agreements. For example, if IHS paid $10 million to frequently used health facilities last year, and $5 million of that amount was paid through reduced rate payment agreements, the percentage calculated would be 5/10, or 50 percent. Why is this such a complex target? According to an IHS executive, IHS leadership felt external pressure to tie outcome data to costs. The executive stated, "These linkages are hard to come by because there are too many intervening variables, such as other federal programs." But where there are opportunities to identify savings and make them a basis for performance indicators, it is difficult to see why they are not included in the performance plan. The same data required to calculate existing CHS measures could be used to identify the actual savings that result from the agreements, rather than merely identifying the percentage paid to facilities with agreements. For instance, reduced rate agreements accounted for more than $200 million in savings in FY 1998 and $182 million in 2001. Given the pressure to develop measures that identify actual savings, it is difficult to understand why this indicator is selected rather than the actual savings achieved.

GPRA AND THE IHS MANAGEMENT CHALLENGE

What are the challenges associated with AI/AN sovereignty as IHS attempts to implement GPRA? For the 44 percent of the IHS budget that is spent on providing grants to tribes, the tribes have control over all aspects of data collected and the choice of what and whether to collect or report at all. Without data, there can be no performance measures that meet GPRA requirements. One IHS official indicated that, initially, the tribes that most resisted performance measurement were the smaller ones with fewer resources. They make what one IHS executive interviewed for this research accepts as a persuasive argument—that all their health care resources should go to patient care. When they fail to cooperate, they sometimes do so by not participating in an audit, by being unwilling to put data in a compatible format, by failing to send data to IHS headquarters, or by sending data that are not in a compatible format.

IHS has approached the formidable challenges of data collection on three fronts. IHS hired a contractor to "sell" GPRA to tribal leaders. A well-respected opinion leader among his peers, this contractor previously served in a prominent tribal leadership position in a self-governing tribe. Because of his efforts, and despite the absence of requirements, many tribes are not only participating (submitting the GPRA data needed by IHS) but also encouraging other tribal programs to participate.

Another approach has been to include the provision of performance data requirements in the grant agreements with the tribes. Each of IHS's twelve area directors includes performance data requirements in the grant agreements signed by tribal leaders. Technically, the only legal requirement on the part of tribes is to get clean audit opinions, but the inclusion of performance data requirements in grant agreements does create among tribes an attitude of obligation rather than a legal requirement.

A final approach to obtaining performance measurement data from tribes that receive IHS grants is to offer something akin to a cafeteria plan. If the tribes choose, they can buy back the information technology and the accompanying data collection and reporting services. For instance, if a tribe's grant for a range of health care and support services is $10 million for a year, and the information technology, data collection, and reporting services portion of that grant is $500,000, the tribe would accept only $9.5 million. In this way, although the tribe still administers and contracts for all the health care services, IHS retains and manages the information technology, data collection, and reporting services.

For the following reasons, when they are taken together these three methods of securing tribal cooperation for GPRA's immense data requirements amount to a success story. As a result of IHS efforts to work with the tribes on their terms and in the spirit of partnership and consultation, tribal cooperation, as defined by submitting the required data on time and in the right format, has increased significantly. In FY 1999, just fewer than 25 percent of the grant-receiving tribes were uncooperative in terms of data collection and reporting. By FY 2002, one IHS executive estimated that the percentage of uncooperative tribes had fallen to below 10 percent.

Tribes can choose whether to have their IHS-financed health services administered and provided directly by IHS or to receive grants from IHS and administer the health care services themselves. This choice is not strategic on the part of IHS, which is to say that IHS does not determine whether direct or contract services would be more effective or economical for certain tribes or geographic areas of the country. Rather, the choice is made on whatever basis the tribes choose. The tribes have increasingly chosen to receive the IHS grants and administer the health care services themselves. According to IHS, "In 1990, 90 percent of IHS health care services were provided directly by IHS." By 2002, that figure had dropped to 37 percent (U.S. Government of Health and Human Services, Indian Health Service 2002).

Even with greatly increased total cooperation in the provision of annual GPRA performance data, there is the problem of rather wide variation in the quality of those data. According to an IHS official, "Not only do we lose economies of scale (with data collection) with more services being devolved to tribes, but our data collection starts to look like Swiss cheese. We made concessions to some tribes, who received the tribal shares of programs that really should not have been divisible. This has adversely affected other tribes where IHS still runs the show." The variation in data quality is influenced by another classic problem associated with grant and contract management—low wages and less-than-competent workers. According to the same IHS official, "One of the difficulties is the tremendous turnover of staff at the local level. This is partly due to non-competitive wages. For instance, in 1999 IHS paid dentists approximately $35,000 per year and paid approximately $50,000 per year for doctors."

Although IHS senior management has been generally supportive of GPRA, an IHS executive said, "Half of the four FTEs dedicated to working on GPRA were never directly asked to help with GPRA. The FTEs were made up from among 8 to 10 employees in the field who give part of their time, about 10 to 20 percent, to GPRA efforts. GPRA work is not part of their job descriptions, but they have received support from their bosses to help out with GPRA."

Support for GPRA from IHS leadership was also tempered by the concern that the performance information could be used as an excuse to cut the IHS budget. One top official said, "There was initially some fear on the part of IHS leadership that using GPRA could backfire if the IHS is seen as not meeting standards. There is a strange combination of appeal and repulsion. How do you use GPRA strategically to leverage more funding and avoid getting beat up in the appropriations process for setting poor goals or goals that are too high?" Another IHS representative expressed concern about the argument made to many tribes that if the GPRA reports demonstrate good IHS performance, it would likely lead to increased funding. This argument worked while trying to secure the FY 2000 budget, when "GPRA-related stuff was seen to bring about more funding." But, the IHS representative noted, if the "tribes get burned, it could be all over." Nevertheless, this method of encouraging the tribes to participate will not likely end soon. The tribes are more interested in spending priorities than in data priorities. And the best way to encourage GPRA participation and compliance is to connect the two.

The IHS federally administered activities and the IHS Sanitation Facilities Construction Program have been "PARTed," with federally administered activities scoring 77 points and the Sanitation Facilities program scoring 80 points. Both are comparatively solid scores, and both programs are rated "moderately effective." Despite the fears at IHS that GPRA and PART would be used to justify budget cuts, the president's FY 2006 budget proposed an essentially flat-line continuation of present funding. So, at least at IHS, performance budgeting as presently projected is neither the horror its detractors feared nor the blessing its advocates imagined.

SOME CONCLUSIONS

This chapter began with these questions: Does it matter in GPRA implementation when policy implementation is carried out by sovereign third parties? How is performance measurement influenced by the use in a single agency of different policy tools to carry out the same activities? What can be learned about GPRA implementation in settings in which agencies can choose among direct services, grants, and contracts to do the same task or believe the same objective?

Although the goals of the IHS are general and applicable to each of its programs, the tools of policy implementation vary. In other words, IHS has not chosen to have different goals for those aspects of its programs that are directly provided, provided by contract, or provided through grants to tribes. As figure 7.1 indicates, accountability to the purpose of federal Indian health policy is somewhat greater when policy is directly implemented by IHS. The variation does not appear to be great, however, and IHS programs generally, whatever the

FIGURE 7.1

KEY VARIABLES IN THE SYNTHESIS OF THE INFLUENCE OF PERFORMANCE MEASUREMENT IN THE INDIAN HEALTH SERVICE

A. The Level of Third-Party Policy Implementation

    IHS(g)   *IHS(d)*

hollowed out   *direct government*

B. Accountability to Federal Program Purposes

                        IHS(g)   *IHS(d)*

attenuated   *strict*

C. The Nature and Quality of Network Articulations

    IHS(g)   *IHS(d)*

remote control   *managed network*

D. The Characteristics of Goals

                    IHS(g) IHS(d)

processes   *outputs*   *(POM) outcomes (HOM)*

E. The Level of Goal and Policy Agreement

                                IHS(d) IHS(g)

disagreement   *agreement*
incongruence   *congruence*

F. The Level of Centralization of Policy Implementation

             IHS(g) IHS(d)

decentralized   *centralized*
fragmented

G. The Precision and Characteristics of Performance Measures

                                IHS(d) IHS(g)

qualitative   *quantitative*
descriptive   *precise*

H. The Level and Character of Client and Stakeholder Support

             IHS(d) IHS(g)

weak   *divided*   *strong*

I. Professional Identity

                             IHS(g)   *IHS(d)*

low   *high*

IHS(g), Indian Health Service grants to tribes; *IHS(d),* Indian Health Service direct services; *POM,* program outcome measure; *HOM,* health outcome measure.

policy implementation tool, tend to be accountable to federal program purposes. The use of third parties in policy implementation does not appear to seriously diminish accountability.

Because IHS policy implementation is highly decentralized and programmatically fragmented, patterns of agency–third-party articulation are rather like federal–state federalism. When IHS provides services directly, principal–agent articulations are obviously tight. In the case of grants to sovereign tribes, however, principal–agent articulation is loose, showing rather wide variations in the detailed characteristics of policy implementation from tribe to tribe. IHS has relatively successfully practiced a form of network management not unlike the forms of diplomatic relations seen in grant-based federal–state relations as a way to deal with GPRA data consistency and management problems associated with such loose third-party articulation. IHS has, in much the same way as HRSA and Medicaid, built parts of the imperatives of GPRA into the details of its management of grant-based, cooperative federalism.

Tribal sovereignty appears in the IHS example to be rather like state autonomy and to resemble such health agencies as HRSA or Medicaid that rely on states and territories to carry out their policy. Also, like the other agencies studied here, IHS has chosen to emphasize management process and agency outcome goals and attendant measures in its implementation of GPRA. The health outcomes goals have been selected carefully as to avoid those health outcomes where there is still considerable disparity between the AI/AN population and the broader U.S. population. This notably cautious approach has even avoided comparisons of Indian health outcomes at one point in time and improvement in those outcomes at a later point in time. Not using measures of improvement over time, and there are such measures, appears to be because such measures might lead to comparisons between changes in health outcomes of Indians and non-Indians, a considerably less favorable story. This same caution is displayed in the IHS approach to an attempt to build bridges between performance measurement and performance budgeting. There is evidence of suspicion on the part of IHS officials regarding the intent of performance measures being connected to appropriations. Thus far there is no evidence in the implementation of either GPRA or PART to support this suspicion.

The careful approach to GPRA at IHS might also be understood on the basis of the lack of influential stakeholders. As clients, Indian tribes see their influence as based less on their political clout, money, or organizational skills and more on the salience of tribal treaties and on lawsuits and court decisions that support Indian tribal rights based on those treaties. In the absence of mobilized clients and influential stakeholders, it is no wonder that IHS leaders exhibit a certain sense of budgetary vulnerability. The response by IHS leaders to the performance measurement movement generally and GPRA specifically is, therefore, risk averse.

Not all agencies of the Department of Health and Human Services rely on third parties for policy implementation. One, the Food and Drug Administration, is a regulatory agency with all the special characteristics of regulatory agencies. We now turn to the implementation of GPRA in a regulatory context.

8

PERFORMANCE AS REGULATION
The Food and Drug Administration

On September 30, 2004, Merck & Co. Inc. voluntarily withdrew Vioxx from the market, and then, on April 7, 2005, Pfizer withdrew Bextra from the market. Vioxx and Bextra are "Cox-2 inhibitors" anti-inflammatory drugs effective in the treatment of chronic joint pain caused by arthritis and in the treatment of menstrual pain. FDA had approved Vioxx in 1999 at about the time two other Cox-2 inhibitors, Celebrex and Bextra, were also approved. Two others are presently in the FDA drug approval pipeline, Prexige and Arcoxia. It was hoped at the time of approval that Vioxx and Bextra would have a lower risk of one of the primary side effects of other pain medicines such as aspirin and ibuprofen, gastrointestinal ulcers and bleeding. It turned out that Vioxx did demonstrate a lower rate of these side effects. But, on the basis of the medicine's continued use after market trials and tests, in June 2000 Merck determined that an increased probability of heart attacks and strokes was a side effect of taking Vioxx. In April 2002 FDA implemented labeling changes to reflect these findings so as to put persons using Vioxx on notice. Other studies were also indicating increased risk of cardiovascular events associated with taking Vioxx as well as the other Cox-2 inhibitors. While FDA was in the process of reviewing these tests and their results to determine whether further labeling changes were warranted, Merck informed the agency of the results of new trials and its decision to withdraw Vioxx from the market.

The Merck Vioxx announcement was headline news in newspapers and led the evening television news shows on September 30, and the story continued to be a news feature for several days. Also on September 30 Dr. David J. Graham, associate director for science of the Office of Drug Safety in the Center for Drug Evaluation and Research of FDA, sent a long memorandum to Dr. Paul Seligman, the acting director of the Office of Drug Safety. This memorandum was a summary of several studies sponsored by or connected to FDA in different ways, all of which determined increased risk of heart attack and stroke for those taking Vioxx. This memorandum, as usually happens in Washington, found its way to Congress, and congressional hearings were scheduled.

On November 18, 2004, Senator Charles Grassley opened the hearing with a statement that FDA had ignored danger signals and failed to take appropriate actions. He further stated that FDA had failed to heed the words of its own scientists. Finally, he stated that FDA had allowed itself to be manipulated by Merck. Dr. Graham was then asked to testify. He said that Vioxx was a medicine disaster unparalleled in U.S. history. He estimated that between 88,000 and 139,000 Americans experienced additional heart attacks and strokes because of taking Vioxx. To dramatize this claim, he compared this estimate to the rough equivalent of 500 to 900 fully loaded jetliners dropping from the sky.

The top FDA official present, Dr. Sandra Kweder, took strong issue with both Senator Grassley and Dr. Graham. First of all, she said, these were not deaths, they were estimates based on assumptions and models worked out on a spreadsheet. These estimates, Kweder said, ignored the benefits of Vioxx; because of the Cox-2 inhibitors, Vioxx was the only one that had a clear-cut gastrointestinal safety benefit. One could not just look at the cardiovascular risks of this drug, she said; one had to look at the full spectrum of risks and benefits.

Merck's chief executive officer, Raymond Gilmartin, then testified that he believed wholeheartedly in Vioxx and that his wife was taking the drug. He denied that Merck had emphasized the benefits of Vioxx while deemphasizing its negative side effects. Indeed, he said, it was Merck who, on the basis of their own after-market research, raised red flags, and, in the end, it was Merck who voluntarily withdrew the drug.

Senator Max Baucus then asked whether FDA had sufficient resources, authority, and independence to ensure that the drugs it approved were safe. He also asked whether FDA should be doing more to monitor drug safety after a drug had been approved.

Senator Grassley asked about separating the two FDA offices involved in new drug approvals and drug safety because witnesses such as Dr. Graham claimed that their safety warnings were too often overruled by FDA officials who had been involved in approving those same drugs. He said that it did not make sense from an accountability standpoint to have the office that reviews the safety of drugs already on the market under the thumb of the office that puts the drugs on the market in the first place.

The next day the acting director of the Center for Drug Evaluation and Research at FDA issued a statement that Dr. Graham's testimony did not reflect the views of the agency. The statement said that "FDA's Office of Drug Safety (ODS), in the Center for Drug Evaluation and Research (CDER), is already an independent office separate from the Office of New Drugs (OND), the office that reviews new drug applications. Both the Office of New Drugs and the Office of Drug Safety report to me as the Director of the Center for Drug Evaluation and Research" (*New York Times*, January 17, 2005). When Bextra was withdrawn from the market in April 2005, the announcement received less media attention, in part because the statement was made the day prior to Pope John Paul II's funeral.

FDA was selected as a subject for this book because of its use of regulation as a policy tool. We seek to determine how performance is measured when the purpose of an agency is regulation rather than research, service provision, or financial assistance. Relationships between regulatory agencies and their third parties are unique. At one level the companies regulated by FDA are its clients. At another level, as we shall learn, regulated companies have unique partnerlike relationships with FDA. Regulated companies are, therefore, both FDA clients and third-party partners. How has GPRA been implemented in a regulatory context, a context in which FDA third parties are both partners and subjects of regulation? How has the application of PART to FDA influenced that agency?

FDA serves the purpose of improving the nation's health and reducing its health risks through regulation. Although each regulatory agency is different, an examination of FDA's GPRA implementation helps to identify the characteristics and qualities of performance measurement and performance improvement likely to be found in other federal regulatory agencies. Using FDA as a subject for this research also serves to illuminate patterns of interaction between an agency and its clients in the development of regulatory performance measures. As our work on FDA unfolded, it became increasingly clear that the nature of coordination with third parties is different in both quantity and quality from the coordination found in the development of performance measures at such health agencies as HRSA, NIH, and IHS, whose service delivery models involve grant making or contracting.

FDA does, however, share an important characteristic with the other agencies considered here—politics. FDA third parties, specifically the industries they regulate, play important political roles not only in the development of regulations but also in regulatory implementation. FDA's unique approach to performance measurement and GPRA implementation has been heavily influenced by external political factors, particularly the power of large drug manufacturing companies on the one hand and the power of certain categories of drug customers, such as the elderly, on the other. The influence of external stakeholders, for example, even extends to powers delegated by FDA to third parties to negotiate specific performance measures that ultimately appear in FDA performance reports.

THE FOOD AND DRUG ADMINISTRATION

FDA, part of the U.S. Public Health Service, monitors and enforces federal regulations for foods, human drugs, biologics (vaccines, blood, blood products, and so forth), animal drugs and feeds, medical devices, radiological health, and toxicology. It is charged with enforcing the Federal Food, Drug, and Cosmetic Act and several related federal public health laws. Its primary charge is to ensure that the food, cosmetics, medicines, and medical devices sold in the United States are safe and effective. FDA is also responsible for the safety of radiation-emitting products, such as cell phones, lasers, and microwaves, and for the safety of food and drugs for animals. And, in recent years, FDA has certain responsibilities regarding the prevention of terrorism.

For GPRA purposes, the formal FDA mission statement is as follows: "The FDA is responsible for protecting the public health by assuring the safety, efficacy, and security of human and veterinary drugs, biological products, medical devices, our nation's food supply, cosmetics, and products that emit radiation. The FDA is also responsible for advancing the public health by helping to speed innovations that make medicines and foods more effective, safer, and more affordable; and helping the public get the accurate, science-based information they need to use medicines and food to improve their health" (U.S. Department of Health and Human Services, Food and Drug Administration 2002, 1).

Pursuant to this mission, FDA objectives are to further the following:

1. Efficient Risk Management
   a. Provide timely, high-quality, cost-effective process for review of new technology/premarket submissions.
   b. Provide high-quality, cost-effective oversight of industry manufacturing, processing, and distribution to reduce risk.
   c. Assure the safety of the U.S. food and cosmetics supply to protect consumers at the least cost for the public.
   d. Develop methodological strategies and analyses to evaluate options, identify the most effective and efficient risk-management strategies, and optimize regulatory decision making.
2. Empower Consumers
   a. Develop an FDA-wide consumer communications infrastructure.
   b. Enhance the FDA's effort to help ensure that industry communications to consumers and health care providers are truthful and not misleading, provide information about product risks and benefits, and appropriately convey the degree of scientific uncertainty associated with such product messages.
   c. Improve and increase FDA-initiated health benefit-risk information.
3. Improve Patient and Consumer Safety
   a. Enhance the ability to quickly identify risks associated with FDA-regulated products.
   b. Increase the capacity to accurately analyze risks associated with medical products, dietary supplements, and food.
   c. Take appropriate actions to communicate risks and correct problems associated with medical products, dietary supplements, and foods.
4. Protect America from Terrorism
   a. Facilitate the development and availability of medical countermeasures to limit the effects of a terrorist attack on the civilian or military populations.
   b. Enhance the agency's emergency preparedness and response capabilities to be better able to respond in the event of a terrorist attack.
   c. Ensure the safety and security of FDA personnel, physical assets, and sensitive information.
   d. The FDA must uphold its responsibility for ensuring the safety of approximately 80 percent of the nation's food supply.
   e. Protect the safety and security of human drugs, biologics (vaccines, blood and blood products, gene therapy, human tissues, and cellular therapies), medical devices (including radiation-emitting and screening devices), veterinary drugs, and other FDA-regulated products.

5. More Effective Regulation through a Stronger Workforce
   a. Ensure a high-quality, diverse and motivated workforce.
   b. Increase efficiency and effectiveness of agency management.
   c. Ensure effective communication and working relationships with key external stakeholders to enhance U.S. and global health outcomes.
   d. Transition information technology from an enabler to a strategic tool for realizing the FDA's policy goals and objectives.
   e. Provide a consolidated FDA headquarters campus to improve operations for employees. (U.S. Department of Health and Human Services, Food and Drug Administration 2002)

These FDA responsibilities are the backdrop for the formulation of GPRA goals and objectives and the performance measures they use to determine the extent to which those goals and objectives are achieved.

FDA carries out its mission in a number of ways. Of the 10,000 FDA employees, 1,100 are investigators and inspectors who inspect approximately 15,000 facilities each year, or about 15 percent of the 100,000 FDA-regulated businesses in the United States. FDA ensures product safety through various levels of sanctions, including requests for voluntary compliance, product recalls, and fines and legal sanctions applied on manufacturers whose products are found in violation of the laws FDA enforces. FDA employs more than twenty-one hundred scientists who examine food, drug, cosmetic, and additive samples to monitor their safety and effectiveness. In addition to this research, these scientists oversee the evaluation of new drugs. In-house and external FDA research is a complex responsibility carried out in the context of ongoing controversies over the need to balance the competing objectives of speedy drug, food, food additive, and biologics approval, on one hand, and consumer safety, on the other. Competing objectives, or goal incongruence, make for a particularly difficult environment within which to establish and implement performance measures because competing goals are particularly common in regulatory contexts (Heimann 1998).

FDA AND THE PROBLEM OF COMPETING GOALS

FDA's mission includes health promotion, on one hand, and health protection, on the other. FDA's health promotion mission centers on bringing new health care and food products and technologies to the market, whereas its health protection mission centers on ensuring the safety of health care and food products in the market. The competing nature of these missions is played out politically as well as administratively. These politics to an important degree influence FDA's general functioning as well as the development and implementation of FDA's GPRA and PART performance measures and the strategies used to improve agency performance.

The competitive characteristics of FDA goals are described in a broad advocacy literature, a literature that gives FDA a much higher political profile than the other four agencies considered in this book. One stream of this literature is represented by James S. Turner's *The Chemical Feast: The Ralph Nader Study Group*

Report on Food Protection and the Food and Drug Administration. This book, like similar literature, argues that FDA fails to protect consumers from the chemicals and additives put into food products. On the other side is a larger advocacy literature that refers to FDA as a "monopoly over drug regulation that threatens the nation's health" (Hawthorne 2005) and as "FDA Follies" (Burkholz 1995). This is a free-market, antiregulation literature that is in some cases friendly to the pharmaceutical industry and in other cases simply against the federal government telling people what they can or cannot eat or which medicines they can or cannot take. For example, the producers of herbal medicines have effectively lobbied to lessen the powers of FDA regarding the control of such medicines, and the HIV/AIDS lobby has successfully caused FDA to speed up the process of new AIDS drug approvals.

Of the five agencies we evaluated, FDA was the last to develop a GPRA strategic plan. According to a top FDA official, FDA's slowness in implementing GPRA can be explained by the politics associated with competing goals. Technically, to fulfill GPRA's requirements, the Department of Health and Human Services must have a strategic plan only at the departmental level. Most HHS agencies have, however, elected to have their own GPRA strategic plan. Before GPRA, FDA periodically developed and adopted some initiatives similar to strategic plans, but these plans were not as wide ranging as the strategic plans required by GPRA. This same official indicated that in the late 1980s and the early 1990s, FDA hired a consultant to develop a strategic plan along the lines of GPRA requirements. This initiative failed because FDA's management was not able to come to an agreement with the consultant or among themselves as to the contents of the proposed strategic plan. This experience left such a bad taste for such exercises that an FDA-level strategic plan was not adopted until late 2000, fully seven years after the passage of GPRA.

The role national politics plays in FDA affairs is reflected in the unique challenges of applying performance measures to goals that are politically in play. Shifting political dynamics and events alter the cues FDA receives regarding preferred directions and leave it in the context of the competing purposes of health protection and health promotion. Below, for example, are two of FDA's strategic goals in its FY 2003 performance plan in the order in which they are presented:

☐ Assure Medical Product Safety—FDA will assure that products are safe by conducting plant and product inspections to ensure that products are manufactured and distributed under safe conditions, and by developing surveillance systems to monitor the safety of the products themselves, their use and consumption.

☐ Bring New Technologies to a World-Wide Market—FDA will assure that the products of new technologies are available to U.S. consumers. Because of the Agency's timely, science-based decisions, millions of Americans can get the medicines and medical devices they need and be assured of safe and effective products (U.S. Department of Health and Human Services, Food and Drug Administration 2002, 17–19).

In previous FDA performance plans, the placement of health promotion versus health protection strategic goals was reversed. For instance, the FY 2000 FDA performance plan lists its first two strategic initiatives in the following order:

☐ Reduce review time for important new products.

☐ Assure safety of products on the market.

Although the placement of the health protection strategic goals ahead of the health promotion strategic goal in the FY 2003 performance plan cannot be taken to mean that FDA places greater importance on the former than the later, it is symbolic of renewed attention to health protection in Congress. This symbolic placement comes after a decade of intense industry pressure, congressional oversight, and federal laws stacking the deck in favor of health promotion over health protection.

The reversal of the placement of the two goals can also be explained by a number of events. The terrorist attack on September 11, 2001, resulted in a new emphasis on terrorism—specifically, preparing for possible bioterrorism attacks. Indeed, the first sentence in the FY 2003 performance plan indicates that it is "a blueprint for action that will protect U.S. citizens in light of new and ongoing challenges to their health and safety." In addition, the entire first section of the FDA's FY 2003 performance report is dedicated to "countering the terrorist threat" (U.S. Department of Health and Human Services, Food and Drug Administration 2002, 2). Of the thirty-four performance measures related to countering the terrorist threat, twenty-nine of them were new in either FY 2002 or FY 2003. These measures cover the areas of food safety deterrence, detection, investigation, and interdiction; medical product availability and safety; emergency preparedness and response (focusing on internal security); and radiation safety.

The new prominence of goals and measures to counter terrorism and the reversal of the placement of the health protection and health promotion strategic goals demonstrate how responsive FDA is to two laws passed in the last decade, laws that have had a profound effect on FDA's attempts to balance competing objectives. The first of these laws is the Prescription Drug User Fee Act of 1992, which authorizes FDA to collect drug safety analysis fees from pharmaceutical companies. These fees finance FDA's prescription drugs authorization process. Specifically, the fees are used by FDA to hire scientists and support staff and to improve the information technology infrastructure to support a more-efficient drug application review process. Prior to PDUFA, FDA drug reviews were paid for entirely out of appropriations. In return for these fees, FDA agreed to meet certain performance targets that emphasize a more rapid drug and human biologics review process.

The second of these laws is the Food and Drug Administration Modernization Act of 1997. In addition to reauthorizing PDUFA, FDAMA emphasized the promotion aspect of FDA's strategic objectives. Congress took the unusual step of dictating to FDA elements of its mission and codifying those elements through the passage of FDAMA. The law instructs FDA to promote the public health by promptly and efficiently reviewing clinical research and taking appropriate action on the marketing of regulated products in a timely manner. The law instructs FDA to protect the nation's health. The placement of promotion before protection was neither coincidental nor accidental. If there was any question where Congress stood on the matter of promotion versus protection, FDAMA resolved that question. Promoting health through quick product review times was to be FDA's first order of business.

Not only did PDUFA and FDAMA ensure that promotion supplanted protection as FDA's primary objective, but also PDUFA has considerably altered both the FDA structure and its budget. Prior to PDUFA, for example, 1,277 FDA FTEs were dedicated to the review of human drugs and biologics. Since its passage and the availability of PDUFA fees, the number of reviewers has nearly doubled. The addition of these new reviewers has been a zero-sum game; the user fees to support the salaries of the new reviewers are built into the existing FDA budget rather than added to that budget. As a result, an ever-increasing percentage of the FDA budget is made up of industry-supported drug reviewers, and the overall budget to support the rest of FDA's activities has suffered in real terms.

Under the authority of PDUFA, FDA collects user fees from the pharmaceutical industry. The law indicates that these funds may be used only to expedite the premarket review of new drugs and biologics. As drug review revenues have increased they have accounted for a greater proportion of FDA's budget. As a result, the proportion and number of FDA employees who are dedicated to meeting FDA's other goals and objectives have decreased. Since PDUFA passed, these user fees have paid for 840 FDA employees who work exclusively to bring pharmaceuticals more rapidly to the market. During the same period, however, the number of FDA employees increased from 8,868 to 8,908 FTEs, an increase of only 0.5 percent. In the years since PDUFA's passage, employees whose salaries were paid from these user fees went from 0 percent to just under 10 percent of the agency's workforce. In other words, given the slight increase of forty FTEs during the same period, the PDUFA-purchased employees do not represent new FTEs, but resources redirected from other FDA activities, particularly from consumer protection.

PDUFA has also had a significant impact on FDA performance goals. As one FDA representative claims, "PDUFA was GPRA before GPRA was ever instituted." As table 8.1 indicates, PDUFA reflected a GPRA perspective not only in terms of the establishment of performance measures and accountability but also in terms of the importance of stakeholders in the development of those measures. The same representative notes, "We made performance commitments to [the drug and biologics] industry before the industry would agree to pay money for these applications. They [industry] didn't want to just throw good money after bad."

This preference for promotion over protection is also evident in the rules that govern the purposes for which PDUFA fees can be used. In the first ten years of the act, PDUFA fees were used to double the number of product review scientists, but their use was limited to premarket, clinical reviews of drugs. They could not be used for after-market studies on the safety or effectiveness of drugs already

TABLE 8.1

FOOD AND DRUG ADMINISTRATION REPRESENTATIVE PERFORMANCE MEASURES

Representative Performance Measures	*Measure Category*
Reduce time to marketing approval for new drugs and biologics.	POM
Percentage of new drugs and biologic product reviews completed within 10 months.	POM
Inspect medical device manufacturing establishments each year.	OM
Reduce administrative staff.	PM
Increase by 10 percent the percentage of American consumers who correctly identify that saturated fat increases the risk of heart disease.	POM
Improve by 10 percent the percentage of American consumers who correctly identify that omega-3 fat is a possible factor in reducing the risk of heart disease.	POM
Number of labs to address surge capacity in the event of terrorist attack on the food supply.	OM
Inspect blood banks and biologics manufacturing establishments each year.	OM
Percentage of medical device submissions that will receive final decisions within 320 review days.	POM
Percentage of FDA reviews of new medical devices completed within 180 days.	POM
Reduce time to marketing approval for generic drug applications.	POM
Percentage of new generic drug application reviews completed in 6 months.	POM
Reduce medication errors in hospitals.	HOM
Increase by 40 percent the percentage of American consumers who correctly identify that trans fat increases the risk of heart disease.	POM

POM, program outcome measure; *OM*, output measure; *PM*, process measure; *HOM*, health outcome measure.

being prescribed. "The result is that our workforce and real resources for most programs other than PDUFA have contracted each year since 1992 while we struggle to assure that enough funds are spent on the drug review process to meet this PDUFA requirement. Several consecutive years of operating in this way have made it difficult to continue to further reduce staffing levels in FDA programs other than drug review" (U.S. Department of Health and Human Services, Food and Drug Administration 2002).

According to a recent GAO study, the impact of PDUFA's user fees on FDA is not limited to its budget and structure (the number of drug review scientists as a percent of total FDA FTEs). GAO calculates that the number of after-market safety-related drug withdrawals from the market has increased since PDUFA's passage, with the Vioxx and Bextra withdrawals being most visible. The GAO study found that "a higher percentage of drugs have been withdrawn from the market for safety-related reasons since PDUFA's enactment than prior to the law's enactment" (U.S. General Accounting Office 2002.) The GAO report found that in the two four-year periods preceding (1989–1992) and immediately following (1993–1996, before the act had time to impact drug review times substantially), the market withdrawal rates were 1.96 percent and 1.56 percent, respectively. During the next four-year period, 1997–2000, the drug withdrawal rate rose to 5.34 percent. The GAO report also indicates that some consumers' and patients' interest groups argue that PDUFA's emphasis on faster review times, specifically the importance given to meeting the stringent performance goals for reducing review times, has compromised drug safety.

FDA has challenged the methodology GAO used to determine post-PDUFA drug withdrawal rates, because they separated out the years after PDUFA's passage into two groups of four years. FDA contends that the eight years before PDUFA's passage should be compared to the eight years after its passage. When this comparison is made, the size of the increase in drug withdrawals diminishes substantially. With the use of this method, withdrawals increased from 3.10 percent to 3.46 percent. Nevertheless, the GAO report and the need in FDA to defend its practices are indicative of the ongoing politics of drug approval, drug withdrawal, and consumer protection.

An interesting illustration of the challenges associated with GPRA implementation at FDA is the transition of responsibility for seafood inspection from FDA to the industry itself. The program is called the Hazard Analysis Critical Control Point, or HACCP, a system of process controls designed to prevent food safety hazards. The implementation of the HACCP program represented a move away from traditional FDA inspection as a means of detecting food-borne hazards and toward industry self-regulation, coupled with a system of FDA audits for monitoring purposes. The problem, however, is that the HACCP auditing portion of the FDA budget is chronically underfunded.

While Congress demands greater accountability, on the one hand, on the other hand FDA now has a much-reduced ability to monitor and assure industry compliance to FDA standards. In the case of the application of the HACCP program to the seafood industry, the agent is entrusted to serve as its own principal. The relationship between FDA and the seafood industry was delicate to begin with; now that arrangement is open to conflicts of interest. It is unclear whether politics or mixed messages have led to inadequate funding for HACCP auditing. One FDA employee explained that both the logic and strategy of reporting for accountability (such as is required by GPRA) differs from the logic and strategy used for budget justifications. Accountability concerns might lead to portraying compliance rates in the best light; justifications for appropriations increases, however, might lead to the opposite, as agency officials try to give the impression that they do not have sufficient funds to do their jobs. What is clear is that shifting from FDA inspections to industry self-regulation, coupled with a chronically underfunded auditing system, is an open invitation to industry noncompliance with FDA regulations.

PERFORMANCE MEASUREMENT AND FDA OUTCOMES

The GPRA and PART preference for output measures is especially obvious in FDA appropriations hearings (see table 8.1). According to one FDA manager, the following exchange in recent appropriations hearings is typical. "How come the number of inspections you're doing is going down? And how come it costs so much for each inspection? I see here you have a budget of X amount, and you've done only this many inspections. Well, those are pretty expensive inspections." FDA's typical response to that line of questioning is that "much of what we spent wasn't on actual inspections, but on education and trying to develop new kinds of working relationships with industry." The problem is that "when they [legislatures] hear 'regulatory agency,' they think of an activity that is traditionally associated with a regulatory agency: inspections. Sometimes they'll try to understand by asking, 'Well, if you're switching to the new direction—education and cooperation—then what's your indicator of effectiveness in that area?' Then we have to tell them that we're still in the process of developing it. So that pushes them back to saying, 'Okay, well how many inspections . . . ?'"

The second factor that leads to the prevalence of output goals and the lack of outcome goals in FDA's performance plan is found in a series of negotiated agreements and codified performance requirements. The negotiated performance agreements reached between FDA and the drug industry are distinctly output in nature, measures of FDA's efficiency in reviewing drugs and differentiating between drugs in priority, standard, and generic categories. The performance agreements were codified by PDUFA and are explicitly referred to in the FDA performance report as "PDUFA goals." The presence of these negotiated output measures does not preclude the use of outcome goals; outcomes themselves—improved health resulting from drugs and vaccines, or reductions in the number of unsafe drugs and vaccines—were not the impetus for the passage of PDUFA. The explicit goal of PDUFA is to have "industry provide the funding in exchange for FDA agreement to meet drug-review performance goals, which emphasize timeliness" (U.S. Department of Health and Human Services, Food and Drug Administration 2002).

The third factor that leads to the prevalence of output goals in the FDA performance report is the recognition that FDA is only one of many parties responsible for food and drug safety. FDA is reluctant to be singled out as accountable for a responsibility that is shared among several parties. According to an FDA official, "The question has often been put to us, 'Why don't you set goals that do not just say how fast you review the product, but what's your health impact or the economic impact?' We're unwilling, so far, to commit to impact goals like fewer sick people or lower mortality rates as a result of more firms being in compliance or being inspected. We can't get the data to establish a baseline very well, and we're not willing to commit to a sickness or mortality goal that we're only one party in making it happen. How many people get sick and die is a function of us, the states, the people, and the industry."

One confounding characteristic of performance measurement occurs when there are statutory mandates for a regulatory agency to produce certain output levels, with no specific attention to eventual outcomes. This is the context within which FDA must perform. For example, Congress's mandate with respect to FDA's statutory site-inspection requirements explicitly focuses on immediate outputs rather than on long-term outcomes. To meet Food Safety Assurance statutory requirements, FDA has to inspect 80 percent of sites semiannually. The agency's strategy, however, puts an emphasis on visits to the most risky sites rather than on broader site coverage stipulated by statutory requirements. Because risky sites take longer to inspect, attention to them comes at the expense of the broader site coverage mandated by statute. Indeed, FDA could meet its statutory requirements for the Food Safety Assurance program only if it were to ignore the more risky, time-consuming sites in its visitation plans. In fulfilling their oversight responsibilities, appropriators do not hesitate to take agency officials to task for their failure to meet statutory output objectives.

Evidence of continuing pressure to develop outcome measures is found in appendix B of the 2004 FDA annual performance plan. In that appendix, under the title "FDA Progress Measuring Long Term Outcomes Goals" is the indication that the agency "is attempting to strengthen its outcome measurement and achievement capability through the following efforts." To achieve these objectives in 2005, FDA proposed a "links to outcomes" scheme, which creatively parses outcomes. Table 8.2, taken from appendix B, shows the scheme.

A number of reasons account for the struggle to develop genuine outcome goals at FDA. As with other health care agencies, the methodological challenges associated with pointing to the specific contribution of FDA's programs and regulations to an improvement of the health of Americans are daunting. In addition

TABLE 8.2

FDA LINKS TO OUTCOMES

FDA Activities	Outputs	Initial Outcomes	Intermediate Outcomes	End Outcomes
Application Reviews	Approval Decisions	Product Availability	Informed Product use	Improved health outcomes:
Inspections	Enforcement actions	Safe, affordable products	Access by target populations	• Mortality • Morbidity
Surveillance reports	Educational efforts	Industry compliance	Consumer confidence	• Health
Research efforts	Product standards	Consumer health professional awareness of risk information		

to the methodological concerns, three other factors have pushed FDA away from outcome goals in the direction of output goals. These factors are as follows:

1. For regulatory agencies, Congress is used to output goals and the language of processes and outputs.

2. Negotiated agreements with the industries it regulates (that later become codified) and other statutory requirements mandate specific output performance levels.

3. FDA recognizes that their work represents only one force in the overall determination of health outcomes. Health outcomes are a complex function of the more general forces of economic, social, and political circumstances and the work of regulatory agencies.

Among FDA's strategic goals is the intent to "provide consumers quicker access to new food ingredients, bioengineered foods, and dietary supplements, while assuring their safety" (U.S. Department of Health and Human Services, Food and Drug Administration 2002, 4). This goal is achieved through the "premarket" food review program, which focuses on food and color additives, dietary supplements, substances that are "generally recognized as safe" (GRAS), and bioengineered foods. Prior to FDAMA, the premarket review program consisted exclusively of industry petitions to FDA before the manufacturers and distributors of these products could market them. These petitions would then be reviewed by FDA to determine whether they were sufficiently safe and effective. Under the petition rules, the petitioning company had to receive an explicit response from FDA in order to begin marketing and selling its product. The absence of a specific response from FDA was effectively a "pocket veto," using one FDA executive's terminology.

Under FDAMA, FDA was directed to alter its premarket review process by establishing a premarket notification program. Premarket notification would allow certain products to be designated as GRAS and some food additives to be categorized as "indirect food additives" and by this mechanism bypass the lengthy review process. Under the notification procedures, companies determine whether their premarket products qualify as GRAS or indirect food additives, and they notify FDA that they intend to market the product. The notification a company provides to FDA includes information that is intended to demonstrate that the product qualifies as GRAS or as an indirect food additive. FDA's FY 2003 performance plan reflects this change. Of FDA's five indicators related to premarket review, four of them relate to notification. An example of such an indicator is to "complete processing of 80 percent of GRAS notifications within 180 days." The last remaining premarket GPRA goal relating to petitions demonstrates the increased pressure to expedite food products to the market even when they do not qualify as GRAS or an indirect food additive: "Complete the safety evaluation of 65 percent of the number of food and color additive petitions that were under review for more than 360 days at the beginning of the fiscal year" (U.S. Department of Health and Human Services, Food and Drug Administration 2002, 114–18).

The FY 2003 performance indicator for petition safety reviews is to complete 65 percent within 360 days. In 1999, that prescriptive performance measure was 30 percent. More important than the more aggressive prescriptive measure for FY 2003 is that it falls well below the statutory requirement under FDAMA. FDA is statutorily required to complete the petition reviews in 90 days, extendable to 180 days. The addition of the notification program has made it more difficult to meet this statutory requirement, even though there are now fewer petitions to review. The reason there are fewer petitions to review is that many of the products that would have previously required a petition and review are now designated as GRAS or an indirect food additive and now only require notification. This makes it more difficult to meet the statutory petition review time requirements because the remaining petitions are more complex. Products that would have previously taken the least amount of time to review have been selected out of the petition process and put into the notification process by their companies. So FDA has petition review goals that are much more aggressive, while the petitioned products it is reviewing are more challenging. In its FY 2003 performance report, FDA is candid about these challenges: "It is widely recognized that meeting the current statutory time frame is an unrealistic goal for all food and color additive petitions, especially the more complex ones. . . . Since the remaining petitions are likely to be more complex and take more time to review, the agency performance on this goal may decline initially" (U.S. Department of Health and Human Services, Food and Drug Administration 2002, 13).

The fundamental changes with regard to the addition of the notification process happen on several levels. The first change is that under the petition rules, industry was essentially seeking permission from FDA to market its food additive and supplement products. Now, for the majority of these new products, industry no longer asks for permission, but rather informs FDA that it intends to market a product. An FDA manager notes that under the notification process the new products are "innocent until proven guilty." Originally, new food products required specific and explicit approval from FDA before they could be marketed to the public, but the presumption of innocence refers to tacit rather than explicit approval required before these products go to market. All that is now required for an industry to begin marketing and selling a product is the passage of time (a different number of days depending on the product) after the notification or petition it has sent to FDA.

A second and related change brought about by FDAMA's and FDA's move toward deregulation is FDA's commitment to cooperate more fully with industry to expedite the premarket review process (for both petition and notification products). The FDA FY 2003 performance report repeats this commitment by stating that it will "work closely with petitioners before they file premarket approval applications, to avoid or quickly resolve problems" (U.S. Department of Health and Human Services, Food and Drug Administration 2002, 31). Taken together, these two FDAMA-based changes, reinforced by FDA's performance measures, represent a substantial shift toward promotion in the struggle between FDA's competing goals.

Although federal agencies are often caught in the middle of several congressional committees with different responsibilities and constituencies, FDA appears to get pulled in more directions than most. The House Energy and Commerce Committee and the Senate Health, Education, Labor and Pensions Committee have ownership over matters related to FDA deregulation, organization, and general oversight. They were both heavily involved in the passage of both PDUFA and FDAMA, and their interests and concerns have been reflected in FDA's performance measures. General ownership of GPRA belongs to the Government Reform Committee in the House and the Government Affairs Committee in the Senate. Authorizing committees are more inclined toward substantive oversight, whereas compliance with generalized GPRA requirements and FDA responses to PART tend to be found in the executive branch.

The goals and objectives set out in the FDA response to GPRA requirements are a rather good reflection of both the competing nature of its goals and the shifting emphasis from one set of goals toward another. In simplified terms, FDA has moved somewhat away from consumer protection goals and toward somewhat more industry-friendly, market-driven goals. Following the logic of the overall theoretical explanation of GPRA application as federal government strategic goals and the measurement of agency performance in pursuit of these goals through articulated networks of third parties, we can understand this review of FDA as describing a patterned adjustment of FDA–third-party articulation. Food and drug companies, FDA's third parties, were at one time essentially the subject of regulatory oversight, a form of articulation that fits the general pattern of regulatory agencies (Hedge and Johnson 2002). In this articulation, the agency is an independent, objective, arms-length regulator of industry for purposes of protecting consumers or some generalized notion of the public interest. With the passage of PDUFA and FDAMA as well as other recent legislation, FDA would now be described, at least to some extent, as being in a series of industry-agency partnerships. Drug companies both pay for and carry out, under FDA direction, the reviews of new drugs, subtly changing the relationship between the two. From the third-party perspective, their articulation with FDA moves, however slightly, from being regulated to being a customer and a partner (Heimann 1998).

In a detailed analysis of FDA's response to political charges, C. F. Larry Heimann found that, at least as far as new drug appraisal is concerned, FDA has moved away from its earlier objective of minimizing "type I errors." A type I error would be the approval of a new drug that proved to be dangerous, as in the thalidomide case, or the failure to prevent the marketing of dangerous food additives. FDA has moved in the direction of minimizing "type II errors," which is understood to mean that a reliable or needed drug is either slow to get to market or not allowed to be marketed, thereby causing those needing the drug to suffer or die. A similar shift can be seen in food regulation, a shift minimizing type II errors on the basis of the argument that the burden of risk should be shifted toward the food customer or the herbal medicine customer (Heimann 1998).

The issue here, according to Heimann, is a determination of acceptable risk. In the matter of AIDS, he claims that "the notion of acceptable risk is particularly salient to testing and review of AIDS as an infectious and terminal disease that is spreading across the United States and other parts of the world. FDA officials recognize that they must be willing to allow for greater risks than the agency had traditionally accepted. Risks are an inescapable part of the FDA's drug approval process. Determining acceptable bounds for these risks is important to the FDA as it is to NASA" (Heimann 1998, 164).

What constitutes acceptable risk is very difficult to define. Measures of FDA output can be useful to policy makers as they attempt to determine what ought to be an acceptable risk. But FDA output measures do not answer questions of acceptable risk; they only sharpen those questions and serve as data in debates over which risks are to be preferred—type I or type II.

FDA's changing approach to the regulation of food and drugs is part of a larger pattern of regulatory change in American government. The modern approach to regulation is described as "management-based regulation whereby the regulator seeks to embed within the management practices of firms being regulated a consciousness of public goals. What is distinctive about management-based regulation is that it compels regulated firms to engage in planning and decision making in a way that identifies both the technology and performance targets needed to achieve socially desirable goals" (Coglianese and Lazer 2002, 201).

The passage of both PDUFA and FDAMA is clearly in the spirit of the movement toward management-based regulatory strategies. In addition, the adoption of HACCP strategies for the regulation of food processing now is used in both FDA and the Department of Agriculture. The HACCP strategy is used to accommodate the very high heterogeneity of food-processing systems, ranging from making fruit juice to processing frozen fish. The HACCP program implements protocols requiring all food processors to "perform rigorous hazards analysis of risks at every stage of production; identification of critical points in the production process at which hazards identified in the first step can be managed," and so forth (Coglianese and Lazer 2002, 214). These HACCP protocols are put in place as replacements for FDA and USDA detailed food-processing steps written by the agencies for every variety of food processing. In the logic of the HACCP program, the fruit juice makers know their technology best and can best determine how to implement general HACCP protocols. This would, at least in theory, reduce the need for inspections, particularly because HACCP protocols require careful record keeping at each step in food processing. Both the U.S. Department of Agriculture and FDA claim to have made impressive improvements in the safety of food processing as a result of the HACCP program, but GAO has been harshly critical of FDA programs because of what it claims to be a lack of industry compliance with HACCP rules (U.S. General Accounting Office 2001).

Despite the unique challenges of implementing GPRA in the context of a regulatory agency under intense political pressures, FDA has done an admirable job both in implementing GPRA and in meeting the performance requirements established by Congress. For example, under an accelerated approval program, FDA took only 5.8 months to approve Ziagen, a drug used in the treatment of HIV-1 infection in adults and children. In addition, the median approval time for generic drugs was reduced from an average of 19.6 months in 1997 to 17.3 months in 1999. Finally, FDA set a goal to review 90 percent of priority new drug applications within six months.

FDA PERFORMANCE MEASUREMENT AND BUDGETING

The central questions in the logic of performance budgeting deal with how agency performance is to be correlated with agency appropriations. Will good performance be rewarded with increased appropriations, or will it indicate that an agency can get by with less? Will poor performance be penalized by decreased appropriations, or will poor performance be an indicator of inadequate funding and the need for appropriation increases?

Performance information presented to an external audience and particularly to Congress might differ from performance information used internally to manage an agency's programs. According to one FDA executive, the main problem is that "when GPRA becomes visible to the outside world, its purpose is either to get more money or to not look bad. And those objectives can distort the facts." Accordingly, this executive states, "some of the information that we present in the name of GPRA is an attempt to secure the budget. This information does not necessarily conform with the information that they're going to actually use to manage the program because they're always going to make conservative estimates based on the need for more money."

An example of this conflict is found in measuring the performance of industry compliance through a technique described as "passive surveillance systems." Compared with active regulatory surveillance systems such as inspections and interviews, passive surveillance systems are regulatory schemes that rely primarily on non-FDA health professionals, patients, and consumers to report adverse reactions to foods, vaccines, and other regulated products. One FDA representative reports, "I've done some surveys on how compliant the industry is to some of our new kinds of passive [surveillance] programs, where the FDA is leading the industry into compliance. As a result of this survey FDA managers concluded that to improve compliance they wanted to focus on the tougher parts of the industry first, and they didn't want to spread their resources too thin. The strategy to get this approach approved internally would be to make the argument that for the most part the industry is in compliance so we should focus on the tougher nuts."

A different strategy is required, according to an FDA official interviewed for this research, when discussing the passive surveillance systems program externally. The conflicting objectives of using performance information for accountability purposes versus using performance information in the hope of securing increased appropriations are evident. "When you're making the argument to Congress that you need more money, you may tend to make the argument that . . . well . . . not very many of them are in compliance. How are they not compliant? You can always go into a plant and say, you know, you should be keeping your record books in a safe and they're lying on the counter. That's not a safety hazard, but it is still not complying with the letter of the law. So, in an attempt to get more resources, you can make your compliance rate very low in order to show a need for more."

One FDA representative states that the "marketing of performance interferes with the management of performance." Presenting performance information in a manner that will lead (at least according to FDA's logic) to stable or increased appropriations "makes you conservative in what you say." When presenting performance information where accountability is the primary focus, however, the first objective "is to not look bad." According to this FDA representative, "Both of those responses to the outside world tend to be in conflict with the good management of the program."

The different audiences for performance information are the same constituencies from which FDA receives much of its direction. As mentioned earlier, in matters related to its authorization and oversight, FDA answers to the Health, Education, Labor and Pensions Committee in the Senate and the Energy and Commerce Committee in the House. With regard to FDA, one insider describes "regulatory reinvention" as the chief emphasis of these committees in the 1990s: "The FDA is being challenged along with other regulatory agencies with regulatory reinvention. In the last five years, legislation which calls for regulatory agencies to 'reinvent' and 'modernize' themselves has happened at FDA, Customs, and several other regulatory agencies. And with a Republican Congress, reinvention means deregulation. It means think of ways so that you're not bothering industry so much."

The logic of reinvention and deregulation is antithetical to the notion that more inspections mean better oversight. Inspections are easy to count and hence lend themselves to measurable performance goals and indicators. Following Congress's lead and in conjunction with its implementation of FDAMA, FDA is attempting to move away from "a performance as number of inspections" mentality toward a more cooperative and a more educational approach.

OMB has assessed FDA through PART. FDA PART information, including its performance against GPRA goals and targets, is included in FDA's FY 2006 budget request. Most of the performance measures are of the process and output type—the percentage of medical-device submissions that receive final decisions within 320 reviewed days, with a target of 80 percent in 2006 and 90 percent in 2007, for example. Although most studies of FDA describe it as having competing objectives, PART indicates that "FDA has a clear mission and a unique Federal Role in protecting public health" and gives them 100 percent of the points available in Section I, for program purpose and design. FDA also received 100 percent of the points for Sections II and III of PART, the strategic planning and management sections, respectively. In the final section (IV), where program results and accountability are assessed, FDA receives just over half the points available, or 54 percent. Overall, FDA fared well in its PART assessment, with a rating of "moderately effective," and a total score of 77, considerably higher than the average PART score of 64 and the average PART score for regulatory programs, 70. Even with competing objectives and the regulation of food and drugs in a highly political context, the FDA budget has steadily increased. For FY 2006 the president's budget recommended a 9 percent budget increase for FDA.

CONCLUSIONS

Do regulatory agencies, and particularly regulatory agencies in politically sensitive settings, respond to GPRA differently from agencies that implement policy through third parties? The answer is yes. Because FDA is the only regulatory agency studied here, its profile in the synthesis of variables that have influenced the application of GPRA requirements is very different from those of the other four agencies considered.

First, as figure 8.1 indicates, FDA is less hollowed out than the other health agencies considered in our analysis. Nevertheless, in the past ten years FDA has moved steadily in the direction of greater third-party involvement through the logic of the regulated paying the costs of the work of regulation and even through some self-regulation. Reason suggests that it is harder for a regulatory agency to protect consumer interests when the regulated are essentially their customers. FDA does pay for some independent, technical, and external review of food and drug products, but the extent of third-party food-and-drug-policy implementation is not very great. Therefore, unlike the possible problem of independence in their relations with companies paying for the trials of their own prospective drugs, organizations that contract with FDA appear to be effectively managed.

Second, the form and level of FDA accountability to federal goals are, however measured, very high. The problem is this: Competing goals and accountability to one set of goals can reduce accountability to the other set of goals. This problem is treated at greater length below.

Third, the nature and precision of FDA performance measures are also high. The problem is that most of the goals and their attendant measures are either process or output measures. FDA is remarkably candid regarding the agency's unwillingness to make assertions of causality between the regulatory process and the status of health in the United States. As they point out, health is influenced by many factors, including the work of other government agencies. Because almost all these factors are beyond FDA control, it is unreasonable to connect the state of overall health—real outcomes—to FDA. Even in the face of high political rhetoric about curing diseases and protecting the quality of food, FDA sticks with process, output, and program outcome measures. Although the nature and precision of FDA performance measures required by GPRA and PART are high, these performance measures do not meet the idealized standard of health outcomes measures. Nevertheless, they are solid performance measures, measures that facilitate annual comparison of goal accomplishment.

Fourth, the nature and quality of FDA network articulation lean rather strongly in the direction of the managed network. The FDA regulatory process is highly structured and serialized.

> The most salient feature of the FDA's drug approval process is the extremely serial nature of the system. Beginning in the manufacturer's lab, progressing through several stages of clinical trials, and contingent to final review at the FDA, the structure accommodates the agency's desire to protect against the possibility of type I failure. . . . [Eighty] percent of all proposed drugs fail to make it through the entire approval process. The serial nature of the system prevents many harmful drugs from getting into the market, but it no doubt allows some good drugs to be eliminated in the process. (Heimann 1998, 153)

FIGURE 8.1

KEY VARIABLES IN THE SYNTHESIS OF THE INFLUENCE OF PERFORMANCE MEASUREMENT IN THE FOOD AND DRUG ADMINISTRATION

A. The Level of Third-Party Policy Implementation

FDA

hollowed out   *direct government*

B. Accountability to Federal Program Purposes

FDA

attenuated   *strict*

C. The Nature and Quality of Network Articulations

FDA

remote control   *managed network*

D. The Characteristics of Goals

FDA

processes   *outputs*   *(POM) outcomes (HOM)*

E. The Level of Goal and Policy Agreement

FDA

disagreement   *agreement*
incongruence   *congruence*

F. The Level of Centralization of Policy Implementation

FDA

decentralized   *centralized*
dispersed, fragmented

G. The Precision and Characteristics of Performance Measures

FDA

qualitative   *quantitative*
descriptive   *precise*

H. The Level and Character of Client and Stakeholder Support

FDA

weak   *divided*   *strong*

I. Professionally Identity

FDA

low   *high*

POM, program outcome measure; *HOM,* health outcome measure.

Several FDA process and output goals are essentially measures of the effectiveness of the serial process.

Fifth, both the level of FDA goal congruence and policy agreement among principals are less than for other agencies. The FDA GPRA goals and measures avoid overt emphasis on competing objectives, but there is little doubt that FDA's permanent bureaucracy of professionals and scientists leans in the direction of consumer protection values and toward a skepticism regarding the food and drug industry (Heimann 1998). But agency goals clearly move in response both to cycles of failure and to political influence. FDA goals and measures "are subject to the oscillation that naturally occurs within the American political system. . . . Analysis of . . . the FDA seems to suggest this is the case. I would argue that these cases are not exceptions; agency failures cycle regularly between type I and type II errors, with major accidents (or failures) occurring periodically" (Heimann 1998, 168). In the early years of the agency the emphasis was heavily on consumer protection and a generalized public interest. Over time, however, as the pursuit of consumer protection began to appear obtrusive, to run counter to freedoms, or to be too expensive, the political pressure mounted to move toward the market and individual freedoms. The passage of both FDAMA and PDUFA is evidence of the trend away from what is thought among dominant political principals to be a bureaucratic and slow food and drug regulatory process, a process that is unfriendly toward business. The threat of biological terrorism and the Vioxx and Bextra cases appear to be early signs of a possible shift back toward tighter regulations and a greater emphasis on consumer protection.

Goal incongruence at FDA is part of a larger finding of "predictable incoherence" in regulatory systems (Sunstein et al. 2002). Predictable incoherence is a policy implementation phenomenon tracing to high jurisdictional fragmentation, layer after layer of sometimes contradictory legislation, extended vertical federalism, and divided systems of executive management and legislative oversight (Coglianese and Lazer 2002). Predictable incoherence has also to do with the fragmentation and compartmentalization of decision-making authority that, when all is summed up, does not "make sense" because of incoherence in terms of the use of different policy instruments and the logic associated with those instruments, because of competing objectives, and because of unintended consequences made increasingly likely because of incoherence (Coglianese and Lazer 2002).

The staff of FDA has been shown to be politically responsive. As political values oscillate, FDA responds, but this response could best be characterized as moving as far in the direction of speeding up drug approval, and relaxing oversight over food and drug business, as can be done without jeopardizing our core responsibilities to protect the consumer. This is a kind of bureaucratic moderating weight softening the influence of political swings. But to be this moderating weight, FDA must appear to embrace, simultaneously, competing values and the goals that reflect those values. The day-to-day work of FDA is, however, an iterative process of goal balance and reconciliation.

Sixth, the level of FDA centralization of policy implementation is mixed. As the emphasis has shifted toward relaxed oversight, drug companies have become customers and partners in the drug approval process. FDA policy implementation has been, to some extent, decentralized. Still, of the agencies studied here, FDA is the most centralized because it does not rely primarily on grant or contract third parties.

Seventh, the plausibility of the FDA program goals is rather realistic, inasmuch as the agency has chosen to emphasize process and output goals. In addition, the agency has essentially said to Congress that it will try to meet legislative drug-approval deadlines; however, in difficult cases, it is likely not to meet them.

The biggest dilemma in the application of performance measurement logic to a regulatory agency such as FDA is this: How do you measure something that does not happen? We know, for example, that only about 20 percent of proposed new drugs make it through the application process. We also know that "safety" is cited as the reason in only about 20 percent of rejections. Drug companies withdraw drugs from the process about twice as often as FDA disapproves a drug because of no commercial interest or because of an imbalance between costs and benefits. Is there any way to estimate catastrophes that might have happened if approval rates for safety purposes were, say, 15 percent rather than 20 percent? Because we will never know the negative effects of an unapproved drug, FDA can only estimate the number of avoided catastrophes.

Eighth, the level of FDA client and shareholder support is mixed. Support almost certainly varies depending on where clients and shareholders stand regarding FDA regulation. "People who are aware of agency decisions and expect to lose from such a policy typically rebel against such action; they often seek to reverse the policy through their activity in the political process" (Heimann 1998, 165). There are continuing strong clients or shareholders for FDA, such as the big drug manufacturing companies in the same way that, for example, universities are supporters of NIH or the American Association of Retired Persons is a supporter of Medicare. But unlike the political support of other agencies from their stakeholders, the articulation between FDA and the drug companies is best thought of as a form of mutual interdependence. This interdependence is described in the standard research literature on regulatory agencies and the companies they regulate as iterative patterns of review and approval on the part of FDA and the use of FDA approval as certification of product safety on the part of drug companies (Heimann 1998).

Ninth, the possible applicability of FDA performance pressures to performance budgeting is thought, among FDA officials, to be a rather dangerous idea. Put in simplified terms, the fear is that the more performance measures show FDA to be doing well, the greater the likelihood of reduced budgets. The reasons have to do with cycles from an emphasis on possible type I failures—such as an approved drug discovered to be harmful or a food product with a harmful additive left on the market—to an emphasis on possible type II failures. Measures that indicate that FDA is especially effective in the hands of the food and pharmaceutical industries could be used to bring Congress to spend less on food and drug oversight rather than more. This is a common paradox in regulatory regimes.

An overview of the comparative location of FDA along the continua describing variables that explain the agency's response to GPRA shows that FDA is high in the following characteristics:

- ☐ measured accountability to realistic federal objectives in terms of processes and outputs
- ☐ retention of most of the characteristics of direct and centralized government while moving in the direction of managed regulation
- ☐ carefully articulated relations with regulated industries, the third parties of FDA

FDA is low in terms of goal congruence and policy agreement and is at the center of shifting values and goals. This suggests that effective public management in the context of goal incongruence and policy disagreement and oscillating values requires exactly the kind of response to GPRA found here. In broad terms this response could be described as the FDA application of GPRA as part of a wider approach to the management of contextual ambiguity.

9

MEASURING PERFORMANCE AND RESULTS IN THEORY AND PRACTICE

To its advocates the passage of the Government Performance and Results Act of 1993 was thought to be among the most sweeping and enduring reforms of management in the modern history of federal government administration. It has been more than a decade since the passage of GPRA, a long enough time to determine reasonably how it has been implemented and what have been the results. To modify a borrowed phrase from a synthesis on the subject of performance management, the question is: How well has GPRA performed (Jennings and Haist 2002)?

Because of the vastness of the federal government, in both programmatic scope and size, to analyze the implementation of GPRA effectively it was necessary to limit the number of agencies examined. The Department of Health and Human Services is an ideal agency for the analysis of GPRA implementation because of its size and particularly because HHS includes a diverse range of types of agencies. After a review of the range of HHS agencies, we selected the following five for in-depth analysis on the basis of variations in their missions, policy tools, and third-party implementers:

☐ Health Resources and Services Administration

☐ Centers for Medicare and Medicaid Services

☐ National Institutes of Health

☐ Indian Health Services

☐ Food and Drug Administration

The detailed study of the implementation of GPRA performance regimes in these five agencies appears in chapters 4 through 8. The purpose of this chapter is to present a cross-case analysis and comparison and a theoretical consideration of the practices of performance measurement in these five agencies. This cross-case analysis is based on the key variables that emerged during the course of our field-work. On the basis of fieldwork using grounded theory, we determined that the primary explanatory variables that influence how performance measurement is implemented in the five agencies are the following:

- [ ] level of third-party policy implementation
- [ ] accountability to federal program purposes
- [ ] nature and quality of network articulations
- [ ] characteristics of goals
- [ ] level of policy agreement
- [ ] level of centralization of policy implementation
- [ ] precision and characteristics of performance measurement
- [ ] level and character of client and stakeholder support
- [ ] level of professional identity

These variables are identified and described in chapter 2 and presented as heuristic continua used in the analysis of each case. Based on our analysis, figure 9.1 indicates where each of the five agencies is located along each continuum. Using these agency locations on each continuum, this chapter is a detailed cross-case comparison of the agencies we reviewed. After the presentation of these detailed findings, GPRA implementation will be considered in terms of the theory and practice of government performance measurement.

THIRD-PARTY GOVERNMENT AND NETWORK ARTICULATION

In our study of these five health agencies it was determined that the most important influence in their implementation of performance measurement is the extent to which their programs are carried out by third parties. In these agencies, third-party policy implementation is the rule rather than the exception; only the direct service of IHS and the intramural research in NIH are not provided by third parties. As the management literature indicates, in the context of third-party policy implementation, management changes from the traditions of bureaucracy and hierarchy in the direction of the management of networks (Agranoff and McGuire 1998, 2001; Radin 2002). The five agencies we studied are so hollowed out that their organization and administration is almost entirely based on network management.

In many ways this is a redefinition of management and public administration. Much of what has traditionally been thought to be public administration, such as record keeping, hiring, promoting, supervising, contacting clients, budgeting, and the like, are now exported to third parties. The meaning or understanding of modern public administration changes to new processes variously described as contract management or network management.

FIGURE 9.1

A SYNTHESIS OF THE INFLUENCE OF PERFORMANCE MEASUREMENT ON FIVE FEDERAL HEALTH CARE AGENCIES

A. The Level of Third-Party Policy Implementation

MCD	IHS(g)				
HRSA	MCR NIH		FDA		IHS(d)

hollowed out ←——————————————————————————→ *direct government*

B. Accountability to Federal Program Purposes

						MCR	
	IHS(g)		MCD	FDA	IHS(d)	HRSA	NIH

attenuated ←——————————————————————————→ *strict*

C. The Nature and Quality of Network Articulations

IHS(g) NIH	MCD	HRSA	MCR	IHS(d)
			FDA	

remote control ←——————————————————————————→ *managed network*

D. The Characteristics of Goals

MCD		IHS(g) IHS(d) NIH	FDA HRSA	MCR

processes ←———————— *outputs* ————————→ *outcomes*

E. The Level of Goal and Policy Agreement

		IHS(d) IHS(g)	
FDA	MCD	MCR NIH HRSA	

disagreement incongruence ←——————————————————————————→ *agreement congruence*

F. The Level of Centralization of Policy Implementation

HRSA	IHS(g) IHS(d)	NIH FDA MCR
MCD		

decentralized fragmented ←——————————————————————————→ *centralized*

G. The Precision and Characteristics of Performance Measures

		IHS(d) IHS(g) NIH(PART)	
NIH(GPRA)		FDA MCD HRSA MCR	

qualitative descriptive ←——————————————————————————→ *quantitative precise*

H. The Level and Character of Client and Stakeholder Support

		FDA	
	IHS(d) IHS(g)	MCD	HRSA MCR NIH

weak ←———————— *divided* ————————→ *strong*

I. Professionally Identity

		IHS(g) IHS(d)	
MCD	MCR	HRSA NIH	
		FDA	

low ←——————————————————————————→ *high*

IHS(g), Indian Health Service grants to tribes; *MCD,* Medicaid; *MCR,* Medicare; *IHS(d),* Indian Health Service direct services.

Previous studies of third-party government and network management have tended to generalize about third parties, putting them into a single category for purposes of classification. Our examination of performance measurement in the five agencies we studied indicates that the range of types of third parties is very important. The two most important distinctions are between contract third parties and grant third parties (Salamon 1989). Even within each category there is a wide variation of characteristics; for example, categorical grants such as Medicaid to the states on one hand and NIH grants to university medical research centers on the other hand are very different, and these differences influence how agencies implemented GPRA and how they practice performance measurement (Cooper 2003). Although the wide variation in types of grants and contracts, and therefore the wide range in types of third parties, has long been understood, the authors of GPRA evidently did not take these variations to be important. Our research has determined that the influence of the variation in types of third parties has influenced in important ways how agencies and their third parties have implemented GPRA. Figure 9.2 captures these variations by setting out two continua, the level of third-party policy implementation and the nature and quality of network articulations and arranging our five agencies along these continua.

The fact that an agency is hollowed out and relies entirely on third parties for policy implementation is, by itself, significant. But how an agency is hollowed out is even more significant because it matters who the third parties are. For example, states and territories receiving either block or categorical grants may use their grant money directly, disperse the money to counties, or contract with profit or nonprofit organizations to implement federal programs. Through grants, Medicaid relies on the states, territories, and sovereign tribes to implement its policies. Medicare, however, uses large private contractors as their third parties. NIH uses medical researchers as their third parties. FDA both regulates the pharmaceutical companies and partners with them in the drug approval process. This variation

FIGURE 9.2

THIRD-PARTY POLICY IMPLEMENTATION AND NETWORK ARTICULATION CONTINUA

A. The Level of Third-Party Policy Implementation

NIH IHS(g) MCD MCR HRSA	FDA	IHS(d)
hollowed out		direct government

C. The Nature and Quality of Network Articulations

IHS(g) NIH	MCD HRSA MCR	FDA	IHS(d)
remote control			managed network

IHS(g), Indian Health Service grants to tribes; MCD, Medicaid; MCR, Medicare; IHS(d), Indian Health Service direct services.

in the characteristics of third parties is described in continuum C in figure 9.2 as ranging from managed network at one pole to remote control at the other.

Figure 9.3 summarizes findings presented in chapters 4 through 8 that relate to the extent to which the agencies considered are hollowed out (vertical axis) and the articulation of third-party networks (horizontal axis) expressing the range between loose coupling, described as remote control, and tight coupling, described as managed networks. Articulation describes tightness or looseness of couplings between agencies and third parties. Coupling can occur through agency oversight programs, auditing procedures, carefully drafted contracts, negotiated shared understandings between agencies and third parties, and so forth. The five agencies studied cluster at the hollowed-out (vertical) axis, but vary considerably in terms of how their networks are articulated. Variations in network articulation can be understood in these three groups, each group exhibiting a distinct approach to network articulation and to GPRA implementation.

First, agencies with states, territories, and tribes as their third parties tend to use a negotiated management approach to network articulation. Negotiated management is a form of partnership federalism or fiscal intergovernmental relations in which third parties have some level of autonomous standing, such as states rights or tribal sovereignty. Under such circumstances many of the details of performance measurement, such as goal definitions, data definitions, data-gathering protocols, data management and presentation formats, and the like, conform gen-

FIGURE 9.3

THIRD-PARTY POLICY IMPLEMENTATION AND NETWORK ARTICULATION CONTINGENCY TABLE

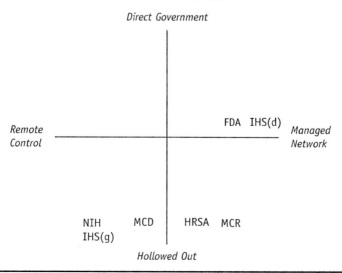

IHS(d), Indian Health Service direct services; IHS(g), Indian Health Service grants to tribes; MCD, Medicaid; MCR, Medicare.

erally to GPRA specifications but are established through a process of negotiation, not unlike diplomacy, between the agencies of the federal government and grant-receiving third parties. Many of the agencies of HRSA use a conscious negotiating strategy in their implementation of GPRA, as do IHS and Medicaid in CMS.

Second, agencies with contractor third parties use a procedural, rules-based contract approach to network articulations. Rules-based contract third parties are best understood as agents in principal–agent relationships. In such relations the goals, expectations, procedures, and services required by federal agencies are made specific in contracts and are responded to by contractors competing for these contracts. GPRA goals, data requirements, and the like are often built into the contracts and are increasingly used as metrics by which to evaluate contract effectiveness. Such contracts may be used to detail services and service levels or to control costs, the case of Medicare in CMS being especially illustrative.

Third, agencies with third-party researchers will use open-ended delegated discretion. Easily the best example of this form of vertical network articulation is the relationship between NIH and their third parties—medical research groups. The open-ended discretion approach to contract grant management, such as research and development projects in the Department of Defense or research projects funded by the National Science Foundation, initially solved this problem by using qualitative performance measures, a GPRA implementation approach found acceptable by OMB. With the application of PART, NIH no longer uses qualitative descriptions of its performance and is now exclusively using quantitative measures. In addition, NIH now uses precise and time-specific performance targets.

As figure 9.2 illustrates, agencies may be hollowed out and primarily reliant on third-party policy implementation, yet vary widely in terms of the nature of their third-party relations. The grant-based operations of IHS, NIH, and Medicaid tend in the direction of loose couplings with their third parties. Medicare, HRSA, FDA, and the direct service activities of IHS tend toward the network management approach and somewhat tighter couplings. HRSA and Medicare are both almost hollowed out, but through negotiated performance expectations with their third parties, as in the case of HRSA, or through contract specifications and continual oversight and adjustment, as in the case of Medicare, tend toward tighter couplings. More traditional hierarchical governmental arrangements are illustrated by FDA and the direct services of IHS. These variations influence GPRA goal descriptions, approaches to performance measurement, and patterns of accountability and are influenced by levels of stakeholder support and power. These are the subjects to which we now turn.

THIRD-PARTY GOVERNMENT AND AGENCY GOALS

GPRA tied the logic of strategic planning to the logic of performance measurement. Because of this, the formulation of agency goals is central to performance measurement and to GPRA implementation. We found that agency goals varied widely both in terms of the level of goal specificity and in terms of performance of their measurement type—including process measures, agency output measures, program outcome measures, and health outcome measures. We found that agencies will, first, favor management process and agency output goals, as figure 9.4 indicates. This finding generally matches the conclusions of the research literature on performance measurement (Jennings and Haist 2002; Forsythe 2001; Morini and Wolf 2002; Radin 1998b, 2000). In each of the cases and for each of the agencies studied, agency officials were reluctant to claim that the work of their agency would, all by itself, bring about significant changes in the quality of health among Americans. The tendency, therefore, was to focus on the quality of health care, the quality of research, the volume of services on management processes, and agency outputs. When it was using qualitative descriptions of its performance, NIH was the boldest in terms of claims for outcomes, but only in their long-range, multiyear, qualitative-descriptive approach to their health quality goals. With their recent move to the exclusive use of quantitative GPRA and PART measures, NIH has moved in the direction of measures of agency outputs. At the other extreme, Medicaid focuses almost entirely on process measures. Overall, in the agencies we considered, GPRA goals tend to be agency outputs and program outcomes. Our findings indicate, however, that what constitutes a management process or an agency output or outcome is very much subject to definition.

Second, agencies tend to define outputs as outcomes, very likely in response to the pressure to measure outcomes. The best example of this finding is the claim by Medicare that the level of beneficiary coverage are outcomes. At the time GPRA agency goals were approved, it appears that this rather slippery definition of Medicare outcomes was tolerated. PART has raised the stakes for not using outcome measures. We attempted to account for these distinctions by using two types of outcomes, program outcomes and health outcomes.

Third, agencies avoid being held responsible for health circumstances over which they believe they have little influence. Agencies vary in their language re-

---

FIGURE 9.4

THIRD-PARTY POLICY IMPLEMENTATION AND AGENCY GOALS CONTINUA

A. The Level of Third-Party Policy Implementation

MCD MCR			
NIH IHS(g) HRSA		FDA	IHS(d)
hollowed out			*direct government*

D. The Characteristics of Goals

		IHS(d) FDA	MCR	
	MCD	IHS(g) HRSA	NIH	
management process		*agency outputs*	*program outcomes*	*health outcomes*

MCD, Medicaid; *MCR*, Medicare; *IHS(g)*, Indian Health Service grants to tribes; *IHS(d)*, Indian Health Service direct services.

garding how they resist the assignment of responsibility for health outcomes. FDA is blunt about it, whereas the other four agencies engage in indirect means by which to avoid being held accountable for health outcomes. The tendency to not claim responsibility for health conditions is subtle, informal, and seldom in writing. The reason is obvious, because the language of GPRA is replete with claims that agencies should have health outcome goals and should measure health outcomes. The implication is, of course, that health conditions can be directly and causally linked to the actions of federal agencies. It is no wonder that agencies are careful not to appear to fly in the face of GPRA language. Nevertheless, these agencies tend to select output goals and measures and to describe them in terms of outcomes.

Fourth, agencies tend to select goals that will ensure favorable annual performance, in some cases "softballs," or easy goals, all of which are output goals. NIH's previous approach is perhaps the best example of an agency that has used GPRA processes effectively to essentially set itself up for success. But all five agencies do it. This finding generally matches the argument in the bureaucratic-behavior literature that agencies are advocates for their programs, seek to protect their interests, and work to have favorable public images (Aberbach and Rockman 2000). The application of PART came about because of a desire by OMB to "set the bar higher" and to force agencies to adopt higher targets or accomplished agency objectives in less time.

Fifth, the GPRA officials in all five agencies indicate that the annual data-gathering and performance-reporting requirements are excessive and not entirely useful. Annual changes in metrics are, they claim, minor, and significant trends or directions take many years to see.

In the implementation of GPRA performance measurement regimes, does it make any difference if an agency operates primarily on the basis of third parties? As figure 9.5 shows, the level of third-party policy implementation appears to make little difference in agency goal selection behavior. For example, NIH is somewhat hollowed out and has managed to claim that performance measures of basic research achievement result in improved health outcomes. Likewise, Medicare has managed to generally define its goals to be the financing of its beneficiaries rather than either the level of coverage of the eligible population or the quality of health among their eligible population. By so limiting their purposes, Medicare can claim that financing beneficiaries is an agency outcome. Medicaid has a similar narrow definition of its goals and has developed performance measures distinctly in the direction of management process and agency outputs.

One particularly interesting approach to goal selection is the pattern of using departmental or agency goals, rather than program-level goals, because agency or departmental-level goals tend to be more general. Program purposes are often rather specific, and if goals and performance measures were tied to them, performance measures might reflect unfavorably both on the program and on the agency. Perhaps the best example is the shift from overall and general NIH goals in the early GPRA years to the more-precise and program-level NIH goals under the PART approach to GPRA.

It is not only the performance measurement approach to goal categorization that matters; goal and policy agreement can also be important. Three of the

FIGURE 9.5

THIRD-PARTY POLICY IMPLEMENTATION AND THE CHARACTERISTICS OF AGENCY GOALS CONTINGENCY TABLE

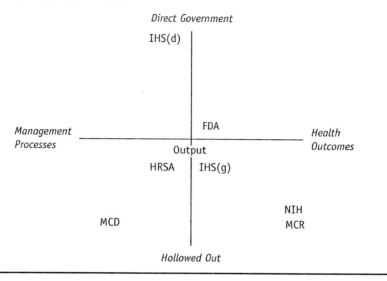

IHS(d), Indian Health Service direct services; *IHS(g)*, Indian Health Service grants to tribes; *MCD*, Medicaid; *MCR*, Medicare.

agencies or programs covered by this book are notable in this regard. FDA is at the center of competing health care goals and policy conflict. Both of the programs in CMS, Medicare and Medicaid, are the subjects of intense policy debate. The other agencies we studied generally enjoy goal congruences and relatively high levels of policy agreement. Our findings indicate that agencies or programs in the context of policy disagreement or goal incongruence will tend toward cautious approaches to performance measurement, emphasizing management processes and agency output goals and measures, the best example being FDA. To respond to GPRA, FDA found it necessary to navigate carefully between the goals of consumer protection on one hand and the promotion of drug safety in the drug industry on the other hand. Caution and prudence regarding goal choices and performance metrics in such circumstances is understandable.

When PART was introduced in 2002, the emphasis on outcome goals increased dramatically. To satisfy PART requirements, FDA, for example, had to change its goals and their attendant measures of performance away from agency outputs in the direction of agency outcome and health outcomes because PART "will track FDA on new long-term outcome goals" (U.S. Office of Management and Budget 2005, 155). This pressure is necessary, according to a leading OMB management official, "because agencies will always tend to set goals that can be easily achieved. PART gives us [OMB] the leverage we need to force agencies to emphasize outcomes."

THIRD-PARTY POLICY IMPLEMENTATION AND CENTRALIZATION

There appears to be an association between third-party government and the decentralization and fragmentation of the federal government. As figure 9.6 shows, patterns of policy implementation that are centrally funded and locally managed and delivered are now deeply established in contemporary federalism. In the health fields, the states and territories, as well as Indian tribes, constitute decentralized governmental third parties. In addition to geographic decentralization, federal program fragmentation is evident in the health fields; each state and territory operates dozens of federally funded programs. Much of the actual operation of these programs at the street level is contracted to private nonprofit or for-profit third parties by the states and territories. In every state and locality, federally funded health contractors operate as financial intermediaries or carriers, as health researchers, or as providers of direct health and hospital services. Third-party government, decentralized federalism, and program fragmentation, it could be argued, are nearly the same thing, as figure 9.7 indicates.

How does this correlation between third-party government and decentralization influence GPRA performance measurement, or vice versa? The study of GPRA implementation indicates, first, that agencies with state, territorial, or tribal third parties will build performance measurement into more general patterns of negotiated cooperative federalism or federal–state mutual adjustment. In this context third parties participate in goal setting and performance measurement decisions

FIGURE 9.6

THIRD-PARTY POLICY IMPLEMENTATION AND CENTRALIZATION CONTINUA

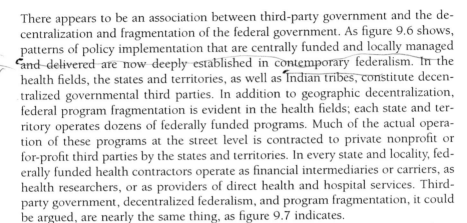

A. The Level of Third-Party Policy Implementation

MCD MCR
NIH IHS(g) HRSA   FDA   IHS(d)

hollowed-out   direct government

F. The Level of Centralization of Policy Implementation

MCD MCR
HRSA IHS(g) IHS(d) NIH   FDA

decentralized   centralized
fragmented

MCD, Medicaid; MCR, Medicare; IHS(g), Indian Health Service grants to tribes; IHS(d), Indian Health Service direct services.

FIGURE 9.7

THIRD-PARTY POLICY IMPLEMENTATION AND CENTRALIZATION CONTINGENCY TABLE

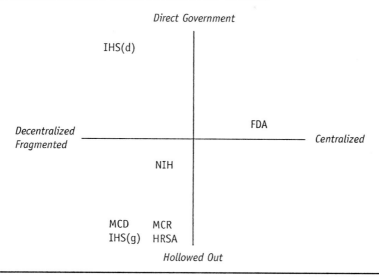

IHS(d), Indian Health Service direct services; MCD, Medicaid; IHS(g), Indian Health Service grants to tribes; MCR, Medicare.

and become partners in GPRA implementation. HRSA is the best example. The most volatile examples are Medicaid and Medicare, both exhibiting constantly changing and churning granting or contracting relationships between CMS and the states.

Most of the GPRA-related elements of agency-state grant relations tend to be among top executives at each level and among GPRA implementation specialists. The rank and file in the state agencies that implement federal programs know little of GPRA.

Second, research third parties will insulate themselves from both agency goal setting and performance measurement. NIH has entirely walled off their grant recipients from any participation in performance measurement and has developed an effective and centralized GPRA compliance system in the context of a decentralized and fragmented medical research model. This NIH finding suggests that under loosely coupled arrangements GPRA is treated by the agencies as Washington-level bureaucratic requirements rather than important elements of their contract and grant management of third-party policy implementation. What may, in Washington, be thought to be essential features of good management may not be reflected down loosely articulated chains of third-party implementers.

Third, nonprofit or for-profit contractors will be obliged to build data and other performance measurement requirements into contracts. In ordinary contract circumstances third parties will be required to keep certain records and aggregate certain data. Contractors may or may not know the connection between what they are obligated to provide as a part of contracts and how that data might be used in measuring agency performance. Such contract regimes are principal–agent models that assume it to be possible to formalize reliable and consistent data requirements and expectations through contract compliance language.

THE PRECISION AND CHARACTERISTICS OF PERFORMANCE MEASURES

In the run-up to full annual implementation of GPRA, as each department and agency prepared its goals and attendant measures, in almost all cases the measures were quantitative, albeit mostly measures of management processes and agency outputs. NIH, however, was a big exception. NIH also carefully arranged its goals in such a way as to essentially guarantee that annual performance "measures" would "exceed targets." Based on the earlier use of narratives in NIH appropriation presentations, its use of narratives as performance measures also appears to have received favorable treatment in the appropriations process. It is not possible to know whether the use of qualitative performance at NIH is the factor that explains its appropriations success or whether that success is a function of its mission, standing, prestige, or a combination of all these. What is clear is the preference PART gives to quantitative outcome measures. The NIH performance bar has been raised, and NIH has turned to the application of quantitative measures to their goals. Even in this new regime, NIH has fared well both in terms of its PART evaluation of its performance and in congressional appropriations.

The precision and characteristics of performance measures turn on the quality of annual data used in those measures. It is evident that the process of agreement on data definitions, the procedures for gathering, managing, and analyzing data, and the use of that data in performance measurement has proved to be difficult in the context of third-party government. In all five agencies the complexity of GPRA compliance, particularly associated with data and with annual performance measurement, has been daunting. GPRA requirements assume the availability of already gathered data and the reliability of those data. Furthermore, it had been assumed that agencies would require little, if any, additional funding to implement GPRA, that data would be annually available, and that annual increments were informative regarding changes in agency performance. After a decade of GPRA implementation, some agencies are still ironing out data issues associated with their performance measures. This is an especially acute issue in Medicaid and Medicare, as is evidenced by the challenges associated with measuring something as seemingly simple as Medicare beneficiary telephone customer service levels.

Many programs, agencies, and third parties have been slow in developing agreed-on data for annual performance measures. In the agency and third-party trenches, data development and performance metrics are moving slowly, their employees arguing that the primary responsibility of agencies and third parties is to deliver services, not to measure their performance.

To comply with GPRA and yet not be held responsible for health outcomes, agencies and their third parties will measure management processes and outputs—the measurable—and either avoid outcome measures or attempt to define outputs to be outcomes. As noted earlier, the stakes for failing to adopt outcome performance measures have increased with the advent of PART. Accordingly, there has been a gradual shift, in the agencies studied for this research, toward more outcome measures.

THIRD-PARTY GOVERNMENT, STAKEHOLDER SUPPORT, AND PERFORMANCE MEASUREMENT

The agencies studied here range from having relatively weak client or stakeholder support, as in the case of IHS, to very strong support, as in the cases of NIH, CMS's Medicare program, and HRSA. Two other entities—CMS's Medicaid program and FDA—have strong but divided stakeholders or clients, as figure 9.8 indicates.

It appears, as figure 9.9 shows, that the third-party characteristics of agencies enhance, or at least do not detract from, the quality of the agencies' level of support. It is not a surprise to find that large-scale and decentralized federal program investments in states and territories and with contractors that operate in states and territories are sources of continuing political support for those programs.

If third-party government is generally supportive of the development and maintenance of client and stakeholder support, how does that appear to influence an agency's approach to the implementation of GPRA performance measures? In the case of NIH, there is little doubt that its initial use of qualitative performance measures and its very broad definition of goals are in part based on its stake-

FIGURE 9.8

THIRD-PARTY POLICY GOVERNMENT AND STAKEHOLDER SUPPORT CONTINUA

A. The Level of Third-Party Policy Implementation

MCD MCR HRSA NIH IHS(g)	FDA	IHS(d)
hollowed out		direct government

H. The Level and Character of Client and Stakeholder Support

	IHS(d) IHS(g)	MCD FDA HRSA	MCR NIH
weak		divided	strong

MCD, Medicaid; *MCR*, Medicare; *IHS(g)*, Indian Health Service grants to tribes; *IHS(d)*, Indian Health Service direct services.

FIGURE 9.9

THIRD-PARTY GOVERNMENT AND CLIENT AND STAKEHOLDER SUPPORT CONTINGENCY TABLE

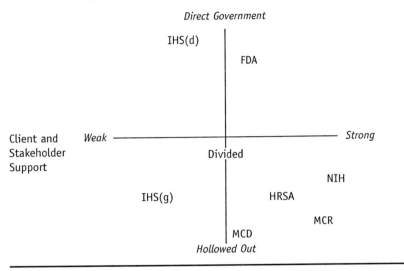

IHS(d), Indian Health Service direct services; *IHS(g),* Indian Health Service grants to tribes; *MCD,* Medicaid; *MCR,* Medicare.

holders' prestige and influence. Medicare's cautious approach to goal definitions and performance measures is also probably made easier by its support among elderly interest groups.

The strong but divided stakeholder support found in FDA and Medicaid is particularly informative. FDA appears to have deliberately developed performance measures to satisfy the requirements of PDUFA and its decreasing time frame for the drug review process. Both Medicare and Medicaid have strong but divided support for different reasons. First, both have competing goals—the imperative both to fund health care to an increasing number of clients and to contain health care costs. Performance measures provide little, if any, illumination on this issue. In the case of Medicare, the stakeholders, primarily the elderly and their interest groups, seek the widest possible definitions of medical services eligible for funding. The large health insurance carriers and health care intermediaries are significant stakeholders, seeking to meet their bottom lines while funding health services within federally defined limited eligibility. GPRA performance measures may exaggerate these vexing policy challenges. The goal to expand SCHIP enrollment adds to the burden of health care costs of Medicaid and reduces the prospects for federal Medicaid and the states and territories funding Medicaid to contain costs.

Our findings indicate that agencies will, in the absence of client and stakeholder support, take a cautious approach to performance measurement. Although the tendency toward caution is general and appears to be mostly independent of the level of stakeholder support, the evidence in these cases runs in the direction of less agency caution if it has strong stakeholder support—the cases of NIH and Medicare—and more caution if it has either weak or divided stakeholder support—the cases of IHS, Medicaid, HRSA, and FDA.

Second, agencies with influential clients and stakeholders will take an approach to performance measurement that is responsive to their stakeholders. In some instances agencies' performance measures reflect mandated responses to stakeholders, as in the cases of IHS and FDA. In other cases client-responsive goals and performance measures appear to be little more than the best efforts of agencies and their third parties to provide services to their clients and to develop performance measures that demonstrate how well they are doing that, HRSA being a notable example.

Third, with influential stakeholders and clients, agencies may take bold approaches to goal setting and performance measurement. The best examples are NIH and its multiyear qualitative performance measures and Medicare's carefully cautious avoidance of performance measures that appear to run counter to the interests of the elderly.

ACCOUNTABILITY TO FEDERAL PROGRAM PURPOSES

A general reading of the rationale for GPRA and of the advocates of federal performance measures would leave one with the impression that comprehensive performance measurement is essential to improve federal accountability (U.S. Congress 2001). As figure 9.10 indicates, each of the five agencies studied here scores relatively high in the accountability continuum.

Agencies with third-party states, territories, and tribes, operating in the form of cooperative federalism, such as Medicaid, HRSA, and grant programs of IHS, are less strictly tied to federal government purposes, having adapted those purposes to local preferences and circumstances. There is little evidence that the states, territories, or tribes can simply ignore federal program purposes or use federal resources in ways other than those intended by the federal government.

FIGURE 9.10

ACCOUNTABILITY TO FEDERAL PROGRAM PURPOSES CONTINUUM

B. Accountability to Federal Program Purposes

	IHS(g)	IHS(d)	
	MCD HRSA	FDA MCR NIH	
attenuated			strict

IHS(g), Indian Health Service grants to tribes; IHS(d), Indian Health Service direct services; MCD, Medicaid; MCR, Medicare.

In Medicare and Medicaid there have been, and continue to be, cases of fraud. In articulated vertical networks of third parties with extensive chains of third parties, the number of financial transactions is so great that the opportunities for fraud are increased (Frederickson 1999). But current Medicaid and Medicare health-financing models are congressionally mandated, which leaves Medicare and Medicaid to manage financial transactions as carefully as they are able, given federal policy and their own limited staff resources. Medicaid has, in its GPRA goals and performance measures, stepped up to the fraud issue with measures indicating progress, or the lack of it, in fraud reduction.

In sum, our findings indicate, first, that agencies with state, territorial, and tribal grant-funded third parties will practice fiscal intergovernmental relations or cooperative federalism and negotiate federal purposes to accommodate local preferences. This finding fits the overall generalization that the operations of contemporary American federalism use a blending of federal purposes with state-level applications. GPRA goals and measures are simply built into that process, the best examples being HRSA and Medicaid.

Second, agencies with nonprofit and for-profit contract-based third parties will attempt to hold contractors strictly accountable to federal purposes. Contract regimes either build in GPRA data requirements or performances reporting expectations, as in the case of Medicare, or hold contractors responsible in relatively loosely coupled research arrangements, as in the case of NIH. To some it may seem counterintuitive that cooperative federalism forms of loosely coupled articulated vertical networks of third parties are at least as accountable to federal program as are contract-based articulated vertical networks of third parties.

Third, there is no evidence in these cases of any variation from generally understood federal purposes. There are compromises between federal and state purposes, and there are agency attempts to satisfy competing purposes, but there is no evidence of a failure to be accountable to federal purposes. This being the case, the argument that GPRA is needed to enforce agency accountability to federal purposes has no supporting evidence in these cases. Indeed, agencies are highly accountable.

Agency accountability is featured as a key element of PART. Each PART evaluation includes a determination, by percentage, of agency clarity of purpose, quality of planning, and quality of management and a percentage labeled "results/accountability." On the basis of programs' scores, PART evaluations are accompanied by a specific overall rating of "ineffective," "adequate," "moderately effective," or "effective." Independent of scores, those programs whose performance measures are deemed to capture their outcomes inadequately and those programs that do not have sufficient outcome performance data are rated as "results not demonstrated." Each PART summary includes a graphically represented continuum ranging from zero to one hundred. PART scores place agencies on these continua on the basis of a summation of the answers given in each PART section. For example, the Medicare program received 80 percent of the points available in the purpose section, 100 percent of the available points in the planning section, 71 percent in the management section, and 67 percent in the results/accountability section. Based on the weighting of the sections, which puts the greatest emphasis on the results section, Medicare's overall PART score is 74, giving it a rating of "moderately effective."

POWER, PRESTIGE, AND PERFORMANCE MEASUREMENT

The prestige of NIH grant recipients and the general prestige enjoyed by the medical research community influence both the quality of articulation between NIH and its grant recipients and the oversight treatment of grant recipients by NIH and the oversight treatment of NIH by Congress. In its initial approach to GPRA, NIH engaged in no goal-setting or data-collection efforts with its grant recipients as a part of its GPRA compliance. In other words, NIH selected a performance measurement scheme that entirely bypassed these challenges. Narratives in the form of "Stories of Discovery," "Science Capsules," and "Science Advances" were "data" that served as proxies for measuring NIH's outcomes. The methods of analyzing these qualitative data consisted of the judgment of NIH-selected experts as to whether the narrative data demonstrate that the performance target is "substantially exceeded," "met or successfully met," "active," "not met and extended," or "not met." Although both the long-range nature of scientific research and the importance of objectivity certainly play a role in this hands-off approach, the prestige of NIH and of NIH grant recipients no doubt contributed as well.

NIH's stated mission is to "uncover new knowledge about the prevention, detection, diagnosis, and treatment of disease and disability" (U.S. Department of Health and Human Services, National Institutes of Health 2002). One NIH manager indicated with regard to NIH's responsibilities that "our goal, then, is not to improve health, per se, because we cannot be directly responsible for that. It is to generate knowledge and then real approaches to developing things like treatments and preventive methods that can later lead to better health." That NIH was initially allowed to measure its performance quantitatively is a testament to its prestige and its unique standing as a federal agency. It is also recognition on NIH's part that both policy and appropriations are more likely to be moved by rhetoric than by data (Hood and Jackson 1991). It is telling that the kind of narrative performance data prepared by NIH for GPRA purposes have been used for budget justification in the appropriations process for several years. Nevertheless, for FY 2004, NIH decided to drop its qualitative performance measures and adopt a battery of quantitative measures.

CMS is at the opposite end of the prestige continuum. Little of the prestige of the broader medical community appears to pass to CMS. The public perception is that NIH and the medical research communities are engaged in a noble venture. The same cannot be said of public perception of CMS. When matters relating to CMS are brought to the public's attention, they usually have to do with disagreements over expanded coverage or cost containment or as a result of actual or alleged mismanagement of Medicare or Medicaid claims. The treatment of CMS in congressional hearings is indicative of its low prestige. At a recent hearing of the U.S. House Committee on Small Business, Chairman Manzullo (R-IL) said:

But as a result of the inefficiency of HCFA [now CMS], health care costs more. The agency itself is the most egregious offender of waste, fraud, and abuse, all to the detriment of the American people at large and medical providers in particular. . . . To them it is simply not worth wading through a morass of red tape to obtain paltry payments that fail to meet their costs and then have their integrity second guessed in the guise of protecting against waste, fraud, and abuse. The question remains, who will protect the providers from harassment and unnecessary regulatory burdens? Something must be done and must be done soon. This chairman will do all in his power to help our health care providers, and HCFA [CMS] needs to step up to the plate. (U.S. House of Representatives 2002)

Our findings indicate that CMS's low prestige has affected its implementation of GPRA. The fear that performance data will be used to accuse the agency of mismanagement is real and is identified as one of the reasons past federal performance measurement–related reforms have failed. As Allen Schick has noted, "Nobody wants to load a gun that's pointed at their heads" (2001, 56). In the case of CMS, this is not an imaginary fear. Performance data are just another source of ammunition for its critics, and CMS is not willing to make its critics' job any easier for them. One way to insulate CMS from such criticism is to select goals that cannot be easily used by its critics as ammunition.

ARTICULATED VERTICAL NETWORKS OF THIRD PARTIES

A primary finding of this research is that the goal setting and performance measurement required by GPRA are carried out in the context of articulated vertical networks of third parties. The agencies studied here no longer manage in ways traditionally thought to be public management, as table 9.1 shows. Modern federal management has been transformed into third-party management, and third-party management is best understood as articulated vertical networks of third parties. The quality of articulation has to do with the extent to which separate organizations or institutions in a network are coupled, are fit together, or are linked or combined and the nature of those connections. The quality of articulation affects not only the management and delivery of public health services but also the challenges and impediments encountered in the implementation of GPRA, including the development of strategic plans, mission statements, goals, and performance indicators. The quality of articulation between the agencies we reviewed for this book and the third parties that deliver services is influenced by many forces and factors. The primary factor is the type of third party used in policy implementation: state governments (CMS Medicaid, HRSA), contractors (CMS Medicare, IHS), local governments (HRSA), universities and health scholars (NIH), industry (FDA), and tribes (IHS). Another key factor in agency–third-party articulation is the policy tool that authorizes the transfer of funds and authority to the third parties. These tools include contracts (CMS Medicare), block grants (HRSA), and categorical grants (CMS Medicaid, HRSA). Other tools

TABLE 9.1

AGENCY NETWORK ARTICULATIONS AND PERFORMANCE MEASURES

Agency	Policy Tool	Third Parties	Nature of Network Articulations	Network Coupling	Performance Measures
HRSA	Grants	States and territories Local govts. Profits and nonprofits	Network management Cooperative federalism	Negotiated Loose couplings	Processes Outputs Data problems Annual reporting questioned
CMS: Medicare	Contracts	Insurance and health care providers	Contract details Rules Processes Networks	Moderate to tightly coupling	Processes Outputs Outcomes
Medicaid	Grants	States and territories	Grant management Cooperative federalism	Negotiated Loose coupling	Processes Outputs Fraud control Data problems Annual reporting questioned
NIH	Grants Intramural research	Health research institutions	Partnerships Open Exploratory	Very loosely coupled	Originally qualitative now quantitative
IHS	Grants	Tribes	Negotiated networks Management Oversight	Moderate to tightly coupled	Processes Outputs Data problems Annual reporting questioned
FDA	Regulation	Regulated industries	Procedural Oversight Load Shedding Capture	Moderate to tightly coupled	Process Output Annual reporting questioned

used throughout the federal government include time-and-materials contracts and performance contracts.

Although the foregoing factors are relatively straightforward, their capacity to predict the nature and level of difficulties encountered in measuring and improving performance is not. Theory suggests that establishing performance goals and indicators in a contract environment is markedly easier than in a grant-making environment. As indicated in chapter 5, however, the efforts of CMS to establish performance goals and indicators to measure satisfaction with telephone services did not bear this out. Despite the more clearly subordinate role that Medicare contractors play compared to the partner role played by states in the Medicaid program, it appears that performance measurement, in the context of contract management, can be at least as difficult as negotiating with states. For example, the "developmental" status of the Medicare telephone satisfaction goals, indicators, and targets continues years after the initial CMS GPRA performance plan primarily because of data problems.

Attempts to measure performance are also influenced by a host of federal agency contextual factors. For example, the threat of contract termination is not always available to federal agencies. In the case of Medicare, the agency does not even select many of the contracting third parties. Authorizing-legislation language and program regulations can combine to limit the universe of potential contractors and weaken contract renewal requirements to the extent that contract termination is not a realistic threat, as CMS executives discovered (or discovered anew) when they endeavored to reduce contractor fraud and meet Y2K readiness targets.

IDEALIZED AND LESS-IDEALIZED APPROACHES TO PERFORMANCE MEASUREMENT

As we noted in chapter 1, the dominant literature on performance measurement has a distinct advocacy tone to it. This literature is an idealized conception of how performance measurement can improve government management and make it more accountable to federal purposes. Certainly the logic and substance of GPRA, both in its statutory language and in its implementation, are in the spirit of this idealized view of the potential of performance measurement.

It is useful here to revisit table 2.1 to illustrate the difference between the idealized conception of performance measurement in government and the less-idealized conception of its critics. In general terms our findings tend in the direction of support for the less-idealized approach to performance measurement, detailed in the right-hand column of table 2.1. Shall it be concluded that, because of the differences between idealized and less-idealized approaches to performance measurement, performance measurement is ineffective? No. The problems with performance measurement in government have to do with two key points: (1) expecting too much from it and (2) attempting performance measurement without understanding the third-party nature of the modern federal government and accommodating performance measurement to that reality. The closing section of this chapter addresses the actual potential of federal performance measurement.

IN PRAISE OF OUTPUT MEASURES

The first and primary lesson of this and other empirical research on performance measurement in government is this: Performance measurement has the capacity to tell an agency how well it is doing. Performance measurement has a very limited capacity to tell either an agency or its principals what to do, however.

In the era of third-party government, federal executives, most of whom no longer directly manage their programs, have a limited repertoire of tools by which to "manage" their third parties. One of those tools, and a very important one, is performance measurement. Performance measurement can help fill the space between departmental and agency executives on one hand and agency third parties on the other. This is the natural home of performance measurement. When performance measurement is built into the work of management, both the management of federal agencies and the management of third parties, then performance measurement can contribute in important ways to improved agency and third-party performance.

Measures of management processes and measures of agency outputs are as essential to modern federal management as personnel or human resources administration was to traditional federal management. Modern federal management is almost always now carried out through articulated vertical chains of third-party providers. To make performance measurement work, agency managers and third-party managers up and down these articulated chains must agree on data definitions: the system of data collection, management and analysis protocols, and performance reporting protocols. This management approach to performance measurement can and should be part of a manager's network approach to grant-based federalism. HRSA works as a managed network using an articulated chain approach to performance measurement and is a good example of a performance measurement approach to modern public management. Such a management approach to performance measurement should be a part of contract-based articulations between agencies and contractors. In sum, performance measurement should be understood as part of the contemporary approach to the management of third-party government.

Federal performance budgeting is now rather well developed. The federal budget now includes agency performance measures with each agency's budget request. But performance budgeting is not the same thing as performance-based appropriations. Our findings show little evidence of an association among performance measurement, performance budgeting, and agency appropriation patterns. So long as the expectation that performance measurement leads to performance budgeting, which leads to appropriations decisions as part of GPRA, agency and departmental executives will move very cautiously toward performance measurement. If performance measurement were uncoupled from the hope of performance budgeting, it is likely that performance measurement would be more acceptable to departmental and agency executives and would improve the prospects for performance measurement. The point is simple, based on an early lesson in public administration: part of the job of agency executives is to look after and protect the interests of their agencies and to be dedicated to the purposes of their agencies (Thompson 1967). If performance measurement is thought by agency executives or their third parties to increase the prospects for agency effectiveness, they will embrace it and make it work. But if performance measurement is thought by agency executives or their third parties to be connected to budgeting and appropriations and could be used by those unfriendly to agency interests, federal executives will be less enthusiastic about it. If performance measurement is used to attempt to give administrative answers to inherently political questions, administrators will be very cautious.

Hollowed-out third-party government is here to stay. The development of sophisticated performance metrics must be a significant part of the public management repertoire. The keys to the development of real performance metrics will be found in the recognition that there are many types of third parties, many different ways to implement public policy, and a wide range of agency–third-party articulations and vertical networks of third parties. The effectiveness of network management is dependent on the development of solid performance metrics that are compatible with the details of the modern hollow state.

10

AFTER THE GOVERNMENT PERFORMANCE AND RESULTS ACT

Performance Measurement, Performance Budgeting, and Performance Management

The fortunes of both third-party government and performance measurement have been and will continue to be influenced by GPRA, but the tides of reform roll on (Light 1997). Chapter 9 is a summary and synthesis of our primary findings. The purpose of this chapter is to put these findings into the broader context of public management theory and practice and government performance measurement theory and practice. In this chapter we consider trends associated not only with GPRA but also with ongoing public sector performance measurement reforms, as well as performance budgeting reforms.

GPRA and later PART are part of a broader, worldwide performance measurement reform. Some countries, such as Australia and New Zealand, had national performance measurement programs before GPRA's passage and are much further along in their performance measurement efforts. In the United States, GPRA and PART are just the latest in a lineage of federal reform efforts: performance budgeting; planning, programming, budgeting systems; management by objectives; and zero-based budgeting. In addition, most of the fifty states have implemented performance measurement regimes, including unit costs application of the Governmental Accounting Standards Board's cost accounting requirements. The point is that the language or performance measurement may change, but the central concepts on which the performance measurement movement rests remain the same. Although each specific reform has been relatively short lived, lessons learned from each reform accumulate, and the core concepts of performance measurement are steadily refined. Our consideration of the implementation of GPRA in the context of third-party government adds to the lessons in ongoing performance measurement refinement.

Approaches to performance measurement are of two distinct types—the idealized conception of performance measurement by its advocates and the less-idealized application of performance measurement by empirical researchers or by those with reservations. Several themes run through both of these bodies of literature, themes to which we now return.

GOALS

The first of these themes is our finding that *in the context of either contradictory and/or ambiguous program goals, the measurement of program performance is rendered more difficult and less effective* (Heinrich 1999). Nowhere is this more evident than in the application of GPRA performance measurement expectations to FDA. FDA is expected to enable pharmaceutical and food products to reach market as quickly as possible while at the same time assuring the public that those pharmaceutical and food products are safe. Which of these two goals FDA maximizes, we learned, is a function of many factors—with political forces in the congressional and executive branches of government and the influence of the pharmaceutical industry being the most important.

In the 1990s FDA, along with many other regulatory agencies, was part of a distinct shift in approaches toward federal regulation of business. This shift was toward deregulation and toward a logic of partnerships whereby regulators and regulated industries share regulatory roles. For FDA this meant that pharmaceutical and food companies paid fees for regulatory "services" and expected, in return, timely reviews. In addition, regulated industries such as the seafood industry, using agreed-on standards and reporting protocols, were authorized to engage in self-regulation. But in 2004 and 2005, two drugs approved under these partnership arrangements, Vioxx and Bextra, were found to have previously undisclosed dangerous side effects and were taken from the market. As a result, Congress, FDA, and the administration are openly reconsidering a return to more-traditional forms of food and drug regulations. The tension between FDA's food and drug safety responsibilities and its food and drug promotion responsibilities is played out as political forces shift from one emphasis to the other and back again. Implementation of GPRA and PART at FDA is being carried out in the context of these contradictory and shifting goal emphases. Evidence of the influence of competing FDA goals is seen in the slowness of their performance measurement development and in the ongoing aggregation and then disaggregation of performance measures. The decision to shift between two contradictory emphases is a policy rather than a performance challenge and one which performance measurement is ill-suited to solve.

Medicare and Medicaid also have competing goals. Unlike FDA's regulation/promotion goals, Medicare and Medicaid have financial service goals achieved through articulated networks of third parties—the states and their third-party contractors in the case of Medicaid and large-scale health finance contractors in the case of Medicare. Clients are at the bottom of these vertical networks, clients entitled to Medicare and Medicaid services from doctors, drug stores, hospitals, and nursing homes providing those services. Medicare and Medicaid are expected to finance health care services to those who are eligible and at the same time control health care costs. As is the case with FDA, GPRA performance measurement applied to Medicare and Medicaid attempts to reconcile these competing objectives. Goal conflict and goal ambiguity are less evident at NIH, IHS, and HRSA.

Although goal conflict is evident in the operations of FDA, Medicare, and Medicaid, a review of their GPRA measures and their PART targets and rankings seems to indicate that open considerations of conflicting goals is unacceptable. Agency and program goals are established and described as if they are compatible. Performance measures and the data needed to make them operative are never described in terms of possible goal conflict. Based on reading GPRA and PART reports, it is as if agency goal conflict is the problem that dare not openly speak its name. In interviews with agency officials, however, agency goal conflict is a regular theme. There is some evidence, particularly at FDA and CMS, that performance measures are attempts to pave over goal conflicts, as if to say that really good agency performance will somehow demonstrate that agency goals can be made compatible. This would not be the first time that the answers to vexing questions of conflicting goals would be better management.

OUTPUTS, OUTCOMES, AND DATA

A second theme in the performance measurement and performance budgeting literature is that *even if there is goal agreement, it is often difficult to find measures adequate to the determination of social outcomes* (Joyce 1993; Radin 2006). Agencies and bureaus, we learned, tend to use output measures as proxies for social and economic outcomes (Broome 1995; Cope 1995; McKinney 1996). For the agencies we considered, the majority of performance indicators found in agency GPRA performance plans are output rather than outcome measures. There are good reasons agencies choose to measure outputs rather than outcomes, including statutory requirements (FDA), unique agency purposes (CMS), continuing pressure from OMB, particularly under PART protocols, to develop outcome measures, and, most important, logical and methodological problems. We attempted to deal with this challenge by distinguishing program outcomes from actual health outcomes. The use of output measures as proxies for outcomes is a subject that needs greater attention and development in the performance measurement literature.

Consider this example. General agreement between the federal and state governments regarding the goals of the Medicaid program does not diminish the challenges associated with measuring the impact of Medicaid on overall health outcomes. First, general agreement on the goal of providing health services to lower-income people does not translate into uniform benefits across all states. To develop performance measures that can adequately address the individual Medicaid-funded services authorized by each state is a monumental task. Second, the methodological problems of isolating the impact of federal programs on health outcomes are also daunting. For example, one of the goals of HRSA's Healthy Start program is to reduce infant mortality, and in the 1990s infant mortality steadily declined. But changes in infant mortality rates are the result of many medical, social, and economic factors. Claims that improved infant mortality rates can be reliably traced to the Healthy Start program are difficult to demonstrate. HRSA, in an attempt to identify the impact of the Healthy Start program, contracted with a research firm to determine the link between declining infant mortality rates and the program. The firm was not able to determine the program's impact, independent of other contextual factors. HRSA, nevertheless, used improving infant mortality rates as a Healthy Start outcome indicator, with a carefully worded narrative explaining the complexity of isolating the impact of the Healthy Start program on increased infant mortality rates. Variations on this theme were found in all five of the agencies we examined and in the dozens of programs these agencies operate.

The data challenges agencies face as they attempt to measure their performance are a research subject of some importance. "The GPRA experience indicated that policymakers had an unrealistic picture of the level of data that was already available to use in the process. Agencies were constrained both by the lack of resources for information as well as the requirements found in the Paperwork Reduction Act" (Radin 2006). The problem of data adequate to form the basis of useful performance metrics was found in all five HHS agencies studied here. Only NIH seems to have based its performance measures on data that are reliably available or relatively easy to gather. These data are, interestingly, qualitative rather than quantitative. As explained in chapter 6, NIH has now changed its GPRA-based performance measures from the qualitative approach to the quantitative.

The data challenges encountered by the five HHS agencies we evaluated are certainly not an aberration. Federal programs operating through third parties have a particular handicap in collecting, analyzing, and reporting data. In addition, almost all the HHS programs have geographically dispersed service delivery, which comes with its own data challenges.

Future considerations of problems associated with data in performance metrics should address the following questions:

☐ What challenges do agencies encounter in their efforts to collect performance data?

☐ What are the underlying reasons for these challenges?

☐ What are agencies doing to overcome these challenges?

An especially hopeful avenue for future consideration is the possibility of an open and honest embrace of federal agency output measures as proxies for social outcomes. Performance measurement specialists should explore the reasons public programs use output measures, the causal assumptions linking outputs to desired outcomes, and the costs associated with attempting to measure outcomes rather than outputs. In most cases, programs are, in fact, designed to produce outputs, and these outputs are, in actual detail, the management of contracts and grants. For example, whereas the broader purposes of Medicare and Medicaid are to finance positive health outcomes among the nation's poor, disabled, and elderly, the actual role of CMS is to finance the third parties that actually provide health care services. CMS effectiveness in managing contracts and grants has an important impact on the extent to which the programs meet their objectives;

therefore, CMS defines program output as its outcomes. Although such an argument does not reflect the outcome measure ideal, we find the CMS position both understandable and practical.

In the case of IHS, the complexity and cost of measuring the health outcomes of American Indians and Native Alaskans appear to have initially persuaded IHS to measure outputs rather than outcomes. IHS, however, has carefully selected those outputs that can be causally linked to health outcomes. For each output measure it has selected, IHS provides a detailed explanation of the research that demonstrates how and why an agency output is an acceptable proxy for a desired outcome. Over the last few years, however, IHS has added to its core of performance measures certain health outcome measures. It is unclear whether the adoption of more outcome measures is a function of the PART process or improvements in IHS's ability to collect and report health outcomes.

Our findings suggest the possibility that the future of effective performance measurement is most likely to be found in measuring agency outputs. We may gradually come to understand that, from the agency perspective, the emphasis on attempting to measure health outcomes and attempting to demonstrate definitive links between program outputs and health outcomes may, in many cases, be of limited value.

Performance measurement specialists as well as academics interested in the subject should consider the following questions:

☐ What are the reasons agencies select output rather than outcome measures?

☐ How well do agencies demonstrate that the outputs they measure are reasonable proxies for program outcomes?

☐ What are the relative costs of measuring outcomes versus outputs?

☐ How does the inclusion of third parties in the setting of goals and the delivery of services impact the ease or difficulty—in terms of resources and practicability—of measuring outcomes compared to outputs?

MANAGEMENT, POLITICS, AND PERFORMANCE MEASUREMENT

A third theme found in the performance measurement and performance budgeting literature is that *performance measurement represents attempts to superimpose managerial logic and managerial processes on inherently political processes embedded in the separation of powers* (Wildavsky 1979; Rosenbloom 1983; Aberbach and Rockman 2000; Radin 2006). In the matter of the application of managerial logic to the politics of intergovernmental relations, consider the implementation of a performance measurement system for Medicaid's goal of full immunization for two-year-olds. Managerial logic would have led Medicaid's managers to impose performance targets and definitions that would apply to all states, which would, in turn, have led to consistency, accuracy, and accountability. Instead, CMS executives recognized that Medicaid operates in a system of federalism that requires states to pay for nearly half of Medicaid's services and allows for the varying tastes and preferences of the individual states; therefore, CMS decided to aggregate data from states that have different definitions of "full immunization," different definitions of when a child is "two years old," and different targets that the individual states agreed to meet. The federal-level pressure to adhere more closely to managerial logic does not always translate cleanly when applied to intergovernmental programs, particularly when those programs are carried out by the states and their third parties.

Our findings support the generalization that the logic of performance measurement as well as performance budgeting attempts to superimpose managerial logic on political processes. In addition we find that GPRA-driven performance measurement attempts to superimpose managerial logic on the theory and practices of American federalism and on the politics of intergovernmental relations. One interesting approach to reconcile the management utility of measurement with the flexibility of federalism is found in MCHB, where a set of shared core measures is complemented by a cafeteria of other measures and targets.

External factors beyond agency control may influence performance and impede attempts to improve federal performance measurement. The sources of these impediments are often found in a program's authorizing legislation and in other related legislation. Examples of such impediments include Medicare's authorizing legislation, which prohibits CMS from contracting with any intermediary it wishes and also requires it to contract on a cost basis, prohibiting CMS from entering into fixed-price or performance-based contracts. These impediments are the result of pressure exerted on Congress by politically powerful constituencies. Authorizing legislation often prevents agencies from engaging in good management practices, practices that would enable them to perform more efficiently or effectively.

Impediments to performance and performance measurement are also found in the Paperwork Reduction Act of 1995, an act intended to limit the paperwork burden imposed by the federal government on state and local governments and on the private sector. Federal agencies that wish to collect data from other entities, including third-party contractors, must seek and obtain permission from OMB's Office of Information and Regulatory Affairs to comply with the Paperwork Reduction Act.

PART rates federal programs according to several criteria, one of which is program design. It is clear that the source of many programs' performance difficulties is embedded in authorizing legislation. As a result of PART, the public will soon have the first comprehensive collection of federally imposed impediments to program performance and should be able shine a bright light on a neglected yet critical aspect of federal performance.

Public managers and public administration scholars should address impediments to effective performances metrics by more aggressively asking the following questions:

☐ What are the sources of impediments to effective performance measurement resulting from interest group pressure? Conflicting program goals? Faulty assumptions?

☐ What are program managers doing to respond to these impediments? Are they, for example, making legislative recommendations? If so, how do legislators respond to such recommendations? Do program managers find ways to work around the impediments?

THE COSTS OF PERFORMANCE MEASUREMENT

A fourth theme in the performance measurement and performance budgeting literature is that *performance measurement regimes seldom consider the cost side of the performance measurement equation* (Radin 2006). Our findings support this claim.

Transaction-cost economics is a promising approach to performance measurement. The choice of "make versus buy" in the federal government is generally made without rigorous analysis of the estimated costs of federal service provision versus third-party service delivery. Transaction-cost economics examines the costs associated with delivering services directly versus contracting out for those same services. The costs associated with contracting go well beyond the price paid to a contractor and include costs associated with information asymmetry and moral hazard (postcontractual opportunism). To reduce information asymmetry and discourage moral hazard, those who purchase contracted services must be capable of oversight sufficient to keep both contractors and their clients or service recipients in check. But contract management is not a federal government strength (Kettl 1988). In addition, there is always the possibility that lax and faulty oversight might result in fraud and abuse, a particularly costly "transaction."

The marginal increase in the costs of collecting performance data where third parties are involved is a transaction cost. In recognition of this form of transaction cost, MCHB's Title V program provided $100,000 to each state to assist in collecting performance data. Unfortunately, there are few other examples of the up-front recognition of the costs associated with performance measurement by third parties. Overall, we found that the most significant costs associated with performance measurement are the opportunity costs in time and resources given to performance measurement and taken away from agency performance.

Those using a transaction-cost approach to performance measurement in the context of third-party government should address the following questions:

☐ What marginal increases in costs are associated with collecting performance data where third parties are involved? What are the differences in costs for collecting performance data from different kinds of third parties?

☐ What are the performance differences, in terms of both effectiveness and efficiency, of federal services provided through contractors and grants compared to those provided directly?

☐ Are unique performance measurement costs associated with third-party service delivery? What data cannot be collected and what measures cannot be utilized when services are provided through third parties?

PERFORMANCE MEASUREMENT AND AMERICAN FEDERALISM

The fifth theme in the performance measurement literature and in our findings is that *American federalism is a key feature of the political context in which agencies attempt to measure their performance.* This is particularly true of agencies that operate state grant-based third-party systems of policy implementation. GPRA did not approach the logic of performance measurement from the perspective of third-party government. Nor did GPRA consider the importance of states and their subdivisions as partners in the implementation of federal policy (Agranoff and McGuire 2001; Barnow 1992; Blalock and Barnow 2001; Radin 2002).

The PART initiative is an attempt, in part, to remedy this deficiency in GPRA. With its seven diagnostic tools for competitive grant programs, block grant programs, regulatory programs, direct federal programs, and so on, PART specifically takes into account the differing management challenges associated with third-party government and other service delivery arrangements.

In the agencies considered in this book, we found that successful performance measurement has been most often achieved through the logic of performance partnerships. For example, the metrics for MCHB of HRSA were negotiated with the states. To be successful, other federal programs and agencies have followed suit. Medicaid, for example, is a huge, cooperatively financed federal–state program that could not possibly have sensible measures of performance without the direct involvement of states. In these partnerships it is essential to find agreement as to which performance data are to be collected, how they are to be collected and managed, and how they are going to be used. Radin (2006) describes this process as negotiated performance measurements and claims that such negotiated measures are one of the keys to making performance measurement effective in the fluid context of American federalism. Although GPRA disregarded third-party government in its design, it is evident at the agency level that much of the actual implementation of performance measurement reforms, particularly when that implementation has been effective, involved full recognition of third-party government and the practices of performance partnerships and negotiated performance measurement.

Among the greatest challenges in performance measurement in third-party regimes is the matter of federal agency–level performance expectations in the context of widespread feelings among federal officials that their agencies are being held responsible for the performance of third parties over which they have limited control. The best evidence of this is the results of surveys of federal managers by GAO (2001). When asked whether they were held accountable for performance results, 68 percent of HHS managers said yes. But when they were asked whether they had any decision-making authority over programs for which they were being held responsible, only 43 percent answered yes. The findings for managers in CMS (then HCFA), an agency that is almost entirely hollowed out and reliant on third-party policy implementation, are much more dramatic—43 percent of CMS managers believe they are held responsible for agency performance, and only 28 percent indicate that they have decision-making authority over programs for which they are held responsible. This is a stark recognition on the part of agency managers that they have limited, and in some cases very limited, influence over the performance of their third parties.

As was found in the detailed consideration of CMS in chapter 5, to reduce the uncertainty associated with third-party policy implementation, managers operate on the basis of performance partnerships and negotiated performance metrics. Partnerships and negotiations with third parties are a key feature of grant- and contract-based management and are described widely in the contemporary public administration literature (Kettl 1993; Salamon 1989). The application of this perspective to performance measurement in third-party government puts metrics properly in the context of contemporary understandings of the operations of federalism (Wright 1988; Walker 1995; Fossett, Gais, and Thompson 2001).

PERFORMANCE MEASUREMENT AND THIRD-PARTY IMPLEMENTATION

The final and most important theme in our findings is not based on the performance measurement literature or in its core logic. Instead, our findings indicate that *the factor with the greatest impact on the ability of the five HHS agencies we studied to measure their performance is the modern practice of using third parties to implement federal health policy and programs.*

Our findings generally confirm the point made more than eighty years ago by Mary Parker Follett, who said that "we see that the place in which orders are given, and the circumstances under which they are given, may make all the difference in the world as to the response we get. Hand them down from President or work manager and the effect is weakened. One might say that the strength of a favorable response to an order is in reverse ratio to the distances the order travels (Follett 1926, 157). Follett's hypothesis had to do with giving orders in a standard organizational hierarchy. If one substitutes goals for orders, and if one assumes that Follett's description of a "favorable response" is essentially the same thing as effective performance, then our findings support her hypothesis. On the basis of our findings, and adapting Follett's hypothesis to modern third-party government, we have determined the following: *The strength of agency performance in pursuit of program goals is in reverse ratio to the distances actual implementation travels and the layers of third parties through which implementation travels.*

Modern federal government performance measurement regimes are deeply embedded articulated vertical networks of third parties. We found, as Follett claims, that the length of these articulations matter. We also found that the characteristics of third parties matter. Performance measurement in the context of federal–state intergovernmental relations and state implementation of federal policy is very different from performance measurement in the context of contract-based third-party services providers. We, therefore, add this conclusion: *The strength of agency performance in pursuit of program goals is in reverse ratio to the distances actual implementation travels and to the characteristics of third-party grantees and contractors.*

The most compelling evidence in this research was found at the intersection of the logic of the application of performance measurement and the logic of third-party government. This aspect of performance measurement has been neglected in the literature, a deficiency in both the theoretical understanding of the nature of performance measurement in the federal government and the practices of sound performance measurement methods. These recurring themes in the performance measurement and performance budgeting research literature are found in the detailed treatment of GPRA implementation in chapters 4 through 8.

By mid-2005 PART had completed three years of application, and about 60 percent of federal agencies and programs had been "PARTed," a total of 604 programs. As described in chapter 3, the PART instrument includes ratings of programs according to their purpose and design, their strategic planning, the quality of their management, and their results and accountability. In addition, as described in chapter 3, unlike GPRA, PART distinguishes between types of federal programs, grant programs, regulatory programs, credit programs, direct programs, and so forth. As table 10.1 indicates, with 60 percent of federal programs PARTed, it is now possible to compare the results.

When direct government and grant- and contract-based third-party government are compared, in general terms direct government is given significantly higher overall PART scores and, more specifically, higher scores for the management section of the PART. Research and development programs, which are mostly third-party based, are a marked exception to this generalization. Nevertheless, it appears that these data support our claim that quality of management and the nature of accountability in hollowed-out third-party-operated federal programs are very different from the management and accountability of directly operated federal programs. The accumulation of GPRA- and PART-based performance measurement results shines a strong light on these differences. One might conclude, on the basis of these data, that third-party-operated federal programs are

TABLE 10.1

COMPARISON OF DIRECT AND THIRD-PARTY PART SCORES

Type of Government Programs	No. of programs PARTed	Average Total PART Score, 0–100	Part III Management Score, 0–20
Direct government	188	68	16.8
Regulatory	38	70	16.4
Research and development (third party)	81	81	17.2
Credit	24	65	17.0
Capital asset	60	65	16.4
Block/formula grants (third party)	101	56	15.3
Competitive grants (third party)	112	54	14.5

less accountable and less well managed, or one might conclude that articulated vertical networks of third parties will be inherently, or by their nature, less accountable to federal government objectives and less well managed, at least less well managed in terms of traditional definitions of management. Of the five agencies and many programs evaluated for this book, NIH and FDA are, on the basis of their GPRA and PART measures, more accountable and better managed. We leave to future research and speculation the question of why federal research and development agencies and regulatory agencies do comparatively better in terms of accountability and management than do block-, formula-, and competitive-grant-based agencies. The data in table 10.1 may leave a clue. Is it possible that many of the contract- and grant-based third-party-operated federal programs that are doing less well in terms of performance measurement are attempting to deal with particularly vexing national social and health challenges? Is it further possible that GPRA and PART performance measures thus far indicate that attempting to deal with these challenges through American federalism's unique version of shared power adds to those challenges? Finally, is it possible that the application of performance measurement to federal programs indicates that the federal government is far from mastering the management and accountability issues associated with federal programs operated through articulated vertical networks of third parties?

THE PROSPECTS FOR PERFORMANCE BUDGETING

We close with a consideration of the prospects for performance measurement–based performance budgeting. On GPRA's passage there was great hope that Congress would use performance information in its appropriations deliberations. To most observers, the extensive and sustained involvement of Congress would be necessary if GPRA were to achieve its stated objectives. For some advocates, a high level of congressional involvement was assumed. The potential role for Congress's use of GPRA is not limited to appropriators' use of performance information in making budget allocation decisions. It also includes the authorizing committees, which can use performance information to take performance impediments more consciously into account when programs are reauthorized. Finally, it includes the committees charged with broad government performance oversight responsibilities, such as the House Government Reform Committee and the Senate Government Affairs Committee.

On the basis of an evaluation of the first two full years of PART applications, John B. Gilmour and David E. Lewis claim that "one cannot escape the conclusion that the (PART) scores are correlated with proposed budget increases. . . . Even when accounting for political influence in the determination of the scores themselves, performance information is a significant predictor of budget changes for FY 2005" (Gilmour and Lewis 2006, 22) Matthew Dull, in a somewhat similar review of the connections between PART-based performance measurement and program grading, suggests that PART enhances the potential for budget control and adds leverage to presidential preferences and initiatives (Dull 2006). It appears that the performance budgeting hopes of both GPRA and PART reformers are, at least to some extent, being realized. What we do not know is whether the performance information that makes its way into the president's budget, including proposed program eliminations and reductions based partially on PART scores and ratings, will make any difference in the congressional appropriations process.

As yet, there is little indication that appropriators pay attention to the performance information, much less make appropriations decisions based in part on this information. A study by the Congressional Research Service claims that GPRA was having an influence on congressional decision making based on laws' and committee reports' increased use of language related to GPRA or performance measures (U.S. Congressional Research Service 1999). As Alan Schick dryly notes, "Her data, however, prove only that buzzwords buzz around" (2001, 43). Schick continues, "Once a term gains popularity, smart people make sure to use it. The more talk there is about performance measurement, the more it filters into laws and legislative reports. But verbiage should never be mistaken for usage" (2001, 43). The first extensive opportunity for appropriators to exploit performance information in making budget allocation decisions showed little to no promise. Instead, the new language of outcomes proved foreign to appropriators, whose preference had always been budget justifications filled with workload tables, number of constituents served, fines levied, and so on. Nor was there much indication that authorizing committees took notice of the new performance data in reauthorization debates.

The legislative committees that did pay close attention were the Committee on Government Reform in the House of Representatives and the Committee on Government Affairs in the Senate. The attention these committees did pay, however, demonstrated a compliance perspective, which betrayed the broader concern of improving the performance of federal programs. These committees' use of GPRA solely for the purpose of criticizing agencies runs counter to GPRA's stated objective of improving the public's confidence in government. Although it is difficult to assess definitively GPRA's impact on confidence in government, it is clear that congressional hearings on GPRA do not have citizen confidence as their primary objective. For instance, a hearing held on July 20, 2000, by the Government Management, Information and Technology Subcommittee of the House Government Reform Committee was titled "Seven Years of GPRA: Has the Results Act Provided Results?"

The focus on accountability as a function of GPRA compliance as opposed to accountability as a function of the actual performance of federal programs is not unique to the House and Senate Government Reform and Affairs committees respectively. Once, after a joint hearing, the Senate Appropriations and Governmental Affairs committees issued what could only have been taken as a threat to the former director of OMB, Franklin Raines: "You ought to be on notice that we are going to condition expenditures until the plans are completed and in a satisfactory fashion" (Schick 2001, 52). Other GPRA-related congressional hearings adopt a similar compliance-and-condemnation mentality. Congress is not alone in this approach, however. Although everybody—GAO, George Mason University's Mercatus Center, and the Congressional Institute—assessed and ranked agencies' compliance with GPRA, few spoke about how agencies were performing. The collective voice was to the effect that the federal government was doing a poor job of measuring its own performance. It is only logical to conclude that the impact this assessment has had on the perception of government has been negative. In this way PART is a considerable departure, where programs' actual performance, rather than compliance, is intended to be the primary focus.

Although GPRA may not be contributing to favorable perceptions of government by citizens, our evaluation suggests that GPRA is achieving two other objectives: to improve program effectiveness and to improve the internal management of the federal government. Improvements in these areas might not be definitive, but the potential is clearly present. Perhaps unwittingly, the authors of GPRA have facilitated a means to manage better the extensive and varied network of third-party providers delivering services funded by the federal government. The study of the HHS agencies discussed in this book demonstrates that the performance measurement processes required by GPRA have resulted in new lines of results-oriented communication and improved cooperation with the third parties the agencies rely on to carry out their missions. Better performance-related communication can bring about clearer expectations between agencies and third parties. This advance can lead to improved program effectiveness, accountability, and internal management. This is likely a different kind of accountability than was intended by the authors of GPRA and by performance measurement advocates. But because the federal government delivers the vast majority of its services through or in conjunction with third parties, the process of data-based communication through articulated vertical networks of third parties is a far more important advance than merely gathering and reporting performance information. Indeed, thus far the positive legacy of GPRA performance measurement reform has proved to be found primarily in the patterns of interaction between agencies and their third parties.

The transition from GPRA to PART confirms that the cycles of management reform are associated with changing presidential administrations (Light 1997). What cannot be known is whether the cycles of federal management reform generally, and performance measurements specifically, will, in time, change or modify GPRA or PART. Federal performance measurement, however, will almost certainly be a central feature of the modern management of third-party government, whatever the acronym.

PERFORMANCE MANAGEMENT

Performance measurement in government is increasingly thought to be just one part of a wider performance management reform. Performance management, particularly as advocated by leading and influential management consultants, is an entire public management perspective based on the logic of performance. Like GPRA, performance management places program and agency strategic plans at the starting point. Once goals and missions are clarified and put in priority, then all aspects of management in pursuit of goals and missions are to be data based and data driven. Performance management seeks to tie agency and program costs and revenues measured traditionally (dollars) to precise quantitative agency and program metrics (nondollar performance measures). Performance budgeting is, obviously, a primary form of performance management. So, too, is the logic behind performance auditing, a form of auditing that presumes to evaluate and verify not only the reliability of an agency's or program's finances but also its actual performance. Part of the performance management repertoire is the setting of targets, targets that can only make sense after reliable performance data are available on a regular basis. This feature of the performance management repertoire is seen in the PART approach to federal performance measurement and in the implementation of the President's Management Agenda program in the George W. Bush administration. There are also connections between the key features of performance management and the logic of pay for individual performance. Finally, the word "accountability" is a key feature of the language of performance management as it is of the language of performance measurement. John Mercer, the "father of GPRA" and now a leading government performance consultant, has moved to the comprehensive performance management perspective and describes it thus: "An effective Performance Management system ensures that an agency's administrative and support functions (budget, financial management, human resources, information technology, procurement, etc.) directly and explicitly serve the needs of program managers in meeting the agency's strategic and annual goals" (Mercer 2006, 1).

Performance management, as described here, is now understood to be the preferred approach to the management and oversight of federal third parties, or, to use the preferred contemporary phrase, "federal partners." This is notable because in the initial stages of the federal performance measurement reform, including the wording of GPRA, there was no mention of third parties or partners or the fact that much of the federal government is hollowed out. As we have described, over time it became increasingly clear that the absence of attention to third-party government was a serious flaw in the initial legislation, a flaw recognized in the later development of the PART approach to performance measurement. Today it appears that the performance measurement movement is pointing the way to the preferred approach to the management of federal third parties—performance management.

There are, of course, many ways to "manage" third parties. One of the continua we developed for the analysis of federal program implementation by third parties is a "measure" of "the nature and quality of network articulations" ranging from "remote control" at one pole to "managed networks" at the other. One version of federal third-party performance management can be a form of remote control—the strict specification of federal performance expectations spelled out in requests for proposals and the equally strict holding of contract and grant holders to specifications. Most contracts operated under standard agency procurement procedures fit the remote-control model. This approach is an antiseptic, linear version of third-party management by remote control using the full performance management repertoire. Another version of federal third-party management can be a form of network management involving negotiations with partners, repeated iterations of agency-partner projects, and the development of levels of trust between agency and partner officials. Although less precise and legalistic than the remote-control approach, the network management approach to performance management is probably better suited to, for example, the management of grants to the states and territories.

If performance management is coming to be the primary means by which the federal government manages third parties and partners, the factors we found to influence performance measurement in the context of third-party government will be even more important. For example, as we described in chapter 9, we conclude that agencies with states, territories, and tribes as their third parties tend to use negotiated management approaches to network articulations, and agencies with contractor third parties use a procedural, rules-based, legalistic contract approach to network articulations. This conclusion, and our many other conclusions in chapters 8 and 9, are at least as relevant to the application of performance management as they are to the application of performance measurement to the implementation of federal programs.

Our aim in this book was to correct a glaring shortcoming in the theory and practice of performance measurement in government—the failure to recognize the importance of third parties to the implementation of federal policy. On the basis of our evaluation of the implementation of GPRA and PART in five key health agencies in the Department of Health and Human Services, we believe our findings have corrected that failure. Third-party government and the application of performance measurement to it are primary features of modern federal public administration. We have attempted empirically to inform that application and to describe fairly the strengths, weaknesses, and prospects of federal performance measurement. Issues associated with the application of performance measurement in the context of third-party government were important when we began this project. Now, with the coming of performance management, they are even more important.

APPENDIX A
Discussion Guide

How have agencies successfully negotiated with third-party providers to establish uniform data gathering and reporting efforts?

1. How was the development of your performance plan measurements affected by data availability, accessibility, and/or ease of manipulation?
2. Can you give me an example of one measure critical to assessing your agency's success for which the data are difficult to obtain or manipulate?
    2a. What is/are the difficulty(ies) associated with this measure?
    2b. What specifically did your agency do to overcome these difficulties?
3. Are there any measures you would have liked to include in the performance plan, but did not due to difficulty of data availability, accessibility, and/or ease of manipulation?
4. Have you had to settle for any indirect measures (intermediate outcome measures) or direct measures with poor methodology or data incompatibility?
    4a. Please give an example of such a measure, explaining what ideally should have been done to measure an outcome.
5. Do you have more measures that are collected and stored from one source or more that are collected and stored at multiple sources?
6. Give me an example of one measure that requires you to work with a third-party provider(s) (i.e., an external entity such as a state, business, or nonprofit to either administer/manage or actually provide services). What did you do to work with the third-party providers to ensure that measurement methods, data collection methods, and data storage methods were brought in sync?
    6a. Who were the external providers?
    6b. What difficulties arose from these dealings with external providers?
    6c. Were they primarily political or logistical?
        6c1. Please explain.
    6d. What was done to alleviate or overcome the difficulties? Did you use incentives or the threat of penalties?
    6e. Do you convey the requirements and purposes of GPRA to the external provider, or do you merely detail the data and reporting requirements?
        6e1. Why or why not? How do you convey the requirements? How might you do it differently if given the chance to "sell" GPRA to these external providers again?

7. Are there still measurement methods, data collection methods, and data storage methods problems with external providers that have yet to be resolved?
8. Did you involve external providers in the development of measures and the methodologies used to assess outcomes? How were they used, and how helpful were they?
9. Can you identify actions your office has taken that have led to success in dealing with external providers in GPRA implementation?
10. Can you identify actions your office has taken that have led to failure in dealing with external providers in GPRA implementation?
11. Now that many of the measures have been in place for over a year, what are the primary difficulties you encounter in reporting?
    11a. Can you give any specific examples?
    11b. In retrospect, what might you have done to avoid these difficulties?
        11b1. Can you give any specific examples?

What accounts for the success in developing and meeting sound performance measures across the policy tools?

1. Please identify two measures from your performance plan that you consider to be two of your best measures.
2. How do you define "best" when it comes to performance plan performance measures and explain why the two meet this criterion?
3. Please identify two measures from your performance plan that you consider to be two of your worst measures.
4. How do you define "worst" when it comes to performance plan performance measures and explain why the two meet this criterion?
5. Why did you have to settle for these two measures?
6. What would have to be different for you to:
    6a.   Not include these measures?
    6b.   Improve upon these measures?

APPENDIX B

Science Advance from the National Institute of Mental Health FY2000

IMAGING SHOWS THE BRAIN IS A PICTIONARY PLUS

Background: One of the most remarkable features of our visual recognition system is that we can instantly identify an object, even when we have never seen that specific object before. One explanation for this is that we have information stored in our brains, similar to a mental picture dictionary, about the visual form of different objects. We can recognize a "dog" or a "hammer" that we have not encountered before because past experience has taught us about the appearances of these objects.

Advance: Results of recent functional brain imaging studies suggest that this answer is only partially correct; information about objects is stored in a set of regions that also identify how an object moves or how it is used. The findings suggest that information about the features and attributes of objects are stored in different regions of the brain, close to the areas involved in the perception of those features.

When subjects verbally named specific objects, a number of different regions of the brain became active, depending on the object's features and attributes. Naming a picture of an animal—for example, a dog—was associated with activity in two specific areas of the brain. One region activated during the perception of visual form, and the other during perception of biological motion. In contrast, naming a picture of an inanimate object (e.g., a hammer) also produced activity close to the brain area activated during perception of form, but distinct from the region activated when naming animals. In addition, verbal naming was associated with activity near the regions activated during object motion perception, and when manipulating an object with the right hand. These regions were also activated when subjects read the names and answered questions about these objects.

Implications: These findings are important for a number of reasons. For example, they help to explain why some patients with focal brain damage can lose the ability to name and retrieve information about a single category of objects, such as animals or tools. The findings also suggest that information about object features and attributes are stored in different regions of the brain, close to the areas involved in the perception of those features. In a broader sense these findings provide important clues about how information necessary to understand the meaning of objects and words is stored and organized in the brain. [Biology, Knowledge: Molecular/Cellular]

APPENDIX C

*Science Capsule from the National Institute
of Mental Health FY2000*

EXIT SIGNS HELP TRAVELING NEURONS IN THE BRAIN

How does an exquisitely complex structure such as the human brain develop properly to form a fully functional unit? It has been shown that neurons—cells making up the brain and central nervous system—actually migrate. NIMH-supported investigators demonstrated that the final destination of migrating neurons is influenced by a protein called reelin, which is produced by a special type of cell at the outermost part of the developing brain. When the investigators measured the rate of neuronal migration, they found that reelin acts something like an exit sign, signaling cells to decrease their rate of migration. In addition, reelin added from outside by investigators actually stopped the migration of neurons in developing cerebral cortical neurons in rat embryos. The mechanism by which reelin exerts its actions appears to involve direct interaction with the protein integrin, as reelin was ineffective in directing the exit of neurons in preparations lacking this protein. This work has begun to identify molecular interactions necessary for establishing critical migratory events in the formation of the intricate folds and layers characteristic of the human brain. This is very important because these findings may aid in understanding the role of developmental factors such as reelin and other molecules in the etiology of several developmental disorders, such as autism and schizophrenia, which appear to involve erroneous development of neuronal connections. [Biology, Knowledge: Molecular/Cellular]

APPENDIX D

*Stories of Discovery from the National Institute
of Mental Health FY2001*

IMPROVING TREATMENTS, PREVENTING RELAPSE: ATYPICAL ANTIPSYCHOTIC MEDICATIONS

Schizophrenia, a chronic, disabling illness that affects an estimated 1 percent of the population worldwide, is among the most severe forms of mental disorder. Through much of the 19th and first half of the 20th centuries, patients with schizophrenia typically were locked away from society. In the 1950s, investigators in France chanced upon a class of medications that proved to have a remarkable calming effect on severely psychotic patients. With the new drugs, called antipsychotics, or neuroleptics, patients long thought to be beyond reach of any intervention short of physical restraint were relieved of such disturbing psychotic symptoms as hallucinations—for example, hearing voices that are not connected to a visible source—and delusions—beliefs that are not subject to reason. Many patients appeared able to re-enter society.

Although the immediate clinical effects were dramatic, researchers did not know how the new compounds acted on the brain to affect behavior. At the young NIMH in the United States, and elsewhere, basic science surged as scientists used these and other psychoactive medications as tools to learn about brain mechanisms in illnesses long thought to be incurable. Soon, however, research and anecdotal experience afforded an unsettling perspective on the overall effects of antipsychotics. Although the medications relieved many frightening, visible symptoms of psychosis, large numbers of patients experienced a range of often severe adverse effects—for example, neurologic and neuromuscular effects called extrapyramidal symptoms, or EPS. These appeared as uncontrollable, or spastic, muscular contractions that resemble the tremors and rigidity of Parkinson's disease. Tardive dyskinesia, a condition involving involuntary movements and tics—most noticeably of the face, lips, and tongue—disproportionately affected patients who took antipsychotic medications for many years. Another drawback was the relatively small impact neuroleptics had on symptoms of social withdrawal and apathy. For patients discharged into community settings, these persistent symptoms proved to be as devastating as outwardly psychotic symptoms, given the manner in which they worked against the goal of re-engaging in the activities of daily life.

Over several decades, researchers sought to fine–tune methods of administering various look-alike antipsychotic medications. Other studies led to the development of very useful community treatment strategies and psychosocial treatments to complement medications. In diagnostic research, a useful refinement was the categorization of "positive" and "negative," or deficit symptoms. Hallucinations, delusions, and disorganized thinking were termed positive symptoms, because they represent an addition—albeit an unfavorable one—to normal, healthy behavior. Withdrawal and other symptoms such as loss of motivation to engage in productive behaviors or satisfying social relationships were called negative symptoms because they represent a loss of, or deficit in, behavior that was normal for an individual before the illness occurred.

On a parallel track, the opportunity afforded by psychoactive medications to study the cellular and molecular mechanisms of the brain's operations helped to fuel the explosive growth of neuroscience. Early research findings suggested that the drug's effectiveness pointed to simple excesses or deficiencies in certain brain chemicals called neurotransmitters; this "single neurotransmitter" interpretation proved to be overly simplistic, but led to an increasingly sophisticated appreciation of the complexity of brain systems in mental disorders.

While these multiple strands of research were being pursued, the Food and Drug Administration approved in 1990 a fundamentally new type of antipsychotic drug, clozapine, for use in the United States. The clinical advantages of clozapine were clear: a virtual absence of the most troublesome motor, or movement, side effects associated with conventional antipsychotics and a greater degree of efficacy in addressing negative as well as positive symptoms. Clozapine, however, was not side-effect free. In a small percentage (1 percent) of patients it caused a potentially fatal blood condition: agranulocytosis, a loss of the white blood cells that fight infections, so all patients taking clozapine are required to have their blood tested weekly and discontinue the drug if necessary.

NIH-funded grantees and intramural scientists were at the forefront of efforts to evaluate the clinical and cost-effectiveness of clozapine. Findings that the effectiveness of the new compound in reducing need for repeated hospitalizations and length of inpatient stays largely compensated for its expense gave impetus to efforts, largely undertaken by the pharmaceutical industry, to develop other medications—which would be called atypical antipsychotics because they have a different therapeutic action than their predecessors—with therapeutic benefits that would meet or exceed those of clozapine, while avoiding serious side effects. The eventual success of industry in this quest would prove to have relied heavily on basic NIH funded research.

Initially, the mechanism of action of clozapine was virtually undecipherable. Scientific appreciation of the complex interactions between such neurotransmitters and the specialized molecules called receptors that are found on the surface of neurons and are the sites at which neurotransmitters—and drugs—influence cellular action was relatively primitive. At that time, scientists had identified only two receptors for the neurotransmitter dopamine, and two for serotonin. Over the past decade, researchers have identified as many as five structurally and functionally distinct receptors for dopamine and 14 for serotonin. These discoveries are playing a critical role in determining the action, or effect, of clozapine; as importantly, they afford specific, and increasingly well-characterized, novel targets for drug development research.

Brain imaging also is beginning to play an increasingly prominent role in medication development efforts. Using newly identified radioligands—molecules that bind to the same receptors that medications do—NIH-funded research now under way is using positron emission tomography, or PET scanning, to examine regional differences in how conventional and atypical medications work. This information opens another window on the therapeutic actions of atypical antipsychotics and other medications.

In recent years, the FDA has approved several new atypicals—risperidone (Risperidol), olanzepine (Zyprexa), and quetiapine (Seroquel)—and yet others are in the pipeline. Although first used to treat schizophrenia, the safety and potency of second-generation atypicals has encouraged their use in treating other disorders, including the manic phase of bipolar disorder and behavioral symptoms associated with Alzheimer's disease and other dementias. NIMH is currently conducting the Clinical Antipsychotic Trials of Intervention Effectiveness project (CATIE), http://www.catie.unc.edu/, which is evaluating the effectiveness of atypicals in the treatment of schizophrenia and Alzheimer's disease under real world conditions.

The introduction of atypical antipsychotic medications is noteworthy for the complementary roles assumed by NIH on the one hand, and the worldwide pharmaceutical industry on the other. Most critically, evidence that rigorous scientific study of schizophrenia and other severe mental disorders can lead to effective treatments and allow patients to reenter the community has proven to be our most potent tool for crushing the stigma attached to mental disorders while enhancing opportunities for health and improved quality of life for millions of persons.

APPENDIX E

The Conduct of Research

The research plan for this study is designed to determine: (1) how federal agencies have gone about implementing GPRA; (2) what problems and challenges agencies have faced with respect to data access and reliability, goal congruence, and political and policy conflicts; (3) how agencies have worked with third-party grantees and contractors as they implement agency programs; (4) the overall effect of the strict application of performance measurement regimes on agency leadership and management; and (5) how the study of GPRA implementation advances conceptual understandings of performance measurement in government.

One of the purposes of this study is to answer some practical and applied public management questions in the hope of usefully informing the practices of performance measurement as part of federal agency management. That is the primary subject of chapter 9. The study is designed, however, to address a series of conceptual and theoretical questions associated with the application of performance measurement to government programs. The substance of these concepts and theories is the subject of chapter 2.

A qualitative, comparative case study research methodology is primarily used in this study. Qualitative research techniques were chosen because GPRA is relatively new and because the body of extant research on public sector performance measurement is still relatively limited (Jennings and Haist 2002, 2004). There have simply not been enough aggregated quantitative data over enough years to sustain reliable generalizations based on statistical analysis. Also, because GPRA is comprehensive and general, applied in about the same way to all agencies, and because agency strategic purposes and policy instruments vary widely and resist generalization, an analytic approach that accounts for and explains how agencies have implemented GPRA agency-by-agency proved to be most informative. As anticipated, agencies varied widely in their approaches to GPRA implementation, and the qualitative research approach facilitated descriptions and explanations of those approaches. Finally, each of the five agencies studied is unique, internally complex, and difficult to compare using quantitative methodologies. Through standard qualitative research techniques—guided discussions, the analysis of reports and documents, and generalized observations of each of these agencies—this study tells the story of the implementation of GPRA in each agency, and it explains, using deduction and logic, how and why performance and results measurements are actually done and why.

Selecting an appropriate qualitative research approach requires more than just determining which data are available. This selection requires an inventory of the following: (1) the research questions involved; (2) the level of control the researcher has over actual behavior and events; and (3) the extent to which contemporary versus historical phenomena are observed (Yin 2003).

Qualitative research methodology can be used effectively to provide rich narratives of processes and understanding of contextual influences on programs and people and as a technique to identify unanticipated phenomena (Miles and Huberman 1994; Maxwell 1996). It is the best approach to understanding subtle political power and authority issues within bureaucratic organizations (King, Koehane, and Verba 2001).

The research questions in this study require exploring the "how" and "why" of events. These questions revolve around how and why contextual variables (policy tool choices, differing program objectives, differing organizational structures, differing levels of conflict) affect the implementation of a major management reform such as GPRA. Unlike experimental research, this research cannot manipulate the variables. Whereas research questions and hypotheses are drawn from the knowledge provided in the reform literature, this research is focused primarily on an essentially new and unique phenomenon, the legislative requirements to measure agency performance. This brief inventory suggests that given the research questions' focus on how and why, the lack of control over behavior and events, and the focus on unique phenomena, a qualitative research design is most suitable.

Qualitative methods have a comparative advantage in the study of organizations with multiple and conflicting objectives. Qualitative methods are valuable in the world of practice and application because findings can be expressed in terms that enable policy makers and public managers to improve organizational performance (Maxwell 1996; Miles and Huberman 1994).

The particular qualitative approach used in this study relies on grounded theory, an increasingly influential approach to applied social science (Dey 1999; Strauss and Corbin 1990; Straus 1987). Grounded theory refers to theory that is inductively developed during the course of a study. The term "grounded" suggests that the theory is grounded in the data that are collected and analyzed through systematic processes. Grounded theory represents a departure from deductive or standard social science empirical research in that it does not involve predetermined theories and hypotheses conceptually developed from extant literature and tested against empirical data (Maxwell 1996). Instead of the use of hypothesis-driven sampling schemes based on existing literature and theory to determine appropriate questions, in grounded theory ongoing discussions with interviewees influence the framing and reframing of research questions, research categories, and the nature of data generated during the cycles of data analysis (Miles and Huberman 1994).

Grounded theory that is well constructed from systematically collected data will meet four criteria:

Fit:	Faithful to everyday reality of the substantive area.
Understanding:	Makes sense to those being studied and to those practicing in that area.
Generality:	Data is comprehensive, and its interpretation is sufficiently conceptual and broad so that the theory is abstract,

making it applicable to a variety of contexts related to that phenomenon.

Control: Hypotheses are systematically derived from actual data related to a specific situation, with applicable conditions spelled out.

(Strauss and Corbin 1990)

The primary purpose of grounded theory is to empirically build theory that provides an understanding of the area studied. The research findings of grounded theory "constitute a theoretical formulation of the reality under investigation, rather than consisting of a set of numbers, or a group of loosely related themes" (Strauss and Corbin 1990, 24).

In grounded theory, the aim is to find, develop, discover, or generate hypotheses, concepts, and theories that account for or explain complex phenomena. Grounded theory is best suited to the study of complex and unique social phenomena that have not previously been the subject of systematic field research or that involve complex and intersecting forces (Strauss and Corbin 1990). The passage of GPRA and its implementation by federal agencies could be fairly described as unique and complex, and, although there have been studies of performance measurement in government, many of them summarized in chapter 2, there have been just a few systematic studies of GPRA (Radin 1998b, 2000; Kravchuk and Schack 1996; Morini and Wolf 2002).

In grounded theory the aim is for plausible explanatory concepts and theories to emerge from the processes of field research. As the research proceeds, the informed researcher codes systematically gathered information and then identifies emerging explanatory concepts that guide further research. Through this process, concepts developed at one stage of research guide and direct the researcher to the next stage and so forth. It is not unusual, in grounded theory, for the subject of that research to change somewhat during the course of study, because as research proceeds the researcher is able to identify genuinely salient explanatory concepts as well as concepts with little explanatory power. It is sometimes the case, therefore, that research using grounded methodology ends up identifying key explanatory concepts not understood at the outset of the research. To some extent this study, as explained in chapter 2 and especially in chapters 4 through 8, is an example of how, through the iterative processes of gathering field-based information and concept development, key explanatory concepts emerged (Dey 1999).

As suggested, the principal tool for theory building in grounded qualitative research is through coding and categories. Qualitative research can be contrasted with quantitative research, where coding is used to separate data according to preestablished categories for purposes of counting frequency. In qualitative research, coding is used not for counting purposes but to "fracture" (Strauss 1987) data and rearrange them into categories to aid in the comparison of data within and between these categories for purposes of developing theoretical concepts (Maxwell 1996). Some codes are predetermined, based on existing theory; others develop other codes inductively during data analysis (Miles and Huberman 1994; Maxwell 1996). The categories set out at the end of chapter 2 and applied to the reports of field analysis in chapters 4 through 8 are illustrative of how explanatory categories emerge during the course of study and come together to frame larger explanatory concepts and theories.

Samples in qualitative research are purposive rather than random (Patton 1990; Kuzel 1992). Because the aim of this research is to develop theory that will aid practice, and not to test for statistical significance, the sample size will be small and the sample selection purposive. In this way researchers can analyze information from those key individuals nested in their contexts (Miles and Huberman 1994). The primary data source for this research, therefore, was field interviews with those charged with the implementation of GPRA in the selected agencies. An additional data source was the use of agency performance plans. The final sources of data for this study were telephone interviews and e-mail exchanges. Telephone interviews and e-mail exchanges were used to ask questions of those agency employees who were tangentially involved in the implementation of GPRA and of those who were affected by GPRA but were not directly involved in its implementation. In addition, telephone interviews and e-mail exchanges were used to ask questions and get answers to follow-up questions posed to those who had been interviewed face-to-face. In some instances the opinions of those interviewed are attributed to them by name. In other cases, based on the preferences of the person interviewed, they are not named but are, instead, simply referred to as an official of a particular agency.

The selection of a qualitative research methodology, specifically grounded theory, was not arrived at primarily on the basis of the preferences of the researchers. Nor is it an indication of a rejection of quantitative research methodology. Instead, grounded methodology was chosen because it fit the research questions and available information and data. The questions for this research surround the processes by which federal health care agencies, representing a diversity of policy tools and third-party service providers, either successfully or unsuccessfully develop performance measures and plans to collect data for those measures.

Given this set of questions, the stage of the GPRA implementation process, the limitations of the extant research literature on the subject, and the data currently available, the appropriate research methodology is a qualitative, grounded-theory approach. Although the difficulties of complex variables and processes will not go away, within a few years when there are adequate data on the performance measures and on agency performance, the subject could be ripe for extensive quantitative analysis. The aim of this research is to develop theory that will help guide future qualitative and quantitative research and to be of more immediate help to practitioners in their efforts to develop performance measures and plans to collect data for these measures.

The main purposes for cross-case analysis are to expand the basis of information, to bolster the validity of and add confidence to findings. By selecting agencies with similar and contrasting policy tools, the findings are grounded in the specific *how*, *where*, and *why* agencies responded as they did to GPRA (Miles and Huberman 1994). Multiple cases also add confidence to findings through theoretical replication or through the production of contrasting results based on predictable reasons. In this case, the predictable reasons include the implementation of public policy using different policy tools and different third-party service providers. The intent is to develop theory that is both policy relevant and practical, theory that aids practitioners in their quest to develop and implement performance measures despite the complexity added by varying implementation strategies.

REFERENCES

Aberbach, Joel D., and Bert A. Rockman. 2000. *In the Web of Politics: Three Decades of the U.S. Federal Executive.* Washington, DC: Brookings Institution.

Agranoff, Robert, and Michael McGuire. 1998. "Multi-Network Management: Collaboration and the Hollow State in Local Economic Policy." *Journal of Public Administration Research and Theory* 8, no. 1 (January): 67–91.

———. 2001. "The Big Questions in Network Management Research." *Journal of Public Administration Research and Theory* 11, no. 3 (July): 295–326.

———. 2003. *Collaborative Public Management: New Strategies for Local Government.* Washington, DC: Georgetown University Press.

Barnow, Burt S. 1992. "The Effect of Performance Standards on State and Local Programs." In *Evaluating Welfare and Training Programs,* ed. Charles F. Manski and Irwin Garfinkel, 277–309. Cambridge, MA: Harvard University Press.

Bartik, Timothy J. 1995. *Using Performance Indicators to Improve the Effectiveness of Welfare to Work Programs.* Kalamazoo, MI: W. E. Upjohn Institute for Employment Research.

Berman, Evan M. 1998. *Productivity in Public and Nonprofit Organizations.* Thousand Oaks, CA: Sage Publications.

Blalock, Ann B., and Burt S. Barnow. 2001. "Is the New Obsession with Performance Management Masking the Truth about Social Programs?" In *Quicker, Better, Cheaper? Managing Performance in American Government,* ed. Dall W. Forsythe, 485–518. Albany, NY: Rockefeller Institute Press.

Bouckaert, Geert. 1993. "Measurement and Meaningful Management." *Public Productivity and Management Review* 17, no. 1:31–43.

Bouckaert, Geert, and B. Guy Peters. 2002. "Performance Measurements and Management: The Achilles Heel in Administrative Modernization." *Public Performance and Management Review* 25, no.4:359–62.

Bradley, Robert B., and Geraldo Flowers. 2001. "Getting to Results in Florida." In *Quicker, Better, Cheaper? Managing Performance in American Government,* ed. Dall W. Forsythe, 365–416. Albany, NY: Rockefeller Institute Press.

Broadnax, Walter, and Kevin J. Conway. 2001. "The Social Security Administration and Performance Management." In *Quicker, Better, Cheaper? Managing Performance in American Government,* ed. Dall W. Forsythe, 143–76. Albany, NY: Rockefeller Institute Press.

Broome, Cheryle A. 1995. "Performance-based Government Models: Building a Track Record." *Public Budgeting and Finance* 15 (Winter): 4–18.

Burkholz, Herbert. 1995. *The FDA Follies.* New York: Basic Books.

Casamayou, Maureen Hogan. 2001. *The Politics of Breast Cancer.* Washington, DC: Georgetown University Press.

Cleary. Paul D., and Susan Edgman-Levitan. 1997. "Health Care Quality: Incorporating Consumer Perspectives." *Journal of the American Medical Association* 278, no. 19:1608–12.

Clinton, Bill, and Al Gore. 1997. *Putting Customers First, '97: Standards for Serving the American People.* Washington, DC: Executive Office of the President.

Coglianese, Cary, and David Lazer. 2002. "Management-Based Regulatory Strategies." In *Market-Based Governance: Supply Side, Demand Side, Upside, and Downside,* ed. John D. Donahue and Joseph S. Nye, Jr., 201–24. Washington, DC: Brookings Institution.

Conlan, Timothy J. 1988. *New Federalism: Intergovernmental Reform and Political Change from Nixon to Reagan.* Washington, DC: Brookings Institution.

————. 1998. *From New Federalism to Devolution: Twenty-five Years of Intergovernmental Reform.* Washington, DC: Brookings Institution.

Cooper, Phillip J. 2003. *Governing by Contract: Challenges and Opportunities for Public Managers.* Washington, DC: CQ Press.

Cope, Glen H. 1995. "Budgeting for Performance in Local Government." *Municipal Yearbook 1995.* Washington, DC: International City/County Management Association.

Courty, Pascal, and Gerald Marschke. 2003. "Performance Funding in Federal Agencies: A Case Study of Federal Job Training Program." *Public Budgeting and Finance* 23, no. 3 (September): 22–48.

Dey, Ian. 1999. *Grounding Grounded Theory: Guidelines for Qualitative Inquiry.* New York: Academic Press.

DiIulio, John J., Jr., Gerald Garvey, and Donald F. Kettl. 1993. *Improving Government Performance: An Owner's Manual.* Washington, DC: Brookings Institution.

DiIulio, John J., Jr., and Donald F. Kettl. 1995. *Fine Print: The Contract with America, Devolution, and the Administrative Realities of American Federalism.* Washington, DC: Brookings Institution.

DiIulio, John J., Jr., and Richard R. Nathan, eds. 1994. *Making Health Reform Work: The View from the States.* Washington, DC: Brookings Institution.

DiMaggio, Paul J., and Walter W. Powell. 1983. "The Iron Cage Revisited: Institutional Isomorphism and Collective Rationality in Organizational Fields." *American Sociological Review* 48, no. 2:147–60.

Downs, G. W., and Patrick D. Larkey. 1986. *The Search for Government Efficiency: From Hubris to Helplessness.* New York: Random House.

Dull, Matthew. 2006. "Why PART: The Institutional Politics of Presidential Budget Reform." *Journal of Public Administration Research and Theory.* In press.

Eddy, David. 1998. "Performance Measurement: Problems and Solutions." *Health Affairs* 17, no. 4:7–25.

Follet, Mary Parker. 1926. "The Giving of Orders." Reprint, 1996, in *Classics of Organization Theory,* ed. Jay M. Shafritz and Steven J. Ott, 157–62. New York: Harcourt Brace.

Forsythe, Dall W., ed. 2001. *Quicker, Better, Cheaper? Managing Performance in American Government.* Albany, NY: Rockefeller Institute Press.

Fossett, James, Thomas Gais, and Frank J. Thompson. 2001. "Federalism and Performance Management: Food Stamps and the Take-Up Challenge." In *Quicker, Better, Cheaper: Managing Performance in American Government,* ed. Dall W. Forsythe, 207–44. Albany, NY: Rockefeller Institute Press.

Fox, Claude Earl. 2002. U.S. Health Resource and Service Administration. GPRA Plan 2002, 1.

Frederickson, H. George. 1999. "Public Ethics and the New Managerialism." *Public Integrity* 1, no. 3:265–78.

———. 2000. "Measuring Performance in Theory and Practice." *Public Administration Times.* September 9–10.

Friedlander, Daniel, and Gary Burtless. 1995. *Five Years After: The Long-Term Effects of Welfare to Work Programs.* New York: Russell Sage Foundation.

Gilmour, Robert S., and Alex A. Halley, eds. 1994. *Who Makes Public Policy? The Struggle for Control between Congress and the Executive.* New York: Chatham House.

Gilmour, John B., and David E. Lewis. 2006. "Assessing Performance Assessment for Budgeting: The Influence of Politics, Performance and Program Size in FY 2005." *Journal of Public Administration Research and Theory.* In press.

Glaser, Amihai, and Lawrence S. Rothenberg. 2001. *Why Government Succeeds and Why it Fails.* Cambridge, MA: Harvard University Press.

Gore Al. 1993. *From Red Tape to Results: Creating a Government That Works Better and Costs Less.* Washington, DC: U. S. Government Printing Office.

———. 1995. *Common Sense Government: Works Better and Costs Less.* Washington, DC: U. S. Government Printing Office.

———. 1997. *Putting Customers First '97.* Washington, DC: U. S. Government Printing Office.

Gormley, William T., and David L. Weimer. 1999. *Organizational Report Cards.* Cambridge, MA: Harvard University Press.

Governmental Accounting Standards Board. 2000. *GASB's State and Local Government Case Studies: The Use and the Effects of Using Performance Measures for Budgeting, Management and Reporting.* Norwalk, CT: Governmental Accounting Standards Board.

Grace, J. Peter, 1984. *War on Waste: President's Private Sector Survey on Cost Control.* New York: Macmillan.

Gulick, Luther, and Lyndon Urwick. 1937. *Papers on the Service of Administration.* New York: Institute of Public Administration.

Haider, Donald. 1989. "Grants as a Tool of Public Policy." In *Beyond Privatization: The Tools of Government,* ed. Lester M. Salamon, 93–124. Washington, DC: Urban Institute Press.

Handler, Joel. 1996. *Down from Bureaucracy: The Ambiguity of Privatization and Empowerment.* Princeton, NJ: Princeton University Press.

Hatry, Harry P. 1999. *Performance Measurement: Getting Results.* Washington, DC: Urban Institute Press.

Hawthorne, Fran. 2005. *Inside the FDA: The Business and Politics Behind the Drugs We Take and the Food We Eat.* New York: Wiley.

Heckman, James, and J. Smith. 1995. The Performance of Performance Standards: The Effects of JTPA Performance Standards on Efficiency, Equity and Participant Outcomes. Unpublished manuscript. University of Chicago.

Hedge, David, and Renee J. Johnson. 2002. "The Plot That Failed: The Republican Revolution and Congressional Control of Bureaucracy." *Journal of Public Administration Research and Theory* 12, no. 3:333–51.

Heimann, C. F. Larry. 1998. *Acceptable Risks: Politics, Policy and Risky Technologies.* Ann Arbor: University of Michigan Press.

Heinrich, Carolyn. 1999. "Do Government Bureaucrats Make Effective Use of Performance Management Information?" *Journal of Public Administration Research and Theory* 9, no. 3:363–93.

———. 2000. "The Role of Performance Standards in JTPA Program Administration and Service Delivery in a Government Bureaucracy." In *Performance Standards in a Government Bureaucracy: Analytical Essays on the JTPA Performance Standards System,* ed. James J. Heckman. Kalamazoo, MI: W. E. Upjohn Institute.

Hirst, Paul, 2000. "Democracy and Governance." In *Debating Governance,* ed. Jon Pierre, 13–35. Oxford: Oxford University Press.

Hood, Christopher, and Michael Jackson. 1991. *Administrative Argument.* Brookfield, VT: Dartmouth.

Hooghe, Liesbet, and Gary Marks. 2003. "Unraveling the Central State, but How? Types of Multi-Level Governance." *American Political Science Review* 97, no. 2:233–43.

Ingraham, Patricia W., and Donald P. Moynihan. 2001. "Beyond Measurement: Managing for Results in Government." In *Quicker, Better, Cheaper: Managing Performance in American Government,* ed. Dall W. Forsythe, 309–34. Albany, NY: Rockefeller Institute Press.

Inman, Robert P., and Daniel L. Rubenfeld. 1997. "Rethinking Federalism." *Journal of Economic Perspectives* 11 (Fall): 43–64.

Jennings, Edward T., and Meg Patrick Haist. 2002. Does Performance Measurement Perform? Unpublished paper, Research Workshop on the Empirical Study of Governance. February 21–23. Texas A&M University, College Station, TX.

———. 2004. "Putting Performance Measurement in Context." In *The Art of Governance: Analyzing Management and Administration,* ed. Patricia W. Ingraham and Laurence E. Lynn, Jr., 173–94. Washington, DC: Georgetown University Press.

Joyce, Philip G. 1993. "Using Performance Measures for Federal Budgeting: Proposals and Prospects." *Public Budgeting and Finance* 13 (Winter): 3–17.

Kamensky, John M., and Albert Morales, eds. 2005. *Managing for Results 2005.* New York: Rowman and Littlefield.

Kearney, Richard C., and Evan M. Berman, eds. 1999. *Public Sector Performance: Management, Motivation, and Measurement.* Boulder, CO: Westview Press.

Kelly, Janet M. 2002. "Why We Should Take Performance Measurement on Faith (Facts Being Hard to Come By and Not Terribly Important)." *Public Performance and Management Review* 25, no. 4:375–80.

Kettl, Donald F. 1988. *Government by Proxy: (Mis?)Managing Federal Programs.* Washington, DC: Brookings Institution.

———. 1993. *Sharing Power: Public Governance and Private Markets.* Washington, DC: Brookings Institution.

———. 1994. *Reinventing Government? Appraising the National Performance Review.* Washington, DC: Brookings Institution.

———. 2002. *Team Bush: Leadership Lessons from the Bush White House.* New York: McGraw-Hill.

King, Gary, Robert O. Keohane, and Sidney Verba. 2001. *Designing Social Inquiry.* Princeton, NJ: Princeton University Press.

Klingner, Donald E., and John Nalbandian. 2003. *Public Personnel Management: Contexts and Strategies.* 5th ed. Saddle River, NJ: Prentice-Hall.

Kravchuk, Robert S., and Ronald W. Schack. 1996. "Designing Effective Performance Measurement Systems under the Government Performance and Results Act of 1993." *Public Administration Review* (July/August): 348–58.

Kuzel, A. J. 1992. "Sampling in Qualitative Inquiry." In *Doing Qualitative Research,* ed. B. F. Crabtree and W. L. Miller. Newbury Park, CA: Sage Publications.

Light, Paul. 1995. *Thickening Government: Federal Hierarchy and the Diffusion of Accountability.* Washington, DC: Brookings Institution.

———. 1997. *The Tides of Reform: Making Government Work, 1945–1995.* New Haven, CT: Yale University Press.

———. 1999. *The True Size of Government.* Washington, DC: Brookings Institution.

———. 2002. *Government's Greatest Achievements: From Civil Rights to Homeland Defense.* Washington, DC: Brookings Institution.

Long, Edward, and Aimee Franklin. 2004. "The Paradox of Implementing the Government Performance and Results Act: Top-Down Direction for Bottom-Up Implementation." *Public Administration Review* 64, no.3 (May/June): 309–19.

Marschke, Gerald. 2001."The Economics of Performance Incentives in Government with Evidence from a Federal Job Training Program," in *Quicker, Better, Cheaper? Managing Performance in American Government,* ed. Dall W. Forsythe, 61–97. Albany, NY: Rockefeller Institute Press.

Maxwell, Joseph A. 1996. *Qualitative Research Design: An Interactive Approach.* Thousand Oaks, CA: Sage Publications.

McKinney, J. 1996. "Performance Budget and Accountability." In *Case Studies in Public Budgeting and Financial Management,* 2nd ed., ed. A. Khan and W. Hildreth. Dubuque, IA: Kendall-Hunt.

McNab, Robert, and Francois Melese. 2003. "Implementing the GPRA: Examining the Prospects for Performance Budgeting in the Federal Government." *Public Budgeting and Finance* 23, no. 2 (June): 73–95.

Mercer, John. 2006. "Government Performance Management." http://www.johnmercer.com, 1.

Mihm, Christopher. 2001. "Implementing GPRA: Progress and Challenges." In *Quicker, Better, Cheaper? Managing Performance in American Government,* ed. Dall W. Forsythe, 101–11. Albany, NY: Rockefeller Institute Press.

Miles, Matthew B., and Michael A. Huberman. 1994. *Qualitative Data Analysis: An Expanded Sourcebook,* 2nd ed. Thousand Oaks, CA: Sage Publications.

Milward, H. Brinton. 1996. "Symposium on the Hollow State: Capacity, Control, and Performance in Interorganizational Settings." *Journal of Public Administration Research and Theory* 6, no. 2 (April): 193–95.

Milward, H. B., Keith Provan, and Barbara Else. 1993. "What Does the Hollow State Look Like?" In *Public Management: The State of the Art,* ed. Barry Bozeman, 309–22. San Francisco: Jossey-Bass.

Morini, Joy S., and Patrick J. Wolf. 2002. The Government Performance and Results Act: The More You Know, The More You Wonder. Paper presented at the National Conference of the American Society for Public Administration, Phoenix. March 23–26.

National Academy of Public Administration. 2000. Minutes of the Standing Panel on Executive Organization and Management. Washington, DC. February 18.

Newcomer, Kathryn E., and Amy Downey. 1998. "Performance-based Management: What Is It and How Did We Get There?" *Public Manager* 26, no. 4:37–49.

Newcomer, Kathryn E., and Roy E. Wright, 1997. "Toward Effective Use of Performance Measurement in the Federal Government." *Public Manager* 25, no. 4:31–33.

Oates, Wallace E. 1972. *Fiscal Federalism.* New York: Harcourt Brace Jovanovich.

Osborne, David E., and Ted Gaebler. 1992. *Reinventing Government: How the Entrepreneurial Spirit Is Transforming the Public Sector.* Reading, MA: Addison-Wesley.

O'Toole, Laurence J. 2000, "Different Public Managements? Implications of Structural Contexts in Hierarchies and Networks." In *Advancing Public Management: New Developments in Theory, Methods, and Practice,* ed. Jeffrey L. Brudney, Laurence J. O'-Toole, Jr., and Hal G. Rainey, 19–32. Washington, DC: Georgetown University Press.

O'Toole, Laurence J., and Kenneth J. Meier. 2004. "Public Management in Intergovernmental Networks: Matching Structural Networks and Managerial Networking." *Journal of Public Administration Research and Theory* 14, no. 4:469–94.

Patton, M. Q. 1990. *Qualitative Evaluation and Research Methods,* 2nd ed. Newbury Park, CA: Sage Publications.

Pear, Robert. 1999. "Fraud in Medicare Increasingly Tied to Claims Payers." *New York Times.* September 20.

Perrin, Edward B., and Jeffrey J. Koshel, ed. 1997. *Panel on Reform Measures for Public Health, Substance Abuse, and Mental Health.* Washington, DC: National Academy Press.

Poister, Theodore H., and Gregory D. Streib. 1999. "Assessing the Validity, Legitimacy, and Functionality of Performance Measurement Systems in Municipal Governments." *Public Administration Review* 29, no. 2 (June): 107–23.

Posner, Paul L. 2002. "Accountability Challenges of Third-Party Government." In *The Tools of Government: A Guide to the New Governance,* ed. Lester M. Salamon, 523–51. New York: Oxford University Press.

Pressman, Jeffrey L., and Aaron Wildavsky. 1984. *Implementation,* 3rd ed. Berkeley and Los Angeles: University of California Press.

Radin, Beryl A. 1998a. "Searching for Government Performance: The Government Performance and Results Act." *PS: Political Science and Politics* 31, no. 3 (September): 553–56.

———. 1998b. "The Government Performance and Results Act (GPRA): Hydra-Headed Monster or Effective Policy Tool?" *Public Administration Review* 58 (July–August): 307–16.

———. 2000. "The Government Performance and Results Act and the Tradition of Federal Management Reform: Square Pegs in Round Holes." *Journal of Public Administration Research and Theory* 11:111–35.

———. 2002. *The Accountable Juggler: The Art of Leadership in a Federal Agency.* Washington, DC: Congressional Quarterly Press.

———. 2006. *Challenging the Performance Movement: Accountability, Complexity, and Democratic Values.* Washington, DC: Georgetown University Press.

Romzek, Barbara S., and Melvin J. Dubnick. 1987. "Accountability and the Public Sector: Lessons from the Challenger Tragedy." *Public Administration Review* 47 (May/June): 227–38.

Romzek, Barbara S., and Jocelyn Johnston. 2005. "Social Service Contracting: Exploring the Determinants of Effective Contract Accountability." *Public Administration Review* 65, no. 4:436–44.

Rosenbloom, David H. 1983. "Public Administration Theory and the Separation of Powers." *Public Administration Review* 43, no. 3 (May/June): 219–26.

Rosenthal, Stephan R. 1984. "New Directions for Evaluating Intergovernmental Programs." Public Administration Review 44, no. 6 (November/December): 469–76.

Salamon, Lester M. 1989. *Beyond Privatization: The Tools of Government Action.* Washington, DC: Urban Institute Press.

Savas, Emanuel S. 1987. *Privatization: The Key to Better Government.* Chatham, NJ: Chatham House Publishers.

Schick, Alan. 1966. "The Road to PPB: The Stages of Budget Reform." *Public Administration Review* 26, no. 4 (December): 143–58.

———. 2001. "Getting Performance Measures to Measure Up." In *Quicker, Better, Cheaper? Managing Performance in American Government,* ed. Dall W. Forsythe, 39–60. Albany, NY: Rockefeller Institute Press.

Sclar, Elliott D., 2000. *You Don't Always Get What You Pay For: The Economics of Privatization.* Ithaca, NY: Cornell University Press.

Shaw, Anwar. 2003. "Fiscal Decentralisation in Transition Economies and Developing Countries: Progress, Problems and the Promise." In *Federalism in a Changing World—Learning from Each Other,* ed. Raoul Blindenbacher, 432–60. Montreal: McGill-Queens University Press.

Smith, Dennis C., and William J. Bratton. 2001. "Performance Management in New York City: Compstat and the Revolution in Police Management." In *Quicker, Better, Cheaper? Managing Performance in American Government,* ed. Dall W. Forsythe, 453–82. Albany, NY: Rockefeller Institute Press.

Springarn, Natalie Davis. 1976. *Heart Beat: The Politics of Health Research.* New York: Robert B. Luce.

Strauss, A. L. 1987. *Qualitative Analysis for Social Scientists.* Cambridge, UK: Cambridge University Press.

Strauss, A. L., and J. Corbin, 1990. *Basics of Qualitative Research: Grounded Theory Procedures and Techniques.* Newbury Park, CA: Sage Publications.

Sunstein, Cass R., Daniel Kahneman, David Schkade, and Ilana Ritov. 2002. "Predictably Incoherent Judgments." *Stanford Law Review* 54:1153–1215.

Thomas, Virginia L. 2001. "Restoring Government Integrity through Performance, Results, and Accountability." In *Quicker, Better, Cheaper: Managing Performance in American Government,* ed. Dall W. Forsythe, 113–42. Albany, NY: Rockefeller Institute Press.

Thompson, James. 1967. *Organizations in Action.* New York. McGraw-Hill.

Turner, James S. 1970. *The Chemical Feast: The Ralph Nader Study Group on Food Protection and the Food and Drug Administration.* New York: Penguin.

U.S. Congress. Subcommittee on Governmental Efficiency, Financial Management and Intergovernmental Relations. 2001. 107th Congress Report on GPRA. Washington, DC: U.S. Government Printing Office.

U.S. Congressional Research Service. 1997. *Government Performances and Results Act: Implications for Congressional Oversight,* by Frederick M. Kaiser and Virginia A. McMurty. Report no. 97-382. Washington, DC. March 24.

———. 1999. *Performance Measure Provisions in the 105th Congress: Analysis of a Selected Compilation,* by Genevieve J. Knezo and Virginia A. McMurty. Report no. 97-1028. Washington, DC. March 30.

U.S. Department of Health and Human Services. Centers for Medicare and Medicaid Services. 2002. *Centers for Medicare and Medicaid Services Performance Plan.* Washington, DC: U.S. Government Printing Office.

———. Food and Drug Administration. 2002. *Food and Drug Administration Performance Plan.* http://www.epa.gov. April 18.

———. Indian Health Service. 2002. *Indian Health Service Performance Plan.*

————. National Institutes of Health. 2002. *National Institutes of Health Performance Plan.*

————. Health Resources and Services Administration. 2003. *Health Resources and Services Administration GPRA Performance Plan.*

U.S. General Accounting Office. 1993. *Performance Budgeting: State Experiences and Implications for the Federal Government.* Washington, DC: U.S. General Accounting Office.

————. 1998. *Report to the Committee on Labor and Human Resources.* Washington, DC: U.S. Senate.

————. 1999. *Medicare Contractors: Despite Its Efforts, HCFA Cannot Ensure Their Effectiveness or Integrity.* Washington, DC: U.S. General Accounting Office.

————. 2001. *Managing for Results: Federal Managers' Views on Key Management Issues Vary Widely across Agencies.* Washington, DC: U.S. General Accounting Office.

————. 2002. *Effect of User Fees on Drug Approval Times, Withdrawals and Other Agencies.* Washington, DC: General Accounting Office.

U. S. House of Representatives. Committee on Small Business. 2002. 108th Congress. *CMS: New Name, Same Old Game?*

U.S. Office of Management and Budget. 2005. *Budget of the United States, 2006.* Department of Health and Human Services, PART Rankings, 141–83. Washington, DC: U.S. Government Printing Office.

U.S. Senate. Joint Hearing of the House Government Reform and Oversight Committee and Senate Governmental Affairs Committee. 1996. 102nd Congress. *Hearing Report.* March.

————. Governmental Affairs Committee. 1997. 103rd Congress. *Implementation of the Results Act.* June.

Walker, David B. 1995. *The Rebirth of Federalism: Slouching toward Washington.* Chatham, NJ: Chatham House Press.

Wholey, Joseph S., Harry P. Hatry, and Kathryn E. Newcomer. 1994. *Handbook of Practical Program Evaluation.* San Francisco: Jossey-Bass.

Wholey, Joseph S., and Kathryn E. Newcomer. 1989. *Improving Government Performance: Evaluation Strategies for Strengthening Public Agencies and Programs.* San Francisco: Jossey-Bass.

Wildavsky, Aaron B. 1979. *The Politics of the Budgetary Process,* 3rd ed. Boston: Little, Brown.

Wilson, James Q. 1976. "The Rise of the Bureaucratic State." In *The American Commonwealth—1976,* ed. Nathan Glazer and Irving Kristol, 77–78. New York: Basic Books.

Wright, Deil. 1988. *Understanding Intergovernmental Relations,* 3rd ed. New York: Harcourt.

————. 2000. "Models of National, State and Local Relationships." In *American Intergovernmental Relations,* 3rd ed., ed. Lawrence J. O'Toole, Jr., 74–89. Washington, DC: Congressional Quarterly Press.

Yin, Robert K. 2003. *Case Study Research: Design and Methods,* 3rd ed. Thousand Oaks, CA: Sage Publications.

INDEX

Aberbach, Joel D., 28
accountability
  in the advocacy literature, 17–18
  at FDA, 137, 146
  grants to subgovernments and, 22–23
  at IHS, 125, 127
  implementation of GPRA and, 27–28
  MCHB–third party articulation and, 64
  at NIH, 109
  in performance management, 186
  in smart-buyer literature, 18
  third-party government and, 14, 19, 21
  as a variable in performance
     measurement (*see* accountability
     to federal program purposes)
accountability to federal program
    purposes
  in all agencies, 153
  in CMS, 91
  conclusions regarding, 165–67
  in FDA, 147
  in HRSA, 67
  in IHS, 126
  in NIH, 113
  as a variable in performance
     management, 29–31
Advancement of Telehealth, Office for
    the, 49
Agriculture, U.S. Department of (USDA),
    143
Alaska Native peoples, health services for.
    See Indian Health Service
American Association of Retired Persons,
    81
American College of Cardiology, 83

American Heart Association, 83
American Hospital Association, 83
American Indians, health services for. *See*
    Indian Health Service
American Medical Association, 83
American Indians
  distribution of anti-drug calendars to,
    102
  health care services for (*see* Indian
    Health Service)
  health outcomes, 121–22
articulated vertical networks of third
    parties, 8–9
  goal attenuation, 23, 26
  grant and contract funds, problems
    associated with, 25–26
  in health program agencies, 13
  of HRSA (*see* Health Resources and
    Services Administration)
  for Medicare and Medicaid (*see* Centers
    for Medicare and Medicaid
    Services; Medicare)
  of NIH (*see* National Institutes of
    Health)
  open-ended delegated discretion, 156
  performance measurement and, 13–14,
    168–70, 181–83
  See also network articulations; third-
    party government
Australia, 173

Baucus, Max, 129
Bextra, 128–29, 137, 174
Blue Cross and Blue Shield of Illinois, 89
Blue Cross and Blue Shield of Michigan, 89

Border Health Program, 51
Budget and Accounting Procedures Act of
    1950, 38
budgets
    of CMS, 73–74
    of HRSA, 48
    of IHS, 116
    of NIH, 96
    performance measurement and (see
        performance budgeting)
    rationality in, political vs. managerial,
        24, 45
Bush, George W., 40, 186

CAHPS. See Consumer Assessment of
    Health Plans Systems
CDC. See Centers for Disease Control
Centers for Disease Control (CDC), 76, 79
Centers for Medicare and Medicaid
    Services (CMS)
    agency network articulations,
        performance measures and, 169
    comparisons of Medicaid and
        Medicare, 23–24, 72, 87–91
    data, challenges of collecting, 78–79,
        81, 92
    fraud and contractor compliance,
        performance measurement and,
        89–90
    goal conflict at, 174–75
    GPRA, implementation of, 74–77,
        90–94
    hospital mortality rates, publication of
        data on, 43
    overview of, 73–74
    Peer Review Organizations (Quality
        Improvement Organizations),
        83
    performance indicators for Medicaid,
        third parties and, 77–80
    performance indicators for Medicare,
        third parties and, 80–85
    performance measures, small number
        of, 74
    public perception of, 167–68
    quality care, definition of, 44
    representative performance measures
        for Medicare and Medicaid, 82
    responsibilities, policy tools, and third
        parties, 4

selection of for performance
    measurement study, 4–5
size of, compared to SSA, 21
synthesis of variables related to
    implementation of performance
    measurement, 91 (see also
    continua of performance
    measurement)
telephone customer service,
    performance measures of, 85–87
Y2K compliance, 88–89
centralization/decentralization
    fiscal federalism and, 24–25
    of HRSA, 49
    of NIH, 97
    as a variable in the analysis of
        performance measurement (see
        centralization of policy
        implementation)
centralization of policy implementation
    in all agencies, 153
    in CMS, 91
    IN FDA, 147
    in HRSA, 67
    in IHS, 126
    in NIH, 113
    third-party policy implementation and,
        160–62
    as a variable in performance
        measurement, 30, 32
Challenging the Performance Movement
    (Radin), 16
Chemical Feast, The: The Ralph Nader
    Study Group Report on Food Protection
    and the Food and Drug Administration
    (Turner), 132–33
CHS. See Contract Health Services
    program
client and stakeholder support, level and
    character of
    in all agencies, 153
    in CMS, 91
    in FDA, 147
    in HRSA, 67
    in IHS, 126
    in NIH, 113
    third-party policy implementation and,
        163–65
    as a variable in performance
        measurement, 30, 33